MOUNTAIN BIKE!
Southwestern British Columbia

A GUIDE TO THE CLASSIC TRAILS

D0001597

WARD CAMERON

Library of Congress Cataloging-in-Publication Data:
Cameron, Ward.
Mountain bike! southwestern British Columbia: a guide to the classic trails/
Ward Cameron.
p.   cm. —(America by mountain bike)
Includes bibliographical references and index.
ISBN 1-55068-094-3
1. All terrain cycling—British Columbia Guidebooks.
2. Bicycle trails—British Columbia Guidebooks.
3. British Columbia Guidebooks.
I. Title II. Series: America by mountain bike series.
GV1046.C22B757 1999
917.11'3044—dc21   99-29363
CIP

Photos by the author unless otherwise credited
Maps by Jeff Goodwin
Cover and text design by Suzanne Holt
Cover photo by Dennis Coello

Menasha Ridge Press
700 South 28th Street
Suite 206
Birmingham, Alabama 35233

All the trails described in this book are legal for mountain bikes. But rules can change—especially for off-road bicycles, the new kid on the outdoor recreation block. Land access issues and conflicts between bicyclists, hikers, equestrians, and other users can cause the rewriting of recreation regulations on public lands, sometimes resulting in a ban of mountain bike use on specific trails. That's why it's the responsibility of each rider to check and make sure that he or she rides only on trails where mountain biking is permitted.

CAUTION

Outdoor recreational activities are by their very nature potentially hazardous. All participants in such activities must assume the responsibility for their own actions and safety. The information contained in this guidebook cannot replace sound judgment and good decision-making skills, which help reduce risk exposure, nor does the scope of this book allow for disclosure of all the potential hazards and risks involved in such activities.

Learn as much as possible about the outdoor recreational activities in which you participate, prepare for the unexpected, and be cautious. The reward will be a safer and more enjoyable experience.

To my parents, Bruce and Shirley Cameron. Dad never saw this book published, but he lives forever in the memories of the people whose lives he touched. Mom's strength during his illness made our whole family stronger.

CONTENTS

AMERICA BY MOUNTAIN BIKE MAP LEGEND

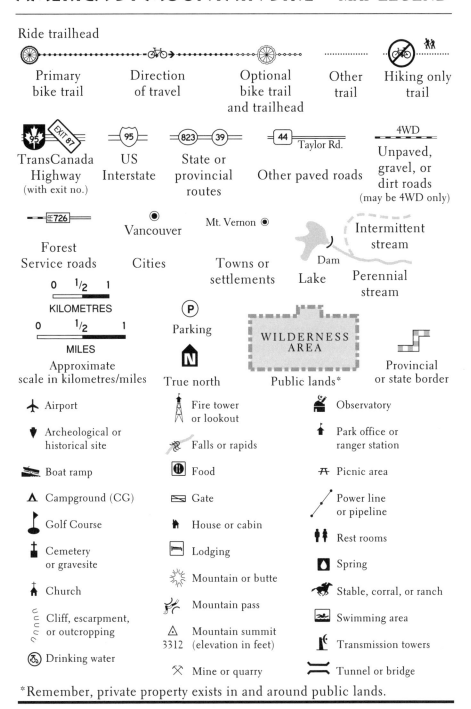

Ride trailhead

Primary bike trail

Direction of travel

Optional bike trail and trailhead

Other trail

Hiking only trail

TransCanada Highway (with exit no.)

US Interstate

State or provincial routes

Other paved roads
Taylor Rd.

4WD
Unpaved, gravel, or dirt roads (may be 4WD only)

Forest Service roads

Vancouver
Cities

Mt. Vernon
Towns or settlements

Dam
Lake

Intermittent stream

Perennial stream

0   1/2   1
KILOMETRES

0   1/2   1
MILES

Approximate scale in kilometres/miles

P Parking

N True north

WILDERNESS AREA

Public lands*

Provincial or state border

✈ Airport

♥ Archeological or historical site

Boat ramp

▲ Campground (CG)

Golf Course

Cemetery or gravesite

Church

Cliff, escarpment, or outcropping

Drinking water

Fire tower or lookout

Falls or rapids

Food

Gate

House or cabin

Lodging

Mountain or butte

Mountain pass

Mountain summit
3312 (elevation in feet)

Mine or quarry

Observatory

Park office or ranger station

Picnic area

Power line or pipeline

Rest rooms

Spring

Stable, corral, or ranch

Swimming area

Transmission towers

Tunnel or bridge

*Remember, private property exists in and around public lands.

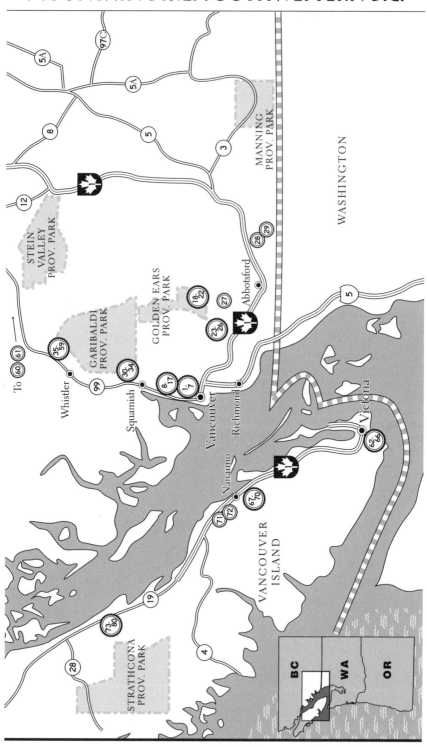

LIST OF MAPS

ACKNOWLEDGMENTS

Special thanks go to Susan Baker. She supported me when things seemed impossible and pushed me when I seemed lazy. Without her strength, I might not have had the oomph necessary to head out day after day in the completion of this book. Even more important, she locked me in my office until I finally completed the manuscript.

During the creation of this book, many people offered support and encouragement. One individual in particular deserves special mention. Aydin Odyakmaz, owner of Trailmasters Mountain Bike Tours in Canmore, Alberta, was kind enough to lend me a mountain bike to use when researching this guide. Without his kindness, it's unlikely this book would have been completed.

Without the help of local bike shops and riders that I met on the many trails, this work would never have been possible. I must also mention the work of associations like the Secret Trail Society, the North Shore Mountain Biking Association, the South Island Mountain Bike Society, and the Arrowsmith Mountain Bike Club. Through these, and many other volunteer organizations, the backcountry of British Columbia is playing host to more and better trails. Areas previously closed to fat-tire travel are being reopened through the lobbying efforts of these groups. It's critical that riders using these trails offer time and support to maintain them. These rides didn't just appear by magic; they are the result to many days of volunteer labour. Regular trail days are a social way to give something back while meeting other local riders.

FOREWORD

Welcome to *America by Mountain Bike*, a series designed to provide all-terrain bikers with the information they need to find and ride the very best trails around. Whether you're new to the sport and don't know where to pedal or an experienced mountain biker who wants to learn the classic trails in another region, this series is for you. Drop a few bucks for the book, spend an hour with the detailed maps and route descriptions, and you're prepared for the finest in off-road cycling.

My role as editor of this series is simple: First, find a mountain biker who knows the area and loves to ride. Second, ask that person to spend a year researching the most popular and very best rides around. And third, have that rider describe each trail in terms of difficulty, scenery, condition, elevation change, and all other categories of information that are important to trail riders. "Pretend you've just completed a ride and met up with fellow mountain bikers at the trailhead," I told each author. "Imagine their questions, be clear in your answers."

As I said, the *editorial* process—that of sending out riders and reading the submitted chapters—is a snap. But the work involved in finding, riding, and writing about each trail is enormous. In some instances our authors' tasks are made easier by the information contributed by local bike shops or cycling clubs, or even by the writers of local "where-to" guides. Credit for these contributions is provided, when appropriate, in each chapter, and our sincere thanks goes to all who have helped.

But the overwhelming majority of trails are discovered and pedaled by our authors themselves, then compared with dozens of other routes to determine if they qualify as "classic"—that area's best in scenery and cycling fun. If you've ever had the experience of pioneering a route from outdated topographic maps, or entering a bike shop to request information from local riders who would much prefer to keep their favorite trails secret, or if you know how it is to double- and triple-check data to be positive your trail info is correct, then you have an idea of how each of our authors has labored to bring about these books. You and I, and all the mountain bikers of America, are the richer for their efforts.

You'll get more out of this book if you take a moment to read the Introduction explaining how to read the trail listings. The "Topographic Maps" section will help you understand how useful topos will be on a ride, and will also tell you where to get them. And though this is a "where-to," not a "how-to" guide, those of you who have not traveled the backcountry might find "Hitting the Trail" of particular value.

In addition to the material above, newcomers to mountain biking might want to spend a minute with the glossary, page 315, so that terms like *hardpack*, *single-track*, and *waterbars* won't throw you when you come across them in the text.

All the best.

Dennis Coello
St. Louis

PREFACE

The west coast of Canada has earned a reputation as one of the premier mountain biking destinations on the North American continent. Photographs in magazines show brightly clad mountain bikers dropping down an inconceivable chute that would terrify most mortals. Other images capture cyclists balancing their way over slippery cedar logs or equally treacherous teeter totters. This is what most of us know about mountain biking on Canada's west coast. Even for expert riders, some rides will strike fear in your hearts and nearly make your lungs explode with effort. Other rides will test your ability to negotiate long sequences of drops, rocks, and roots, any of which could launch you into the realm of bike repair and facial reconstruction.

On the other hand, novices can roll their way through old-growth forests before cresting a mountain pass to have lunch beside a pristine glacial tarn. This is not the image of British Columbia that we see in the media—if it ain't vertical, it doesn't make the magazine. This book reveals rides for all abilities. There is an endless number of rides for beginner and intermediate mountain bikers. British Columbia is a high-impact landscape that relies on its vast natural resources for economic well-being. This leaves a landscape that has been dissected by logging and mining access roads. River banks have been lined with smooth, rideable dikes. One look at a topographic map and most cyclists can find endless opportunities for exploration.

This reliance on forestry and high-impact industries also means that mountain bikers have access to alpine environments they might otherwise be forbidden to enter. Most riders will agree that access should be limited when it comes to sensitive alpine landscapes. In British Columbia, though, you are not leaving any mark on these high-elevation landscapes; in fact, you have wide double-track leading the way. The views stretch for hundreds of miles, and the ocean sits at your feet. Ah, the freedom of the hills.

I had no idea what I was getting myself into when I agreed to write this book. I believed my abilities were the equal of riders everywhere. I had used mountain biking as a means of transportation, a way to access magical mountain landscapes while also getting a great workout. Living in the Rockies, I was used to huge elevation gains and solid technical landscape. For me, this book was a journey of discovery, not to mention a humbling experience. I was repeatedly

Blowdown Creek Trail.

beaten and bruised, and I quickly realized that I had to begin anew. In British Columbia, I was a beginner.

Riding on the west coast requires an entirely different set of skills. Much of it involves limited physical distance, opting rather for a Zen-like approach. You don't ride to go somewhere, you ride to become one with the landscape. You finesse your way over man-made and natural obstacles simply because you can. You begin looking for trails with taller log pyramids, bigger verticals, and narrower, steeper lines. Suddenly, you've dropped your seat, replaced your handlebars with risers, and upgraded your brakes and tires. After a few hard hits, you stop caring about a little blood—heck, you've got plenty more where that came from. You begin to believe that many of the trail builders in British Columbia must be sick individuals. They have to be somewhat demented to think up some of the combinations and lines on trails with names like Sex Boy, Humility, and Kill Me, Thrill Me.

It begins innocently enough. You head out on a ride like Island Highway, a winding gravel road climbing up the side of Grouse Mountain. As you ascend, you notice single-track routes tempting you into the woods. As you pass the first one, you think, "That will be a good place to explore the next time I come up here." By the time you get to the final switchback, you've passed so many trails that you've forgotten why you're riding the wide gravel in the first place. Why are there so many side trails? Where do they go? How tough can they really be? Then it happens . . . something inside of you snaps. You pop into a narrow opening and instantly find yourself leaping off your bike as the line suddenly goes vertical. Your quick reaction was not quick enough, and you find yourself a twisted mass of scratches and bruises. Your bike survives, although your front tire has a new wobble. This can't possibly be a mountain bike trail. As you dust yourself off, a veteran bounces down the drop, flashes you a knowing grin, and disappears into the distance. A few minutes later, a group of three people do exactly the same thing. It's like they are simultaneously part of both the mountain and their bikes.

When you first encounter trails like these, it's easy to discount them as strictly for elite riders, a hard-core minority of slightly brain-damaged individuals with little else to do in their lives. Once you begin to ride, though, starting on easier trails with moderate obstacles, you begin to feel a new rush of adrenaline. Before you know it, you're using expressions like "Go big or go home." Your friends begin to worry about your sanity, especially when you tell them what you've been doing in your spare time. Your paycheck disappears into a new set of wheels and constant upgrades to the latest mountain biking accessories. Soon you're looking for more exhilarating challenges. Before you know it, you'll find yourself chuckling at a novice you see a few feet from the entrance of Kirkwood's Seventh Secret, bent and bruised, and you'll smile at the look on his face as you whiz by. He looks at you, and wonders about your mental health — you've come full circle.

Eventually, you'll find that you outgrow many of the trail guides on the market. This is for good reason. There's an unwritten rule on the coast that authors avoid describing the most severe trails. Because many of these routes are of questionable legal standing, describing them in a book is impractical. After all, the trails may not even be around by the time it's published. In addition, the most radical trails are often in areas very prone to erosion. Sending novices down such trails usually only serves to increase trail damage and reduce the enjoyment of those riders best served by the trail. It also tends to lead to trail braiding as novices look for a safe way to descend. When you are ready for these trails, you will find them. They are well known to local riders and bike shops. In British Columbia, building a relationship with local riders is critical, especially for elite, top-end riders.

Looking at the big picture, British Columbia offers more diversity than almost any other area on the continent. It's impossible to try to quantify the landscape and trails of this amazing area. Riding the coast takes you through a rich history and a landscape that mocks human attempts to civilize it. I remember riding through the Parkhurst ghost town in Whistler and finding a very old butcher knife stuck in a railroad tie. I picked it up, gave it a careless toss, and it lodged itself right back in the tie. As I explored the ghost town, I had a feeling of being watched; though it has been deserted for years, it still had a feeling of life about it. This is a land of stories and legend. If you ride here, it will leave its mark on your soul.

This book will focus on Vancouver and the surrounding area, including the corridor between Vancouver and Pemberton on the Sea to Sky Highway, the Fraser Canyon from Chilliwack to the coast, and the southern part of Vancouver Island, specifically Victoria to Courtenay.

THE LAND

British Columbia is massive, wild, and rugged. In area, it covers 952,263 square kilometres (367,574 square miles) along Canada's western margin. It stretches from the 49th parallel to the 60th, with some of the most rugged mountain ranges on the North American continent. To the south lie the border states of Washington, Idaho, and Montana. To the north are Alaska and the Northwest Territories. The massive character of this immense province has forced us to limit our focus to a small corner of British Columbia, the southwest coast. Centred around the urban hub of Vancouver, the Coast Mountains stretch to the north, south, and east. To the west are the waters of the Strait of Georgia, and beyond, Vancouver Island.

Rising from the frigid waters of the Strait of Georgia, the Coastal Mountains reach skyward, with many summits retaining a veil of snow even through the summer. These mountains were the product of a massive collision as continental plates collided millennia ago. As the North American plate was hit by the Pacific plate, huge compressing forces squeezed the rocks, bending and folding the strata. As one plate was pushed on top of the other, incredible heat was produced. At the same time, molten magma from the earth's core erupted as new volcanoes formed along the plate margins. This combination of compression, mixed with volcanic action, has created the mountains that line the western edge of the continent. Today, these volcanoes persist and may some day awaken to spew fiery magma on the landscape. The modern eruption of Mount Saint Helens, Washington, to the south only reminds us of the molten genesis of these immense peaks.

Land Jurisdictions   While you read through this text, you'll notice numerous definitions of land ownership. These include terms like "Crown land" and "municipal land." Crown land is used to describe land that is outside of normal town and city boundaries but not privately owned. In essence, it is the property of the government, and in Canada it is referred to as Crown land.

Within the boundaries of most cities and towns, some of the land has not been designated for development and remains the property of the town or municipality. This is referred to as municipal land.

Along the west coast, there are two other large landlords. The area around Vancouver is divided into many small cities and towns, and they have banded together to manage their municipal parks as a unit. The Greater Vancouver Regional District (GVRD) is the organization responsible for managing these parks. This centralization helps bring a higher level of consistency in the management of local parks and recreation areas.

On the north shore of Burrard Inlet, British Properties, a private land development company, owns much of the undeveloped land. On many rides—particularly those on the slopes of Cypress Mountain—signs indicate this ownership of the land. They do allow access onto their lands, but signs indicate that hikers and cyclists must accept full responsibility should injuries occur.

Kill Me, Thrill Me Trail.

THE PLANTS AND ANIMALS

This contrast of vertical peaks adjacent to a coastal landscape has created a diverse collection of plants. Ancient forests of western redcedar, western hemlock, sitka spruce, and Douglas fir bask in the steady rainfalls that characterize the coastal landscape. Some of these giants exceed 70 metres (230 feet) in height and more than 2 metres (6.5 feet) in girth. Beneath their dense canopy, huge ferns grow among the vinelike growth of the coastal salal. In moist areas the 2-metre (6.5-feet) leaves of the skunk cabbage soak in whatever sunlight they can gather on their huge surface. Nearby, devil's club, a 2-metre-tall (6.5 feet) plant with huge, maple-style leaves and a vicious armament of razor-sharp thorns, challenges any attempts to pass. The thorns can easily rip through a pair of jeans and leave a nasty wound. It's not B.C. single-track until you've found yourself ejected into a stand of devil's club. Beneath the devil's club, tiny foam flowers soak up any remaining sunlight.

In more open areas, vine and bigleaf maple dominate along with red alder. Along the margins, salmonberry, blackberry, and blueberry plants offer their succulent fruit to tenacious riders. Later in the season, thimbleberry, salal, and Oregon grape fruits add to the wilderness smorgasbord. Plants like ocean spray and goatsbeard round out the picture.

Few plants on this planet have such a two-faced character as blackberry. The fruit is delightful, and cyclists gorge themselves along blackberry-lined trails. However, it quickly shows its nasty side as it begins to reclaim lesser-used trails. As you ride past, its thick spines rip at any exposed flesh unlucky enough to pass within reach of its sharp talons. While researching this book, I took an incorrect turn on a fast, wide double-track only to have it suddenly choke, closed in a dense tangle of blackberry. It was like being attacked by a cougar. In the few seconds it took me to stop, my arms and legs were covered with scrapes and cuts. The scars still remain a year later. In fact, in British Columbia, you can learn to recognize the berries by the scars they leave behind. Thimbleberry lacks thorns, salmonberry can leave many shallow scratches, and blackberry leaves fewer, but deeper, scars from its recurved thorns.

On sun-bathed ridges on Vancouver Island, arbutus trees, with their succulent leaves and peeling red bark, add a splash of colour to the landscape. Although their peeling bark makes them look diseased at first glance, they are indeed healthy and thrive on sunny locales. Also common is the Scotch broom, innocently introduced by settlers from England. Since its arrival, it has taken to the island with a vengeance, often at the expense of native plants.

Local wildlife has developed a close relationship with the rugged landscape of the coastal regions. Countless species of birds thrive in this land of salmon, berries, and other natural foods. Along the coast, waterfowl and surf scoters skim the waves while great blue herons wade the shallows looking for minnows and frogs. In the trees, bald eagles and ospreys watch for larger prey, particularly the formerly prevalent salmon. Belted kingfishers reveal their presence by a rattling call as they fly from point to point, following the rivers inland. Listen for the raucous call of the Steller's jay, a beautiful relative of the blue jay, with blue feathers and a black head.

Bears and Cougars   Of all the wildlife on the coast, bears seem to generate the most fear and concern. Throughout this region, both black and grizzly bears may be encountered. Meeting a bear in the wild can be a terrifying experience or a magical one—it depends on your knowledge and the situation you're in. These magnificent animals need our respect, and a little bit of knowledge goes a long way.

Mountain biking, by its very nature, produces the perfect conditions for meeting bruins. Moving quickly and quietly, cyclists may round a corner and suddenly find themselves face to face with a bear. The most important piece of advice at this point is to prevent this situation from occurring in the first place. Bears, like many other local animals, take advantage of trails just like humans do. If you make a habit of riding very fast down long hills with blind corners, you're asking for trouble. Given the opportunity, bears will always retreat. Attacking is a high-risk response, and the bear would prefer to quietly disappear. By making sure that you let the bear know you are coming—primarily by making lots of noise—you will probably never even see it. It will skulk off to find quieter environs. Sound is your friend, so make lots of it.

It's very easy to tell the difference between black bears and grizzly bears. Ignore the colour, as black bears are often cinnamon-colored or brown, rather than black. Grizzlies have a large hump on the shoulder and a somewhat dished-in face. Black bears lack the hump, and their nose is similar to a dogs, a straight line from the shoulder to the tip of the nose.

If you do meet a bear, try to retreat slowly and avoid making strong eye contact. The idea is to convince the bear that you're not a threat. If the bear begins to move toward you, don't run—you may just trigger an age-old predator-prey reaction. In most cases they will only move a short distance toward you. Continue to move away, but also look for a tree to climb or large trees that you can place between you and the bear. This will also serve to show that you are harmless.

Playing dead is a last resort, and it's not recommended when faced with black bears. More easily frightened than grizzlies, most experts recommend that you fight back rather than play dead. You won't hurt the bear, but you may convince it to move along. In a daytime grizzly encounter, again as a last resort, you can drop down, place your hands behind your neck, and bring your knees up under your chest. This protects your most vulnerable areas. Keep your pack on, as it offers additional protection. This is only a last resort and is no guarantee that you won't be injured. Stay still and wait for the bear to move on. Again, they are generally only attacking out of fear, and this helps them feel safe enough to leave the area.

Another animal of concern in British Columbia is the cougar. These large cats have occasionally attacked people and can cause serious injury. Like bears, they are a majestic animal that requires respect, not fear. Never approach a cougar, and always leave the area if you see one. They are much more shy than bears, so your chance of encountering one is extremely slim.

THE WEATHER

The west coast of British Columbia experiences some of the most moderate weather in Canada. Many of the trails in this book can be ridden throughout the year. In Vancouver, the mean temperature for July is 17°C (63°F) whereas in January, the coldest month, it is only +3°C (37°F). While it does snow in Vancouver and Victoria, it's an uncommon occurrence, often stopping daily life in its tracks. When it does snow, it usually disappears almost as quickly as it arrives.

As you move away from the water's edge and climb in elevation, you begin to see much more snow during the winter months. Driving north from Vancouver toward Whistler, you'll find yourself at skiers' paradise. The season for mountain biking in places like Whistler is limited to the season between April and September.

Whenever you have a range of mountains rising out of an ocean, you also get one other thing—rain. As weather patterns move inland, they are forced to climb over these rocky sentinels. As weather fronts move uphill, the temperature drops, and because cold clouds cannot hold as much moisture as warm clouds, they release it in the form of rain. Be prepared, and make sure you have good rain gear. Vancouver receives 1,117 millimetres (44 inches) of rain annually, whereas Victoria receives 858 mm (33.8 in), Nanaimo gets 1,144.4 mm (45 in), and Hope gets 1,915.7 mm (75.4 in). Most of this rain falls during the winter months, with Vancouver averaging 500 mm (19.7 in) during the three-month period of November to January. This heavy rainfall feeds the dense coastal rain forests through which these rides pass. On one hand, nobody likes a wet ride. On the other hand, no rain also means no rain forest.

Along with this intense amount of moisture comes a high degree of unpredictability. Storms may move in with little or no warning, and you must be on the lookout for changing weather conditions. You don't want to be cresting a mountain pass just as a thunderstorm hits. If you are heading into the high country, be sure to retreat when lightning threatens.

This brings up another issue related to rainfall. Many of the single-tracks in this book pass through habitats that can be severely damaged by heavy use during wet conditions. Please try to reduce your impact by staying off such trails when they are soft and muddy. We all need to do our part to protect the trails we love to ride.

THE PEOPLE

For millennia, the southwest coast of Canada has been a haven for humans, in particular the Coast Salish, the Nootka, and the Kwakiutl. To the north, the Haida and the Tsimshian were dominant. Long before tall ships began to ply the coast in search of the fabled Northwest Passage, these natives hunted and fished throughout the entire area. They collected local berries and built a strong cultural connection to the land and the ocean. Unlike native groups in other areas, they had plentiful food supplies, teeming salmon streams, and an endless supply of nutritious local plants and berries. This freed them from having to move constantly, following herds of wild game. They built stationary communities.

A side benefit of living in such a land of plenty was the freedom of leisure time. They had time to relax, tell the stories of their family history, and record these family histories in fantastic works of art. Totem poles are unique to the west coast. Contrary to popular belief, they were not religious objects, but are better compared to a family crest. Each object (or totem) on the pole represented an individual or a story related to the family's history. Some of these poles were placed at the entrance to a family's longhouse, and this would identify the occupants.

It is believed that as early as 1592, Apostolos Valerianos (Juan de Fuca), a Greek explorer on a Spanish ship, may have been the first to enter the strait that now bears the name Juan de Fuca. This strait separates Vancouver Island from the Olympic Peninsula. Later, as Spain and England competed for title to the vast lands and resources of North America, they began to move farther north. In 1774, Juan Perez of Spain became the first European to trade with the natives of the southwest coast. England's Captain James Cook visited Nootka on the west coast of Vancouver Island in 1778. He traded supplies for sea otter pelts, which fetched a handsome price in China. Suddenly the rush was on, and many ships began to move up the coast looking for furs. In 1792, Captain George Vancouver, who had been with Cook 14 years earlier, returned and circumnavigated Vancouver Island, proving that it was indeed an island.

The following spring, Alexander Mackenzie, an explorer for the Northwest Fur Trading Company, became the first nonnative to cross the Rockies by land — 13 years before the more famous expedition of Lewis and Clark. Finally, in 1846, the Treaty of Washington set the international boundary at the 49th parallel. All of Vancouver Island, though, which extends beyond that boundary, remained in British hands.

A Hudson Bay Company fur trading post, Fort Victoria had been built in 1843, and it quickly became the capital of the territory of British Columbia. Although furs remained the main focus of the Hudson Bay Company, conditions were changing in the eastern political landscape. In 1867, the country of Canada was formed, and it soon began to focus on cementing its claim to the western territories. In an attempt to convince British Columbia to join the confederation, politicians promised to build a railway linking them with the rest of the country. This offer was too good to refuse, and on July 20, 1871, British Columbia officially joined Canada. Fourteen years later, the last spike in the railroad was hammered. The community at its terminus, Vancouver, was destined to become a great metropolis. Today, it's the largest city in British Columbia, with surrounding communities extending up the Fraser River, south to the 49th parallel and north across Burrard Inlet. As the largest port on the Pacific coast, it is the economic hub of the province, although Victoria remains the capital.

HEALTH AND SAFETY

The mountain landscape of British Columbia simply begs to be explored. Towering above the urban landscape of Vancouver, the mountains pull you toward them. For mountain bikers, the mountains have an irresistible magic, something that makes us forgo the security of our home for the call of the wild. However, with this return to the wild country comes some added responsibility. The coastal mountains are dense, wild, and unforgiving. Every year, hikers and cyclists get lost in this sea of wilderness. Even the simple act of following a logging road can get confusing as you pass junction after identical junction. High-quality maps are essential. It's also highly recommended that you carry a compass (and know how to use it). Global Positioning Sensors (GPS) are becoming more popular in the backcountry. These systems, which use satellites to track your position with pinpoint accuracy, are also a great accessory to have along. I also recommend a good bike computer. Many cyclists on the coast avoid them, but the convoluted nature of many trails makes their use critical in correctly selecting junctions on complex routes.

Along with your basic first-aid kit, make sure you pack along a good bike repair kit. You will have to deal with repairs if you ride in British Columbia. The rugged nature of the landscape makes periodic breakdowns guaranteed. A good repair kit can ensure that you still have a functional bike to get back to the road. Mountain bikes allow us to travel farther in a few hours than you could walk in a day, so it is critical that we bring sufficient repair equipment to keep the wheels rolling.

Ticks   Local ticks have been known to carry Lyme disease, so it's critical that you check yourself for ticks after a day's ride. Contrary to popular belief, ticks don't jump on you from surrounding vegetation, nor do they bury themselves under your skin. Ticks climb onto grass and low vegetation and simply grab at unsuspecting hosts as they brush against them. They proceed to climb up your leg to look for a suitable spot to feed. Preferred locations are wet and moist, like armpits, groin areas, and hairlines. When they find just the right spot, they embed their mouth parts—only their mouth parts—under the skin and begin to feed on your blood. Because they tend to wander for several hours before feeding, you should be able to remove most before they attach themselves.

If you are too late and they have begun to feed, removing them is a simple matter of grabbing them firmly and gently pulling until they become detached from your person. Be sure that the mouth parts don't break off and remain in the wound. This can cause severe infection. Once you've checked the wound, a little antiseptic doesn't hurt.

Don't Drink the Water   Even though the trail passes a crystal-clear mountain stream, it's advisable to resist the urge to reach down for a drink of mountain water. As the wilderness of British Columbia becomes increasingly accessible, so does the potential that you will receive more than just water with your drink. The most common water-related problem is giardiasis, also called beaver fever. This unpleasant malady is brought about by a tiny organism, *Giardia lamblia*, that lives in the water; once it enters your body, you will quickly be made aware of its presence. Other than the usual symptoms—gas, nausea, and diarrhea—you may get cramps and other unpleasant symptoms. Treatment includes a strong dose of antibiotics, but the best solution is to simply carry your own water. On an extended trip, you can treat your water with iodine tablets, but be sure to allow suitable time for the tablets to kill the Giardia cysts. This is camelback country, and everywhere you turn you'll see riders with these reservoirs of water strapped to their backs.

RIDE RECOMMENDATIONS FOR SPECIAL INTERESTS

Family

1 Stanley Park Seawall
2 Jericho Beach
23 De Boville Slough/Pitt River Dike
24 Old Poco Trail
26 Hayward Lake Railway Trail
27 Matsqui Trail
29 Vedder Mountain Road Ride
30 Squamish Estuary Trails
48 Valley Trail
51 Brandywine Trail

52 Brandywine–Function Junction
56 Helm Creek Trail
62 Galloping Goose Railroad Trail—
   Victoria to Glen Lake
63 Galloping Goose Railroad Trail—
   Sooke Road Second to Third Junction
64 Galloping Goose Railroad Trail—
   Sooke Road to Terminus
69 Westwood Lake Loop
75 Mount Washington—Discovery Trail

Novice and Beginner

1 Stanley Park Seawall
2 Jericho Beach
3 Pacific Spirit Regional Park—
   Salish/Spanish Loop
4 Pacific Spirit Regional Park—
   Sasamat/Salish Loop
23 De Boville Slough/Pitt River Dike
24 Old Poco Trail
26 Hayward Lake Railway Trail
27 Matsqui Trail
29 Vedder Mountain Road Ride
30 Squamish Estuary Trails
34 Crumpit Woods Network
35 Whistler Mountain Bike Park
42 Whip Me, Snip Me
48 Valley Trail

49 Parkhurst Ghost Town Loop
51 Brandywine Trail
52 Brandywine-Function Junction
55 Riverside Trail
56 Helm Creek Trail
62 Galloping Goose Railroad Trail—
   Victoria to Glen Lake
63 Galloping Goose Railroad Trail—
   Sooke Road Second to Third Junction
64 Galloping Goose Railroad Trail—
   Sooke Road to Terminus
66 Mount Work Park—Hartland Surplus
   Lands
69 Westwood Lake Loop
72 Top Bridge Mountain Bike Park

Intermediate and Advanced (Short Rides)

5 Burnaby Mountain—Cardiac
   Hill/Joe's Trail
6 Burnaby Mountain—Naheeno
   Park/Mel's Trail
7 Burrard Thermal Access
   Plant/Belcarra Trail System
8 Mountain Highway
9 Kirkwood's Seventh Secret and
   Leopard Trails
10 Seymour Demonstration Forest—
   Twin Bridges Loop
15 Fern Trail via BLT
16 Stupid Grouse
17 No Stairs Allowed
19 Golden Ears Park—Alouette
   Mountain/Switchback/Eric Dunning
   Loop

20 Golden Ears Park—Menzies Trail
21 Golden Ears Park—Mike Lake Trail
22 Golden Ears Park—East Canyon Trail
25 Woodland Walk to Coquitlam River
   Loop
33 Powerhouse Plunge Loop
34 Crumpit Woods Network
35 Whistler Mountain Bike Park
36 Cut Yer Bars
38 Shit Happens
39 Section 102
40 Lower Sproat
41 Beaver Pass Trail
43 Danimal North
44 Danimal South
45 Bob's ReBob
46 A River Runs Through It

Intermediate and Advanced (Short Rides) *(continued)*

47 Mel's Dilemma
54 Cheakamus Lake Trail
57 Highline Trail
59 Ancient Cedars
62 Galloping Goose Railroad Trail—
   Victoria to Glen Lake
63 Galloping Goose Railroad Trail—
   Sooke Road Second to Third Junction
64 Galloping Goose Railroad Trail—
   Sooke Road to Terminus
65 Millstream Highlands
66 Mount Work Park—Hartland Surplus
   Lands

67 Ultimate Abyss
68 Humility
70 Westwood Ridge
71 Hammerfest Race Course
72 Top Bridge Mountain Bike Park
73 Monster Mile
74 Mount Washington—Single-Track
75 Mount Washington—Discovery Trail
76 B-21/Boston Main
77 Tomato Creek
78 Bevan Trail
79 Nymph Falls
80 Bear's Bait

Intermediate and Advanced (Long Rides)

11 Cypress Mountain—Old Access Road
12 BLT Trail
18 Golden Ears Park—Alouette
   Mountain Fire Access Road
28 Vedder Mountain Ridge Trail
31 Elfin Lakes (Diamondhead)
32 Ring Creek Rip

37 Kill Me, Thrill Me
50 Microwave Hill
53 Cheakamus Challenge Race Course
58 Black Tusk via Westside Main
60 Birkenhead Loop
61 Blowdown Creek

Extreme

13 Upper Sex Boy
14 Lower Sex Boy
25 Woodland Walk to Coquitlam River
   Loop
53 Cheakamus Challenge Race Course
58 Black Tusk via Westside Main

66 Mount Work Park—Hartland Surplus
   Lands
67 Ultimate Abyss
73 Monster Mile
74 Mount Washington—Single-Track

Loops

3 Pacific Spirit Regional Park—
   Salish/Spanish Loop
4 Pacific Spirit Regional Park—
   Sasamat/Salish Loop
10 Seymour Demonstration Forest—
   Twin Bridges Loop
11 Cypress Mountain—Old Access Road
12 BLT Trail
26 Hayward Lake Railway Trail
28 Vedder Mountain Ridge Trail
29 Vedder Mountain Road Ride
30 Squamish Estuary Trails
32 Ring Creek Rip
36 Cut Yer Bars
45 Bob's ReBob

46 A River Runs Through It
47 Mel's Dilemma
48 Valley Trail
49 Parkhurst Ghost Town Loop
51 Brandywine Trail
59 Ancient Cedars
60 Birkenhead Loop
65 Millstream Highlands
66 Mount Work Park—Hartland Surplus
   Lands
69 Westwood Lake Loop
70 Westwood Ridge
71 Hammerfest Race Course
72 Top Bridge Mountain Bike Park
75 Mount Washington—Discovery Trail

Out-and-Backs

1 Stanley Park Seawall
2 Jericho Beach
8 Mountain Highway
18 Golden Ears Park—Alouette
   Mountain Fire Access Road
23 De Boville Slough/Pitt River Dike
27 Matsqui Trail
31 Elfin Lakes (Diamondhead)

54 Cheakamus Lake Trail
56 Helm Creek Trail
58 Black Tusk via Westside Main
61 Blowdown Creek
64 Galloping Goose Railroad Trail—
   Sooke Road to Terminus
75 Mount Washington—Discovery Trail
76 B-21/Boston Main

Point-to-Points

5 Burnaby Mountain—Cardiac
  Hill/Joe's Trail
6 Burnaby Mountain—Naheeno
  Park/Mel's Trail
9 Kirkwood's Seventh Secret and
  Leopard Trails
13 Upper Sex Boy
14 Lower Sex Boy
15 Fern Trail via BLT
16 Stupid Grouse
17 No Stairs Allowed
19 Golden Ears Park—Alouette
   Mountain/Switchback/Eric Dunning
   Loop
20 Golden Ears Park—Menzies Trail
21 Golden Ears Park—Mike Lake Trail
22 Golden Ears Park—East Canyon Trail
24 Old Poco Trail
25 Woodland Walk to Coquitlam River
   Loop
26 Hayward Lake Railway Trail
27 Matsqui Trail
33 Powerhouse Plunge Loop
37 Kill Me, Thrill Me
38 Shit Happens

39 Section 102
40 Lower Sproat
41 Beaver Pass Trail
42 Whip Me, Snip Me
43 Danimal North
44 Danimal South
50 Microwave Hill
51 Brandywine Trail
52 Brandywine–Function Junction
53 Cheakamus Challenge Race Course
55 Riverside Trail
57 Highline Trail
62 Galloping Goose Railroad Trail—
   Victoria to Glen Lake
63 Galloping Goose Railroad Trail—
   Sooke Road Second to Third Junction
67 Ultimate Abyss
68 Humility
73 Monster Mile
74 Mount Washington—Single-Track
75 Mount Washington—Discovery Trail
77 Tomato Creek
78 Bevan Trail
79 Nymph Falls
80 Bear's Bait

Technical Heaven

7 Burrard Thermal Access
  Plant/Belcarra Trail System
9 Kirkwood's Seventh Secret and
  Leopard Trails
16 Stupid Grouse
25 Woodland Walk to Coquitlam River
   Loop
28 Vedder Mountain Ridge Trail
33 Powerhouse Plunge Loop
36 Cut Yer Bars
37 Kill Me, Thrill Me
38 Shit Happens
39 Section 102

41 Beaver Pass Trail
45 Bob's ReBob
46 A River Runs Through It
47 Mel's Dilemma
53 Cheakamus Challenge Race Course
66 Mount Work Park—Hartland Surplus
   Lands
67 Ultimate Abyss
68 Humility
70 Westwood Ridge
71 Hammerfest Race Course
73 Monster Mile
74 Mount Washington—Single-track

High-Speed Cruising

Wildlife Viewing

Great Scenery

Single-Track

Single-Track (continued)

73 Monster Mile
74 Mount Washington—Single-Track
75 Mount Washington—Discovery Trail
75 Mount Washington—Discovery Trail

77 Tomato Creek
78 Bevan Trail
79 Nymph Falls
80 Bear's Bait

Double-Track

1 Stanley Park Seawall
2 Jericho Beach
3 Pacific Spirit Regional Park—
   Salish/Spanish Loop
4 Pacific Spirit Regional Park—
   Sasamat/Salish Loop
5 Burnaby Mountain—Cardiac
   Hill/Joe's Trail
8 Mountain Highway
10 Seymour Demonstration Forest—
   Twin Bridges Loop
11 Cypress Mountain—Old Access Road
12 BLT Trail
18 Golden Ears Park—Alouette
   Mountain Fire Access Road
23 De Boville Slough/Pitt River Dike
24 Old Poco Trail
26 Hayward Lake Railway Trail
29 Vedder Mountain Road Ride
30 Squamish Estuary Trails
31 Elfin Lakes (Diamondhead)
32 Ring Creek Rip

42 Whip Me, Snip Me
43 Danimal North
44 Danimal South
48 Valley Trail
49 Parkhurst Ghost Town Loop
50 Microwave Hill
51 Brandywine Trail
52 Brandywine–Function Junction
53 Cheakamus Challenge Race Course
56 Helm Creek Trail
58 Black Tusk via Westside Main
61 Blowdown Creek
62 Galloping Goose Railroad Trail—
   Victoria to Glen Lake
63 Galloping Goose Railroad Trail—
   Sooke Road Second to Third Junction
64 Galloping Goose Railroad Trail—
   Sooke Road to Terminus
65 Millstream Highlands
69 Westwood Lake Loop
75 Mount Washington—Discovery Trail
76 B-21/Boston Main

MOUNTAIN BIKE!
Southwestern British Columbia

INTRODUCTION

TRAIL DESCRIPTION OUTLINE

Each trail in this book begins with key information that includes length, configuration, aerobic and technical difficulty, trail conditions, scenery, and special comments. Additional description is contained in 11 individual categories. The following will help you to understand all of the information provided.

Trail name: Trail names are as designated on National Topographic Series (NTS) or other maps, and/or by local custom.

At a Glance Information

Length/configuration: The overall length of a trail is described in kilometres and miles, unless stated otherwise. The configuration is a description of the shape of each trail—whether the trail is a loop, out-and-back (that is, along the same route), figure eight, trapezoid, isosceles triangle, decahedron . . . (just kidding), or if it connects with another trail described in the book. See the Glossary for definitions of *point-to-point* and *combination*.

Aerobic difficulty: This provides a description of the degree of physical exertion required to complete the ride.

Technical difficulty: This provides a description of the technical skill required to pedal a ride. Trails are often described here in terms of being paved, unpaved, sandy, hard-packed, washboarded, two- or four-wheel-drive, single-track or double-track. All terms that might be unfamiliar to the first-time mountain biker are defined in the Glossary.

Note: For both the aerobic and technical difficulty categories, authors were asked to keep in mind the fact that all riders are not equal, and thus to gauge the trail in terms of how the middle-of-the-road rider—someone between the newcomer and Alison Sydor—could handle the route. Comments about the trail's length, condition, and elevation change will also assist you in determining the difficulty of any trail relative to your own abilities.

Scenery: Here you will find a general description of the natural surroundings during the seasons most riders pedal the trail and a suggestion of what is to be found at special times (like great fall foliage or cactus in bloom).

Special comments: Unique elements of the ride are mentioned.

Category Information

General location: This category describes where the trail is located in reference to a nearby town or other landmark.

Elevation change: Unless stated otherwise, the figure provided is the total gain and loss of elevation along the trail. In regions where the elevation variation is not extreme, the route is simply described as flat, rolling, or possessing short steep climbs or descents.

Season: This is the best time of year to pedal the route, taking into account trail conditions (for example, when it will not be muddy), riding comfort (when the weather is too hot, cold, or wet), and local hunting seasons.

Note: Because the exact opening and closing dates of deer, elk, and moose seasons often change from year to year, riders should check with the local fish and wildlife department or call a sporting goods store (or any place that sells hunting licenses) in a nearby town before heading out. Wear bright clothes in fall, and don't wear suede jackets while in the saddle. Hunter's-orange tape on the helmet is also a good idea.

Services: This category is of primary importance in guides for paved-road tourers, but is far less crucial to most mountain bike trail descriptions because there are usually no services whatsoever to be found. Authors have noted when water is available on desert or long mountain routes and have listed the availability of food, lodging, campgrounds, and bike shops. If all these services are present, you will find only the words "All services available in . . ."

Hazards: Special hazards like steep cliffs, great amounts of deadfall, or barbed-wire fences very close to the trail are noted here.

Rescue index: Determining how far one is from help on any particular trail can be difficult due to the backcountry nature of most mountain bike rides. Authors therefore state the proximity of homes or nearby roads where one might hitch a ride, or the likelihood of other bikers being encountered on the trail. Phone numbers of local police departments or hospitals are hardly ever provided because phones are usually not available. If you are able to reach a phone, the local operator will connect you with emergency services.

Land status: This category provides information regarding whether the trail crosses land operated by the Greater Vancouver Regional District (GVRD), British Columbia Provincial Parks Department, or logging companies;

whether it crosses private land whose owner (at the time the author did the research) has allowed mountain bikers right of passage; and so on.

Note: Authors have been extremely careful to offer only those routes that are open to bikers and are legal to ride. However, because land ownership changes over time, and because the land-use controversy created by mountain bikes still has not completely subsided, it is the duty of each cyclist to look for and to heed signs warning against trail use. Don't expect this book to get you off the hook when you're facing some small-town judge for pedaling past a Biking Prohibited sign erected the day before you arrived. Look for these signs, read them, and heed the advice. And remember, there's always another trail.

Maps: The maps in this book have been produced with great care and, in conjunction with the trail-following suggestions, will help you stay on course. But it is strongly suggested that you obtain even more detailed maps of the area you plan to ride.

In Canada, topographic series maps provide the basic guide for route finding. Produced as part of the National Topographic Series (NTS), they are available in a variety of scales. The most useful is the 1:50,000 scale, which provides enough detail to locate most natural features and trails. With these maps, 1 km is represented as 2 cm on the map (1.25 in = 1 mile). This is not as detailed as the maps available in the United States, but for most trails this is sufficient. Unfortunately, many of the maps are badly out of date. Some are based on information from the 1970s. As a minimum, they provide a reliable guide to traditional routes and natural features. They are available from local information centres and map dealers, or can be ordered directly from the Canada Map Office; see "Topographic Maps" below.

Finding the trail: Detailed information on how to reach the trailhead and where to park your car is provided here.

Sources of additional information: Here you will find the address and/or phone number of a bike shop, governmental agency, or other source from which trail information can be obtained.

Notes on the trail: This is where you are guided carefully through any portions of the trail that are particularly difficult to follow. The author also may add information about the route that does not fit easily in the other categories. This category will not be present for those rides where the route is easy to follow.

RIDE CONFIGURATIONS

Combination: This type of route may combine two or more configurations. For example, a point-to-point route may integrate a scenic loop or an out-and-back spur midway through the ride. Likewise, an out-and-back may have a loop at its farthest point (this configuration looks like a cherry with a stem attached;

the stem is the out-and-back, the fruit is the terminus loop). Or a loop route may have multiple out-and-back spurs and/or loops to the side. Mileage for a combination route is for the total distance to complete the ride.

Loop: This route configuration is characterized by riding from the designated trailhead to a distant point, then returning to the trailhead via a different route (or simply continuing on the same in a circle route) without doubling back. You always move forward across new terrain but return to the starting point when finished. Mileage is for the entire loop from the trailhead back to trailhead.

Out-and-back: A ride where you will return on the same trail you pedaled out. While this might sound far more boring than a loop route, many trails look very different when pedaled in the opposite direction.

Point-to-point: A vehicle shuttle (or similar assistance) is required for this type of route, which is ridden from the designated trailhead to a distant location, or endpoint, where the route ends. Total mileage is for the one-way trip from the trailhead to endpoint.

Spur: A road or trail that intersects the main trail you're following.

Ride Configurations contributed by Gregg Bromka

TOPOGRAPHIC MAPS

The maps in this book, when used in conjunction with the route directions present in each chapter, will in most instances be sufficient to get you to the trail and keep you on it. However, you will find superior detail and valuable information in the 1:50,000 scale National Topographic Series (NTS) topographic maps. Recognizing how indispensable these are to bikers and hikers alike, many bike shops and sporting goods stores now carry topos of the local area.

But if you're brand new to mountain biking you might be wondering "What's a topographic map?" In short, these differ from standard "flat" maps in that they indicate not only linear distance, but elevation as well. One glance at a topo will show you the difference, for "contour lines" are spread across the map like dozens of intricate spider webs. Each contour line represents a particular elevation, and at the base of each topo a particular "contour interval" designation is given. Yes, it sounds confusing if you're new to the lingo, but it truly is a simple and wonderfully helpful system. Keep reading.

Let's assume that the 1:50,000 series topo before us says "Contour Interval 20 metres ," that the short trail we'll be pedaling is two centimetres in length on the map, and that it crosses five contour lines from its beginning to end. What do we know? Well, because the linear scale of this series is 1 kilometre to the centimetre (roughly 1 1/4 inches representing 1 mile), we know our trail is approximately 2 kilometres long (2 centimetres × 1 kilometre). But we also know we'll be climbing or descending 100 vertical metres (5 contour lines × 20 metres each) over that distance. And the elevation designations written on occasional contour lines will tell us if we're heading up or down.

The authors of this series warn their readers of upcoming terrain, but only a detailed topo gives you the information you need to pinpoint your position exactly on a map, steer yourself toward optional trails and roads nearby, plus let you know at a glance if you'll be pedaling hard to take them. It's a lot of information for a very low cost. In fact, the only drawback with topos is their size — several feet square. I've tried rolling them into tubes, folding them carefully, even cutting them into blocks and photocopying the pieces. Any of these systems is a pain, but no matter how you pack the maps you'll be happy they're along. And you'll be even happier if you pack a compass as well.

In addition to local bike shops and sporting goods stores, you'll find topos at major universities and some public libraries where you might try photocopying the ones you need to avoid the cost of buying them. But if you want your own and can't find them locally, contact:

Canada Map Office
615 Booth Street
Ottawa, ON K1A OE9
(613) 952-7000

TRAIL ETIQUETTE

Pick up almost any mountain bike magazine these days and you'll find articles and letters to the editor about trail conflict. For example, you'll find hikers' tales of being blindsided by speeding mountain bikers, complaints from mountain bikers about being blamed for trail damage that was really caused by horse or cattle traffic, and cries from bikers about those "kamikaze" riders who through their antics threaten to close even more trails to all of us.

The authors of this series have been very careful to guide you to only those trails that are open to mountain biking (or at least were open at the time of their research), and without exception have warned of the damage done to our sport through injudicious riding. All of us can benefit from glancing over the following International Mountain Bicycling Association (IMBA) Rules of the Trail before saddling up.

1. *Ride on open trails only.* Respect trail and road closures (ask if not sure), avoid possible trespass on private land, obtain permits and authorization as may be required. Federal and state wilderness areas are closed to cycling.

2. *Leave no trace.* Be sensitive to the dirt beneath you. Even on open trails, you should not ride under conditions where you will leave evidence of your passing,

such as on certain soils shortly after rain. Observe the different types of soils and trail construction; practice low-impact cycling. This also means staying on the trail and not creating any new ones. Be sure to pack out at least as much as you pack in.

3. *Control your bicycle!* Inattention for even a second can cause disaster. Excessive speed can maim and threaten people; there is no excuse for it!

4. *Always yield the trail.* Make known your approach well in advance. A friendly greeting (or a bell) is considerate and works well; startling someone may cause loss of trail access. Show your respect when passing others by slowing to a walk or even stopping. Anticipate that other trail users may be around corners or in blind spots.

5. *Never spook animals.* All animals are startled by an unannounced approach, a sudden movement, or a loud noise. This can be dangerous for you, for others, and for the animals. Give animals extra room and time to adjust to you. In passing, use special care and follow the directions of horseback riders (ask if uncertain). Running cattle and disturbing wild animals is a serious offense. Leave gates as you found them, or as marked.

6. *Plan ahead.* Know your equipment, your ability, and the area in which you are riding—and prepare accordingly. Be self-sufficient at all times. Wear a helmet, keep your machine in good condition, and carry necessary supplies for changes in weather or other conditions. A well-executed trip is a satisfaction to you and not a burden or offense to others.

For more information, contact IMBA, P.O. Box 7578, Boulder, CO 80306, USA; (303) 545-9011.

HITTING THE TRAIL

Once again, because this is a "where-to," not a "how-to" guide, the following will be brief. If you're a veteran trail rider these suggestions might serve to remind you of something you've forgotten to pack. If you're a newcomer, they might convince you to think twice before hitting the backcountry unprepared.

Water: I've heard the questions dozens of times. "How much is enough? One bottle? Two? Three?! But think of all that extra weight!" Well, one simple physiological fact should convince you to err on the side of excess when it comes to deciding how much water to pack: a human working hard in 90-degree temperature needs approximately ten quarts of fluids every day. Ten quarts. That's two and a half gallons—12 large water bottles, or 16 small ones. And, with water weighing in at approximately 8 pounds per gallon, a one-day supply comes to a whopping 20 pounds.

In other words, pack along two or three bottles even for short rides. And make sure you can purify the water found along the trail on longer routes. When writing of those routes where this could be of critical importance, each author has provided information on where water can be found near the trail—if it can be found at all. But drink it untreated and you run the risk of disease. (See *Giardia* in the Glossary.)

One sure way to kill the protozoans, bacteria, and viruses in water is to boil it. Right. That's just how you want to spend your time on a bike ride. Besides, who wants to carry a stove or denude the countryside stoking bonfires to boil water?

Luckily, there is a better way. Many riders pack along the inexpensive and only slightly distasteful tetraglycine hydroperiodide tablets (sold under the names Potable Aqua, Globaline, and Coughlan's, among others). Some invest in portable, lightweight purifiers that filter out the crud. Unfortunately, both iodine *and* filtering are now required to be absolutely sure you've killed all the nasties you can't see. Tablets or iodine drops by themselves will knock off the well-known *Giardia*, once called "beaver fever" for its transmission to the water through the feces of infected beavers. One to four weeks after ingestion, *Giardia* will have you bloated, vomiting, shivering with chills, and living in the bathroom. (Though you won't care while you're suffering, beavers are getting a bum rap, for other animals are carriers also.)

But now there's another parasite we must worry about—*Cryptosporidium*. "Crypto" brings on symptoms very similar to *Giardia*, but unlike that fellow protozoan it's equipped with a shell sufficiently strong to protect it against the chemical killers that stop *Giardia* cold. This means we're either back to boiling or on to using a water filter to screen out both *Giardia* and crypto, plus the iodine to knock off viruses. All of which sounds like a time-consuming pain but really isn't. Some water filters come equipped with an iodine chamber, to guarantee full protection. Or you can simply add a pill or drops to the water you've just filtered (if you aren't allergic to iodine, of course). The pleasures of backcountry biking—and the displeasure of getting sick—make this relatively minor effort worth every one of the few minutes involved.

Tools: Ever since my first cross-country tour in 1965 I've been kidded about the number of tools I pack on the trail. And so I will exit entirely from this discussion by providing a list compiled by two mechanic (and mountain biker) friends of mine. After all, since they make their livings fixing bikes, and get their kicks by riding them, who could be a better source?

These two suggest the following as an absolute minimum:

tire levers
spare tube and patch kit
air pump
Allen wrenches (3, 4, 5, and 6 mm)
six-inch crescent (adjustable-end) wrench

small flat-blade screwdriver
chain rivet tool
spoke wrench

But, while they're on the trail, their personal tool pouches contain these additional items:

channel locks (small)
air gauge
tire valve cap (the metal kind, with a valve-stem remover)
baling wire (ten or so inches, for temporary repairs)
duct tape (small roll for temporary repairs or tire boot)
boot material (small piece of old tire or a large tube patch)
spare chain link
rear derailleur pulley
spare nuts and bolts
paper towel and tube of waterless hand cleaner

First-aid kit: My personal kit contains the following, sealed inside double Ziploc bags:

sunscreen
aspirin
butterfly-closure bandages
Band-Aids
gauze compress pads (a half-dozen 4" × 4")
gauze (one roll)
ace bandages or Spenco joint wraps
Benadryl (an antihistamine, in case of allergic reactions)
water purification tablets / water filter (on long rides)
moleskin / Spenco "Second Skin"
hydrogen peroxide, iodine, or Mercurochrome (some kind of antiseptic)
snakebite kit

Final considerations: The authors of this series have done a good job in suggesting that specific items be packed for certain trails—raingear in particular seasons, a hat and gloves for mountain passes, or shades for desert jaunts. Heed their warnings, and think ahead. Good luck.

Dennis Coello

AND NOW, A WORD ABOUT CELLULAR PHONES . . .

Thinking of bringing the Flip-Fone along on your next off-road ride? Before you do, ask yourself the following questions:

- Do I know where I'm going? Do I have an adequate map? Can I use a compass effectively? Do I know the shortest way to civilization if I need to bail out early and find some help?

- If I'm on the trail for longer than planned, am I ready for it? Do I have adequate water? Have I packed something to eat? Will I be warm enough if I'm still out there after dark?

- Am I prepared for possible injuries? Do I have a first-aid kit? Do I know what to do in case of a cut, fracture, snakebite, or heat exhaustion?

- Is my tool kit adequate for likely mechanical problems? Can I fix a flat? Can I untangle a chain? Am I prepared to walk out if the bike is unrideable?

If you answered "yes" to *every* question above, you may pack the phone, but consider a good whistle instead. It's lighter, cheaper, and nearly as effective.

If you answered "no" to *any* of these questions, be aware that your cellular phone does little to reduce your risks in the wilderness. Sure, being able to dial 911 in the farthest corner of the White Mountains sounds like a great idea, but this ain't downtown, friend. If disaster strikes, and your call is routed to some emergency operator in Manchester or Bangor, and it takes awhile to figure out which ranger, sheriff, or search-and-rescue crew to connect you with, and you can't tell the authorities where you are because you're really not sure, and the closest they can come to pinpointing your location is a cellular tower that serves 160 square kilometres of dense woods, and they start searching for you but dusk is only two hours away, and you have no signaling device and your throat is too dry to shout, and meanwhile you can't get the bleeding stopped, you are out of luck. I mean *really* out of luck.

And when the battery goes dead, you're on your own again. Enough said.

Jeff Faust
Author of Mountain Bike! New Hampshire

VANCOUVER AND AREA

Vancouver and its surrounding area represent the most concentrated population centre in British Columbia. Sitting at the mouth of the Fraser River and on the south shore of Burrard Inlet, it is the financial centre of the province. Vancouver first rose to prominence with the building of the Canadian Pacific Railway. During railway construction, a decision was made to extend the western terminus to Burrard Inlet. The tiny community of Granville was rechristened Vancouver and quickly began to grow. Today, the city of Vancouver forms the centre of a region referred to as the Greater Vancouver Regional District (GVRD). This collection of communities is home to 1.7 million people—more than half of the population of the entire province! Adjacent to Vancouver are communities like Burnaby, Richmond, Port Moody, North Vancouver, and West Vancouver. As you radiate further from Vancouver, you visit Delta, Surrey, Port Coquitlam, Langley, Maple Ridge, Matsqui, Abbotsford, Mission, and Chilliwack. These communities hug the mighty Fraser River, the focus of life along this portion of the coast. Down its winding channel, logs are floated to mills and huge booms testify to British Columbia's forest wealth. Along its banks, lush farms give witness to the fertility of the land. The river is the focus of all settlement in this corridor.

The port of Vancouver stretches over more than 276 kilometres (165 miles) of coastline and hosts almost 10,000 ship visits every year, including 3,000 by foreign vessels. It is Canada's largest port and the busiest port on the Pacific coast. Jutting into the mouth of Burrard Inlet, the main entrance to the port, is Stanley Park. This park, named after Lord Stanley (the same Lord Stanley honoured in the name of professional hockey's holy grail, the Stanley Cup), was dedicated in 1887. Its 405 hectares (1,000 acres) has become one of the focal points of Vancouver's urbanites looking for a quick escape from the bustle of city life.

For mountain bikers, the area around Vancouver and the south shore provides a smorgasbord of riding. On one end of the spectrum, you've got the paved roll around the Stanley Park seawall, and the smooth surface of the Jericho Beach ride. The University of British Columbia offers the cultivated double-track of Pacific Spirit Regional Park, and Burnaby Mountain provides more diverse and challenging single-track. There is a little of everything in the area surrounding the city of Vancouver. This is also the corridor where so many riders cut their teeth. They begin rolling along wide city paths and soon graduate to increasingly challenging rides. Many out-of-towners ignore the potential within Vancouver and its environs, opting instead for more adventuresome riding in places like Squamish and Whistler. The rides around Vancouver offer a great diversity in landscape, while also offering challenges for every ability level.

RIDE 1 · Stanley Park Seawall

AT A GLANCE

Length/configuration: 9-km (5.4-mile) loop

Aerobic difficulty: The trail is flat and paved. This is not a trail for those looking to ride fast and hard, as it is quite popular and can be very busy

Technical difficulty: This is a very easy, smooth ride

Scenery: Excellent views of Burrard Inlet and the city of Vancouver

Special comments: Every visitor to Vancouver should take the time to do this ride. It's an excellent way to experience the wonders of Stanley Park and some of the best views of the city

The seawall around Stanley Park offers some of the best views in Vancouver, along with a welcome break from the bustle of city life. The paved loop is approximately 9 km (5.4 miles) in length and has little elevation change. This is one of the most pleasant family rides in the city. As you roll your way around the seawall, take your time. Marvel at the diversity of Vancouver and its many ways of life. After passing the naval base at *HMCS Discovery*, you'll arrive at the nine o'clock gun. Every evening at precisely 9 p.m. this cannon is fired electronically. It was originally cast in England in 1816, and was moved to Stanley Park in 1894. Historically, by firing the cannon at a precise time, mariners were able to set their chronometers, allowing them to navigate more accurately during changing tides. Mistakes in timing could sink a ship, so the cannon was an important part of the marine life in the harbour. Adjacent to the gun, one of the best views of the city is obtained.

As the seawall winds around Brockton Point, views across Burrard Inlet showcase the many products exported from the port of Vancouver. The first lighthouse was built on this site in 1890, while the present structure was completed in 1915. Beyond the lighthouse, the trail winds its way toward the Lion's Gate Bridge. Beyond the bridge, the trail turns south, passes Prospect Point (why not

RIDE 1 · Stanley Park Seawall

stop for an ice cream?), and continues toward the south end of the park and Second Beach. Turn inland and pass Lost Lagoon on the way back to your car.

General location: Within the city of Vancouver.

Elevation change: Virtually none.

Season: Year-round.

Services: All services are available in Vancouver.

Hazards: This paved trail has few obstacles; however, its popularity can be a problem on a busy day. Cyclists compete with in-line skaters, dogs, and walkers. Be courteous of other users and stay on the designated bike trails.

Rescue index: The trail is very popular and help is always close at hand. If passersby are not of sufficient assistance, numerous kiosks and other facilities have staff who can help. From any pay phone, 911 will get an immediate response.

Land status: Vancouver Board of Parks and Recreation.

Maps: The very best map of the trail system in the park is produced by the Vancouver Board of Parks and Recreation. It is freely available at the entrance to the park. The 1:50,000 NTS series topographic map for the park is 92 G/6 North Vancouver, but it is of little use for this ride.

Finding the trail: In Vancouver, follow Georgia Street west until you enter Stanley Park. As the road winds to the right along Coal Harbour, look for a parking lot on the left, near the totem poles. From here, the trail continues along the shoreline and around the perimeter of the park.

Sources of additional information: Contact the Greater Vancouver Parks Department at (604) 224-5739.

Notes on the trail: This trail needs little in the way of description. It is easily followed as it circumnavigates the park. Be careful to watch for signs indicating bike paths as it does leave the main walking path periodically.

RIDE 2 · Jericho Beach

AT A GLANCE

Length/configuration: Up to 20 km (12 miles) out-and-back (10 km [6 miles] each way). Most riders will vary the length based on their interest and a desire to avoid the sections that follow the road

Aerobic difficulty: This trail requires little in the way of fitness. It also has a 15 kmh (9 mph) posted speed limit

Technical difficulty: The trail is very level and has no difficult sections

Scenery: The trail has excellent views across English Bay and the ships anchored offshore

Special comments: This trail is one to reserve for a hot, lazy day. The breeze off the inlet offers a slightly cooler option for scorching summer days. It also gives you the excuse to take a break at the beach

There are days when you feel like bouncing your way down a winding, technical single-track, and then there are days when you just want to get out and roll. The Jericho Beach trail is flat and winding, skirting the south margin of English Bay. It is a 10-km (6-mile) out-and-back trail that follows a combination of good gravel and pavement. It's a perfect ride for families preferring a scenic, seaside roll. Views to the north include English Bay, with many ships anchored offshore. Along the shoreline, eagles, herons, gulls, and crows search for an easy meal at low tide. They can be seen picking at the barnacle-covered rocks or taking advantage of the shallow water to fish. On a hot summer day, the beaches are crowded and noisy. Locals descend on the beaches like the herons to low tide. At this time, the ride can be an obstacle course of joggers, cyclists, and dog walkers. The wind off the water helps to keep the ride a bit cooler in the hot sun.

General location: City of Vancouver.

Elevation change: None.

Season: Year-round.

Services: All services available in Vancouver.

Hazards: The trail has posted speed limits of 15 kmh (9 mph). Because it is very busy on hot summer days, be respectful of other users. Although the cycle trail is kept separate from the walking trail, joggers and dog walkers often ignore this distinction and may be on the cycle path.

You may also find yourself at a nude beach if you don't pay attention. Wreck Beach is a locally well-known nude beach, but the entrance is not designated. The first time I rode this trail, I simply tried to stay on trail and avoid road riding, and found myself at the beach.

Rescue index: You pass numerous concession stands where help can be initiated. In addition, this is a very busy trail, so you are likely to be able to find help at very little notice. The emergency phone number is 911. During the busy summer season, there are also numerous lifeguard stations along the beach, any of which could provide emergency services.

Land status: Greater Vancouver Parks Department.

Maps: You don't really need a map for this trail; however, the City of Vancouver Parks and Recreation Department has a good cyclist's map of Vancouver. The NTS 1:50,000 topographic map is 92 G/6 North Vancouver.

Finding the trail: From downtown Vancouver, take Burrard Street over the Burrard Bridge, and immediately turn right onto Cornwall Avenue. This will wind its way toward Point Grey Road. Near the west end of Point Grey Road, you pass the Royal Vancouver Yacht Club, followed by the Jericho Beach Tennis Club. The road ends at the Jericho Beach parking lot just beyond the tennis club. Park here.

Sources of additional information: Contact Greater Vancouver Parks Department at (604) 224-5739.

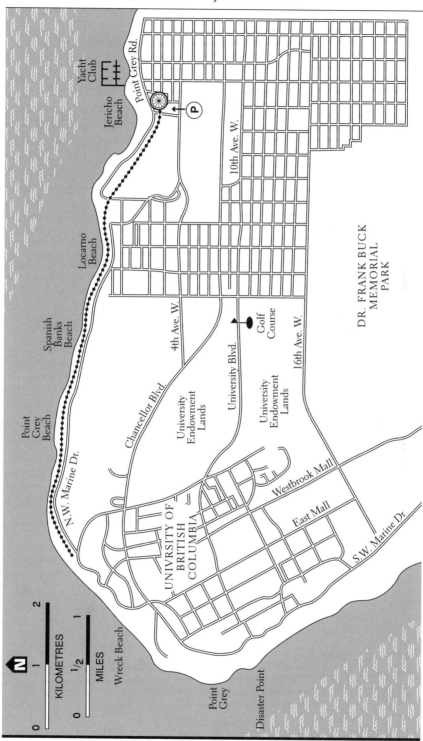

15

Notes on the trail: This ride is flat but exceedingly pleasant. Follow the well-defined path as it winds through Jericho Beach Park along the south shore of English Bay. On certain sections, there are separate trails marked for bicycles. Please obey the signs, although the endless supply of joggers will probably be utilizing the bike trail as well. As you roll along, you'll pass numerous small concession stands and lifeguard stations. At kilometre 3.95 (mile 2.4), the trail joins the road, climbing N.W. Marine Drive, passing the entrance to the University of British Columbia Endowment Lands at kilometre 5.0 (mile 3.0). While you climb the road, stay to the right of the concrete barriers designed to keep cyclists off the actual roadway. Turn around and return to your vehicle at kilometre 10.0 (mile 6.0).

RIDE 3 · Pacific Spirit Regional Park—Salish/Spanish Loop

AT A GLANCE

Length/configuration: 8.5-km (5.1-mile) loop

Aerobic difficulty: The trail drops to the junction with N.W. Marine Drive, then climbs back toward the beginning. It takes a little strength on the climb up

Technical difficulty: This beginner-level trail is well groomed and smooth. A few sections seem to hold water during wet seasons, but they are easily negotiated

Scenery: The trail is largely within forests of vine maple and western red cedar. Beneath the trees, a variety of ferns, salmonberry, Oregon grape, and foam flower bloom

Special comments: Pacific Spirit Regional Park offers cyclists a chance to ride trails within the confines of the city. Although the rides are not technically difficult, they offer mountain bikers a chance to disappear into the woods for a while without having to leave town

This 8.5-km (5.1-mile) loop provides a good cross-section of the trail system provided by the Pacific Spirit Regional Park. It drops from the trailhead to its junction with N.W. Marine Drive and then climbs back toward the trailhead. The trails are wide and smooth, with good surfaces.

Part of the University of British Columbia Endowment Lands, Pacific Spirit Regional Park provides a touch of wilderness in the middle of the metropolis of Vancouver. The trails are all rated as easy and feature wide gradients and well-maintained surfaces. Park managers have been careful to create a network of trails

RIDE 3 · Pacific Spirit Regional Park–
Salish/Spanish Loop

designed to minimize conflicts between users; it is incumbent on mountain bikers to honour these efforts by staying on designated trails and avoiding the temptation to poach some of the narrower single-track hiking trails. Wooden gates have been placed at the entrance to the hiking-only trails to indicate closure to cyclists.

Although largely forested, the trails traverse forests of western red cedar mixed with stands of cottonwood and bigleaf maple. The understory is a mixture of vine maple, salmonberry, and ferns.

General location: University of British Columbia, Vancouver.

Elevation change: From the trailhead at 85 metres (279 feet), the trail drops 45 metres (146 feet) to its junction with N.W. Marine Drive and Spanish Trail. All of this elevation is reclaimed as you ride up Spanish Trail.

Season: Year-round.

Services: All services available in Vancouver.

Hazards: Although the trail surface is consistently smooth and clear, other users are also present on the trails and caution must be advised. Although mountain bikers are allowed to use the trails, increased conflict between hikers and other users could quickly undermine the efforts of local bike clubs in ensuring access. Also, although rideable, there is a set of steps near junction of Salish Trail and N.W. Marine Drive. They are not very difficult, but if you're not expecting them you may find yourself ejected.

Climbing up the Spanish Trail, the route is less clearly marked. There are several unsigned junctions, but if you stay on the main route you'll be fine. Also, sections of this trail hold water after a heavy rainfall. Try not to bypass the puddles, as the trail is beginning to braid from poor riding practices.

Rescue index: The trails are very popular, and help is rarely far away. The route crosses two main roads along with roads at each end of the loop. From any pay phone, 911 will access instant help.

Land status: Greater Vancouver Regional District Parks Department.

Maps: The maps produced by the park are the best guide to the trails of Pacific Spirit Regional Park. They provide details of all the designated trails, along with clearly visible details on which trails are open to cyclists. The NTS 1:50,000 topographic map is 82 G/6 North Vancouver.

Finding the trail: From downtown Vancouver, take Burrard Street, cross the Burrard Bridge, and turn right on 16th Avenue W. Follow the road to the park administration building located on the right side shortly after crossing Blanca Street. Park here. Maps are available in a dispenser just outside the small administration building.

Sources of additional information: Contact the Greater Vancouver Regional District Parks Department at (604) 224-5739.

Notes on the trail: From the trailhead, follow the trail along the left side of the administration building and onto the Cleveland Trail (Trail 2). This will quickly come to a junction with the Heron Trail (Trail 10). Stay straight. At kilometre 0.7 (mile 0.4) the Cleveland Trail ends at a parking lot on University Boulevard. Cross the road, and look for the sign indicating Salish Trail (Trail 21). The trail skirts the university golf course, eventually meeting Spanish Trail (Trail 23) at two junctions, one at kilometre 1.6 (mile 0.96), and the other at kilometre 1.76 (mile 1.06). Stay straight, remaining on the Salish Trail at both junctions. You will later return on the Spanish Trail. Cross Chancellor Boulevard at kilometre 2.16 (mile 1.3) and the trail continues on the opposite side. It follows the road for a short distance, turning into the woods again as you pass a school on the left.

Up to this point the general trend has been a pleasant downhill roll. The final stretch before meeting N.W. Marine Drive has several small wooden steps that are easily negotiated by most riders. Be cautious of them, though, and keep your eyes out for other trail users.

The trail meets N.W. Marine Drive at kilometre 3.0 (mile 1.8). Turn right, and roll down the smooth pavement of N.W. Marine Drive until kilometre 4.5 (mile 2.7), where you will see an information sign to the right. From this sign, take the steep trail up to the right side of the open area, ignoring the lower trail to the left. This is the Spanish Trail (Trail 23). This trail has a confusing sign, making you think it is actually the Admiralty Trail, a hiking-only trail. The true junction with the Admiralty Trail is located partway up the hill. Stay left at the next junction (unmarked).

Cross Chancellor Boulevard at kilometre 5.7 (mile 3.4). On the opposite side of the boulevard, go left, followed by an immediate right onto Spanish Trail. At this point the trail narrows to become a wide single-track. Stay right at an unsigned junction shortly after entering the woods at kilometre 6.0 (mile 3.6), and go left at a second unsigned junction at kilometre 6.1 (mile 3.66). The trail has a tendency to hold water over the next stretch, but try to ride slowly through the puddles rather than riding around. This helps avoid problems with trails widening through erosion.

The junction with the Salish Trail (Trail 21) is at kilometre 6.2 (mile 3.7). Turn left onto the Salish Trail, cross University Boulevard at kilometre 7.56 (mile 4.5), and stay to the left at the junction with Cleveland Trail. Return to the administration building at kilometre 8.5 (mile 5.1).

RIDE 4 · Pacific Spirit Regional Park—Sasamat/Salish Loop

AT A GLANCE

Length/configuration: 7.9-km (4.9-mile) loop

Aerobic difficulty: The trail drops 20 m (66 feet) from the trailhead to the turnaround point at S.W. Marine Drive. It then climbs gradually back to the administration building

Technical difficulty: The trail is very easy with wide gradients and few obstacles

Scenery: Excellent example of western red cedar forests with mixed stands of cottonwood and bigleaf and vine maple

Special comments: This is a fun, fast loop. It can also be ridden in conjunction with the previous trail

The south half of the Pacific Spirit Regional Park offers a wider selection of trails and smoother gradients. This ride circumnavigates the lower section of trails to make a 7.9-km (4.9-mile) loop. It is wide, with little change in elevation, offering a peaceful wooded ride.

South of 16th Avenue, the trail network becomes more convoluted and the options increase. Although this route maximizes the distance on the southern part of the network, one can easily meander for hours without needing to look at signs. When it's time to head home, simply get your bearings at the next sign. You're never far from the road. In every case, it seems that 16th Avenue is the high point of the network, with trails dropping off to the north and south.

General location: University of British Columbia Endowment Lands, Vancouver.

Elevation change: From the trailhead at 85 m (279 feet), the trail drops 20 m (66 feet) to its junction with S.W. Marine Drive. Turn around and the elevation is gradually gained back on the return trip.

Season: Year-round.

Services: Al services available in the city of Vancouver.

Hazards: Although the trails are wide and clear, other users are also wandering along them. Be cautious of others and respect their right to be there. These trails could easily be closed to cyclists if too many conflicts arise.

Rescue index: This trail is very popular, and help is usually close at hand. The adjacent University of British Columbia buildings will also simplify finding help. From any pay phone, dial 911.

Land status: Greater Vancouver Regional District Parks Department.

Maps: The maps produced by the park are the best guide to the trails of Pacific Spirit Regional Park. They provide details of all the designated trails, along with clearly visible details on which trails are open to cyclists.

Finding the trail: From downtown Vancouver, take Burrard Street, cross the Burrard Bridge, and turn right on 16th Avenue W. Follow the road to the park administration building located on the right side shortly after crossing Blanca Street. Park here. Maps are available in a dispenser just outside the small administration building.

Sources of additional information: Contact the Greater Vancouver Regional District Parks Department at (604) 224-5739.

Notes on the trail: From the parking lot at the administration building, turn left onto 16th Avenue and follow the Ivan Mann Walk Trail on the same side as the administration building, crossing at Blanca Street. On the opposite side, turn left onto the Sherry Sakamoto Trail (Trail 30), and then right onto Top Trail (Trail 25) at kilometre 0.7 (mile 0.4). This quickly drops to the signed junction with Sasamat Trail (Trail 22). Turn left at this junction, and then right at an unsigned **T** intersection at kilometre 1.0 (mile 0.6). This will take you around the concrete wall of the drinking water reservoir. This is quickly followed by a left turn at the

RIDE 4 · Pacific Spirit Regional Park–
Sasamat/Salish Loop

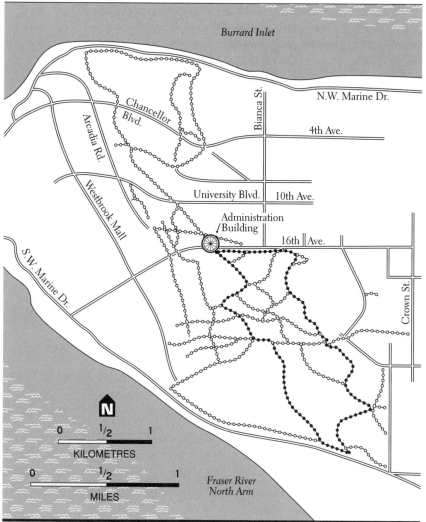

Burrard Inlet

N.W. Marine Dr.

Chancellor Blvd.

Bianca St.

4th Ave.

Arcadia Rd.

Westbrook Mall

University Blvd. | 10th Ave.

Administration
Building

S.W. Marine Dr.

16th || Ave.

Crown St.

N

0   ½   1
KILOMETRES

0   ½   1
MILES

*Fraser River
North Arm*

junction with Huckleberry Trail (Trail 11) at kilometre 1.22 (mile 0.73). Sasamat is a rolling downhill ride, with a slightly rocky double-track. Stay left at all the signed junctions as you descend, until you join Clinton Trail (Trail 3) at kilometre 3.13 (mile 1.9). Turn right onto the smooth surface of Clinton Trail, turning right again at the junction with Salish Trail at kilometre 3.5 (mile 2.2). The trail parallels S.W. Marine Drive for a short distance before turning away from the road and beginning to climb back toward 16th Avenue. The surface is composed of a wide, smooth, gravel carpet, rolling through an understory of cedar and hemlock. The trail borders an ecological reserve where access is prohibited without special permits. At the junction with the Imperial Trail (Trail 12) at kilometre 5.7 (mile 3.5), turn left for a short distance and then right again onto the Salish Trail. Stay straight at the junction with Council Trail (Trail 4), and turn right onto Hemlock Trail (Trail 9) at kilometre 6.5 (mile 4). Shortly after turning onto Hemlock Trail, turn left onto Nature Trail (Trail 15) at kilometre 6.72 (mile 4.2). The character changes as you ride Nature Trail; it begins with a rocky, rooted climb before widening and becoming smoother. Turn left onto Cleveland at kilometre 7.4 (mile 4.6). Stay left on Cleveland at the junction with Salal Trail (Trail 20), and cross 16th Avenue at 7.9 km (mile 4.9). Your car is directly across the street in the Information Centre parking lot.

RIDE 5 · Burnaby Mountain—Cardiac Hill/Joe's Trail

AT A GLANCE

Length/configuration: 3.5-km (2.1-mile) point-to-point trail. Loop options are available using the Gagliardi Way Road or Naheeno Park and Mel's Trails

Aerobic difficulty: This trail climbs 255 m (836 feet) over 3.5 km (2.1 miles), so a strong set of lungs is required

Technical difficulty: The trail is not technically difficult—just challenging due to the constant uphill gradient

Scenery: The trail offers periodic views northwest toward Burrard Inlet and northeast to Port Moody

Special comments: Burnaby Mountain offers a great variety of short rides, making the network perfect for an afternoon diversion. This loop provides an excellent workout, with a great downhill scream along Gagliardi Way back to your car

Cardiac Hill and Joe's Trail takes you up a 3.5-km (2.1-mile) climb along a wide, smooth surface with some views of Burrard Inlet. It ends at the Shell Station on University Drive where you can scream your way back down Gagliardi Way. It is a point-to-point trail; however, the pavement offers a simple, fast coast back to your car.

The rides around Burnaby Mountain, adjacent to Simon Fraser University, provide an ideal proving ground for novices seeking to hone their single-track

RIDE 5 • Burnaby Mountain–Cardiac Hill/Joe's Trail

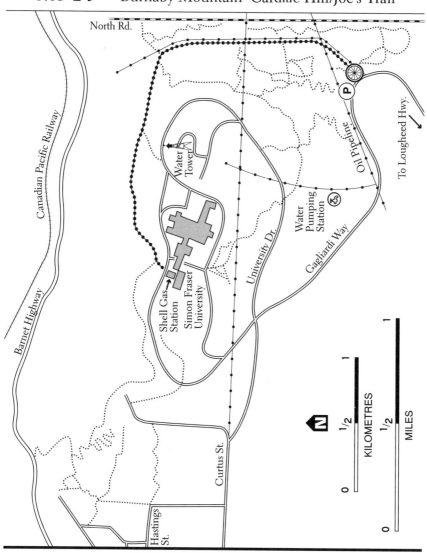

skills. Hard-core riders will enjoy a break from the ruggedness of the north shore. The trail network has been upgraded by the Burnaby Mountain Bike Club, and their efforts have kept this network open and active. Many of the trails run through lands of varying jurisdiction and legal status; only through respect and proper organization will the network continue to be open to riders.

Most of the rides are well groomed, with solid bridge crossings, but they still offer a diversity of difficulty levels. For the beginner, loops like Cardiac Hill and Joe's Trail provide more of a cardiovascular workout than a technical challenge.

Joe's Trail offers a wide, smooth surface. It's a popular trail for riders of all abilities.

From Mel's Trail, several hard-core trails drop down to the right. Each offers numerous sharp drops with steady hits and tight switchbacks.

The network is well contained within the confines of Gagliardi Way, the university, and North Road, leaving the options for exploring wide open. Expert riders can use trails like the Hydroline, Mel's Trail, and Joe's Trail to access a labyrinth of single-track heaven. When you're sufficiently bruised, head downhill to one of the main access points for a quick exit.

General location: Simon Fraser University.

Elevation change: From the trailhead at 75 m (246 feet), climb the power line path to its junction with Cardiac Hill at 185 m (607 feet). Save some energy, because Cardiac Hill climbs toward Joe's Trail, which begins at 290 m (951 feet), and the ride finally finishes at the Shell station at 330 m (1,082 feet)—a total elevation gain of 255 m (836 feet) over 3.5 km (2.1 miles).

Season: Year-round.

Services: All services available in Burnaby.

Hazards: This trail has few hazards in the uphill direction. Lung capacity is the main challenge. If you decide to ride from the Shell station down the trail, the temptation is to ride fast and hard. The trail is popular with hikers, though, and it's critical that mountain bikers respect other users of the trail network. In this direction, the loose rock of the hydroline also offers a few options for unplanned ejection.

Rescue index: Because of its urban setting, help is rarely far away. You'll probably encounter many other riders on this trail, and if need be, you are near the university, where help is close at hand.

Land status: Simon Fraser University land along with a mixture of private and city land.

Maps: The NTS 1:50,000 topographic map for this trail is 92 G/7 Port Coquitlam, although none of the trails are shown on the map. The Burnaby Mountain Bike Club has produced a trail map; it's available on the internet at www.sfu.ca/~michael/bmbc/maps/index.htm, or you can contact the bike club at the number listed below.

Finding the trail: In Burnaby, follow signs to Simon Fraser University. As you cross Lougheed Highway, climb toward the university for approximately 2.4 km (1.4 miles) until the road passes under a power line. There is a pullout to the right just past the power line. Park here. From the pullout, a rough trail heads a few feet into the woods and then turns right, paralleling the road. Take this trail. You can also ride slightly back on the pavement to access the power line trail, but by taking the trail through the woods you cut off some of the climbing.

Sources of additional information: Contact the Burnaby Mountain Bike Club at (604) 936-5172.

Notes on the trail: The trail begins along a bumpy single-track with numerous muddy washouts. From the trailhead, it climbs gradually until its junction with the power line. At this junction, turn left and climb along the power line path toward the junction with Cardiac Hill at kilometre 1.8 (mile 1.06). Ignore all junctions on your way to this point. The trail appears just as the power line crests a small summit. Turn left onto this trail and begin the grind up Cardiac Hill. Stay on this trail as a single-track joins from the left at kilometre 2.02 (mile 1.2). Once you begin climbing Cardiac Hill, the trail enters the dense forest with an understory of devil's club, ferns, bigleaf maple, and alder. After crossing a high-quality wooden bridge, the trail winds around an S-turn with a log breakwall to the right. The junction with Joe's Trail is reached at kilometre 2.2 (mile 1.3). Stay right on Joe's Trail as Cardiac Hill continues to climb steeply up to the left. The upper portion of Cardiac Hill is only recommended for sadistic hill climbers. Joe's Trail offers a more enjoyable ride. Joe's is an excellent double-track trail with a smooth, gravel surface. To the right, views open up toward Burrard Inlet. Several short, steep uphills will get you puffing as you climb Joe's Trail, with a few rutted washouts offering an additional challenge. At kilometre 3.37 (mile 2.02), stay left as the trail climbs toward the Shell station. The trail to the right continues on to Burnaby Mountain Park. You will recognize this junction as the sound of traffic on the road right above you will be very evident. From the Shell station at kilometre 3.5 (mile 2.1), either scream downhill toward your car or make a loop with Naheeno Park and Mel's Trail.

RIDE 6 · Burnaby Mountain—Naheeno Park/Mel's Trail

AT A GLANCE

Length/configuration: 5.1-km (3.05-mile) point-to-point

Aerobic difficulty: The trail gradient is moderate, with little elevation gain

Technical difficulty: This is a challenging, intermediate single-track. It has numerous sudden obstacles and drops

Scenery: The trail stays in the trees and offers little in the way of views

Special comments: This is a great trail for intermediate riders trying to improve their ability to deal with sudden obstacles

VANCOUVER & AREA

This 5.1-km (3.05-mile) point-to-point single-track is a perfect place for intermediate riders looking to hone their single-track skills. Bouncing down a series of sudden obstacles and sharp drops is both challenging and enjoyable. The drops are rideable, and the gradient moderate. Advanced riders will drop off Mel's onto hard-core single-track like Nicole's and Gear Jammer, which bump their way down the lower slopes of Burnaby Mountain. Although not described in detail in this guide, they are two expert single-track chutes.

General location: Burnaby Mountain adjacent to Simon Fraser University.

Elevation change: From the trailhead at 360 m (1,181 feet), the trail drops gradually, finally returning to your vehicle at 75 m (246 feet).

Season: Year-round.

Services: All services available in Burnaby.

Hazards: Although this is an intermediate-level trail, it has a requisite amount of sudden drops, rocks, and root challenges. It does require a rider to be confident with the sudden onset of a drop of up to a metre (3 feet). Also, on the first bridge, several of the boards were broken when I rode it. All the other bridges were in good repair.

Rescue index: Because of its urban setting, help is rarely far away. You'll probably encounter many other riders on this trail; if need be, you're never far from the university, where help is close at hand.

Land status: Simon Fraser University land along with some private and municipal land.

Maps: The NTS 1:50,000 topographic map for this trail is 92 G/7 Port Coquitlam, although none of the trails are shown on the map. The Burnaby

RIDE 6 · Burnaby Mountain–Naheeno Park/Mel's Trail

Mountain Bike Club has produced a trail map. It is available on the Web at www.sfu/ca/~michaec/BMBC/maps/index.htm; or, contact the bike club at the number below.

Finding the trail: From the Trans-Canada Highway, take the Burnaby exit for Gagliardi Way/Caribou Road. Follow Gagliardi Way until you cross under the power lines 2.4 km (1.4 miles) north of the Lougheed Highway. At the pullout along the right side of the road just beyond the power lines, park your car. From here, grind your way up the road toward Simon Fraser University. As you enter the university grounds and begin to pass the buildings, stay to the right at the first junction. After passing a sign indicating CENTRAL STORES FACILITY MANAGE-MENT and several other buildings, you'll pass a small weather station to the right. Immediately beyond this, take the narrow trail to the right. As an alternative, you can create a loop by linking this trail with Cardiac Hill and Joe's Trails.

Sources of additional information: Contact the Burnaby Mountain Bike Club at (604) 936-5172 or by fax at (604) 291-9544.

Notes on the trail: The trail begins on a deeply rutted single-track and drops immediately to meet a large stump that almost blocks the trail. Stay to the right as the trail forks. Just past this stump, the trail makes a sudden drop down a ledge of three logs. The drop is around 1 m (3 feet) and marks the beginning of some moderate technical riding. Obstacles like this abound on the trail, so you have to remain vigilant. Just past this drop, you cross the first of numerous high-quality bridges. One of the boards was broken when I rode the trail, so be cautious of loose woodwork. After the bridge, stay left at a **Y** junction (follow the more well defined trail). This is quickly followed by a **T** intersection. Stay left yet again. You cross another bridge at the 0.25 kilometre (mile 0.15) mark. Go left at the **T** intersection that rapidly follows this bridge, and follow this with a right turn at a junction approximately 100 m (328 feet) further. After a final bridge, the trail drops suddenly to meet East University Drive at approximately the 0.8 kilometre mark (mile 0.5). Cross the road, and Mel's Trail begins with a short, rutted downhill stretch. Stay straight as a trail crosses Mel's Trail at kilometre 1.1 (mile 0.67). After your first bridge on Mel's Trail, the trail climbs sharply to the left while a rough single-track drops to the right. At the top of this hill, stay to the right as another trail joins Mel's. At kilometre 1.4 (mile 0.85), stay left (straight ahead) as a secondary trail drops off to the right. You will know you are on the right trail when you encounter a log pyramid at kilometre 1.53 (mile 0.9). This challenging obstacle will see novices carrying their bikes while more advanced riders will barely even pause. This log pyramid marks the beginning of a stretch of more technical riding.

After crossing two more bridges, watch for a small patch of rotting corduroy trail. Following the next bridge, the trail begins traversing the slopes of Burnaby Mountain with some steep drops down to the right. At kilometre 2.2 (mile 1.3), the trail crosses under a power line. Stay straight on the main trail, ignoring the rough single-track to the left beneath the power line. After a technical descent, the trail meets the lower portion of Cardiac Hill at kilometre 3 (mile 1.8). Stay to the right, and meet the power line at kilometre 3.7 (mile 1.96). Turn right and bounce your way down the power line until kilometre 4.5 (mile 2.68) or the second right-hand turn. Drop down this rutted single-track to get to your car at kilometre 5.1 (mile 3.05).

RIDE 7 · Burrard Thermal Access Plant/Belcarra Trail System

AT A GLANCE

Length/configuration: Network of numerous trails enclosed within a small area

Aerobic difficulty: The trails drop 150 m (492 feet) from the trailhead to the shores of Burrard Inlet. Once you bottom out, there is only one way to go—up

Technical difficulty: Most of the trails in this small area are advanced to expert rides

Scenery: Although largely surrounded by trees, the views of the inlet are quite picturesque

Special comments: Strong riders will want to come back time after time to hone their technical skills

This trail network is more of a state of mind than a single ride. It is a tight, technical network offering riders a diversity of options. It is best suited for strong riders looking to play, rather than mileage mashers looking to cover any significant territory. This is the place to go when you want to practice finessing your way up and down sharp drops and narrow chutes. A huge area of slickrock keeps many riders around for lengthy periods of bounce and balance. Once you've had your fill of the slickrock, there are numerous trails that will offer you a little more challenge. To maximize the distance, I took an outside line following the access road to Ocean Creek, and along Oceanside back to the B.C. Hydro access road. This loop totaled 4.45 km (2.67 miles), so the distance is not great. The challenge is what draws riders to Belcarra time after time.

The great part is that the trails offer quite a variety. Most are rated in the expert category, but patient intermediate riders will find many short stretches on which to test their mettle.

The network is maintained by the Canadian Pacific Trials Association, a group of competitive motorcycle enthusiasts. Unlike the gravel-chewing motocross bikes most of us are familiar with, trials motorcycles keep the rider very close to the ground, allowing them to finesse their bikes up the most improbable lines. To watch these riders make the most difficult route look easy is worth a trip itself.

General location: North shore of Port Moody.

Elevation change: From the trailhead at approximately 150 m (492 feet), the trail system drops right down to the wave-lapped shores of Burrard Inlet at sea

RIDE 7 · Burrard Thermal Access Plant/Belcarra Trail System

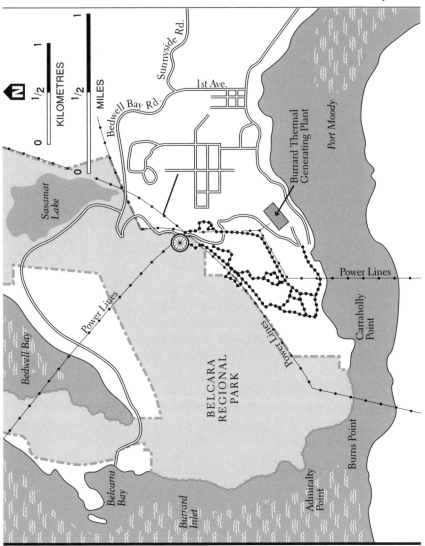

level. Remember, though, because the network begins at the high point, any elevation lost must eventually be regained as you grind your way back toward the trailhead.

Season: Year-round.

Services: All services are available in Port Moody.

Hazards: This trail system has the entire spectrum of narrow drops, chutes, roots, and technical slickrock. Also, be on the lookout for trials motorcycles. They will not hear you coming, so be sure to yield to them.

The Belcarra Trail Network drops down to the shores of Burrard Inlet, offering some pleasant views before the sharp return climb.

Rescue index: The network is quite popular, and other riders, either on mountain bikes or trials motorcycles, are usually nearby.

Land status: The land is owned by the Thermal Access Plant but is maintained by the Canadian Pacific Trials Association.

Maps: The NTS 1:50,000 topographic map for this trail is 92 G/7 Port Coquitlam, but the trails are not indicated on the map in any way. The best way to find your way around is simply to explore. Because the area is bordered on the east by the Thermal Access Plant, on the south and west by Burrard Inlet, and on the north by the power line access roads, you can pretty much explore with impunity.

Finding the trail: In Port Moody, exit Highway 7A, the Lougheed Highway at Ioco (onto Heritage Road). At the second set of lights, turn left, following signs for Belcarra. After 3.1 km (1.9 miles), turn right onto 1st Avenue at the Ioco United Church. It winds to the left and becomes Bedwell Bay Road. After going for 2.7 km (1.6 miles) along this road, you'll pass a sign for Belcarra Park, and Sasamat Lake is soon visible to the right. Turn left at this point and continue as the road makes a sharp switchback to the left. Stay left again at the sign indicating BURRARD THERMAL GENERATING PLANT, After 0.4 km (0.24 miles), you'll reach a spot where there are metal gates on both sides of the road. On the left, a sign indicates CANADIAN PACIFIC TRIALS ASSOCIATION. The gate on the right says NO MOTOR VEHICLES OR DUMPING ALLOWED ON RIGHT OF WAY. This is the trailhead.

Sources of additional information: I was unable to find any additional sources of information.

Notes on the trail: From the parking area, you can cross the road and pass through the gate to warm up on the slickrock. This is a favourite place for trials riders, motorized or not, to show their stuff. Riders new to the area can expect some bruises. When you're ready to move on, you can cross back over the road and follow the fire road as it winds to the southwest. As you ride, Deceptor drops to the left at kilometre 0.36 (mile 0.22). It offers a short access back to the slickrock. Staying on the fire road, the next left junction (kilometre 0.63; mile 0.38) takes you down Herman's Hill, bottoming out along another hydro access road. Taking the next left at kilometre 1.0 (mile 0.6), provides the longest drop as you bounce your way down Ocean Creek. Less technical than either Deceptor or Herman's Hill, Ocean Creek offers a nice technical bounce down toward the inlet and the Oceanside Trail, which runs parallel to the shoreline. The trail joins Oceanside at kilometre 1.82 (mile 1.1). As you ride along the inlet, the forest opens up a little with some vine maple, salal, and Oregon grape. Numerous trails climb up from Oceanside, including Lower Jamtart. If you choose to stay near the water, you can take the wide track of the Crying Climb at kilometre 2.3 (mile 1.4) or continue to the Access Road at kilometre 2.82 (mile 1.7). The climb back up the road brings you back to your vehicle at kilometre 4.45 (mile 2.67). However, if you are not ready to quit yet, take the yellow gate to the left at kilometre 3.57 (mile 2.14) and head back into the network. This road gives you access to the climb up Herman's Hill, but it also allows you a very short, very challenging drop down Stove Top just before you reach the top of the Crying Climb.

THE NORTH SHORE AND
GOLDEN EARS PROVINCIAL PARK

Once you cross the Lion's Gate Bridge toward the north shore, you enter an entirely different world in terms of mountain biking. The communities of North and West Vancouver lie right at the bottom of a rugged landscaped of volcanic peaks and dense rain forest. The north shore, more than any other location, has been responsible for establishing the reputation of west coast mountain biking. It was only a matter of time before the vertical landscape of the coast ranges was cracked by trail builders. Through the work of dedicated trail builders like Ross Kirkwood, the north shore has gained an international reputation.

British Properties, a large land development company, owns a significant portion of the north shore. Periodically, such as on Cypress Mountain, signs indicate this tenure while still allowing access to hikers and mountain bikers. Much of the land owned by British Properties is slated for development over the next few years, so enjoy these rides while you still can.

Cypress Provincial Park is one of the battle fronts of west coast riding. As the area has increased in popularity, so has the tendency to expand networks, add feeder trails, and push the envelope in terms of riding terrain. Much of the area has recently been threatened with closure due to rapid trail expansion and poor maintenance of existing trails. Organizations like the North Shore Mountain Biking Association are working with local land owners to improve trail maintenance and reduce impact on existing trails. They are also trying to impress on cyclists the importance of resisting the temptation to build new trails; rather, they focus on improving existing rides.

Grouse Mountain, with its winding Mountain Highway, forms the primary access for lots of expert verticals. Dropping to the left and right of this wide doubletrack, they include the renowned Seventh Secret and numerous other trails. Like much of the north shore, some of these trails are of questionable legality, particularly those that drop down to the left, toward the Baden Powell Trail. Be sure to check with local authorities and bike shops before riding these trails.

RIDE 8 · Mountain Highway

AT A GLANCE

Length/configuration: 18.8-km (11.28-mile) out-and-back (9.4 km [5.64 miles]) each way)

Aerobic difficulty: The trail climbs moderately but steadily for a total of 560 m (1,837 feet)

Technical difficulty: The trail is a wide double-track for its entire length

Scenery: Excellent views toward the city of Vancouver and the Lion's Gate Bridge

Special comments: Although often used as access to some radical single-track, this is a pleasant ride with some great views near the summit

Mountain Highway takes you 9.4 kilometres (5.64 miles) up a winding double-track ending at the boundary to the Grouse Mountain ski area. Along the climb, as you wind your way through seven switchbacks, a number of single-track runs drop away to the right and left (see Seventh Secret Trail). Once you pass the final switchback, the views begin to open up, with some exquisite views toward Burrard Inlet and Lion's Gate Bridge. Although many riders use this trail strictly as an access to single-track descents, it is a great ride in its own right. It offers beginner and intermediate riders a great workout and rewarding views near the turnaround point. On the way down, you get your own brand of downhill—but avoid going too fast or you'll risk smearing riders grinding their way uphill. This fast downhill stretch brings you back to your car at kilometre 18.8 (mile 11.28).

General location: This trail is located in North Vancouver at the north end of the Mountain Highway.

Elevation change: The trail maintains a constant uphill gradient. From the trailhead at elevation 320 metres (1,050 feet), it climbs via a series of seven switchbacks to a maximum elevation of 880 m (2,886 feet) before a NO TRESPASSING sign beckons you back toward the trailhead.

Season: March through November, varying with snowfall.

Services: All services are available in North Vancouver.

Hazards: As this is a wide access road, there are few hazards. Although the road is gated, occasionally there are vehicles that have access to the road. It would not be advisable to scream blindly down the road. Watch for loose rocks as you grind your way up.

RIDE 8 · Mountain Highway

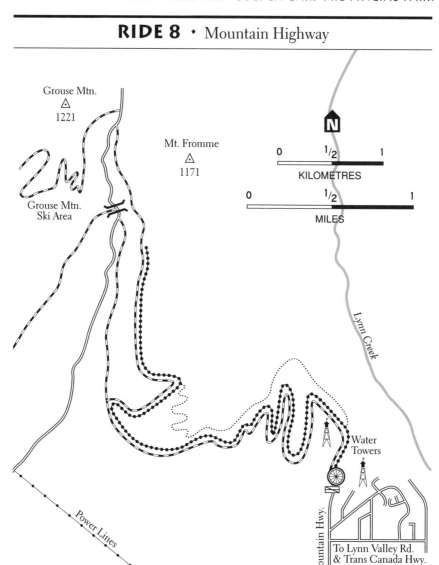

Rescue index: The popularity of this trail helps to make rescue easier than many of the other trails in the book. The grind up the hill historically has formed the main access to a diverse series of radical single-track rides. However, with increasing enforcement on these marginally legal trails, the number of riders may drop as cyclists begin to move to other, more stable networks. Most of the trails drop away to the left between the fifth and sixth switchbacks. Beyond the seventh, you will see fewer riders.

From the summit of the Mountain Highway trail, you are rewarded with unobstructed views of Vancouver and Burrard Inlet.

Land status: The status is a mixture of private land and city park. It is currently under much dispute as mountain biking is becoming more organized. With riders being charged for riding on illegal trails, local bike clubs are trying to work with the Parks Department to ensure access and reduce the impact on existing trail systems.

Maps: The NTS 1:50,000 topographic map is 82 G/6 North Vancouver.

Finding the trail: If you are coming from Vancouver on the Trans-Canada Highway, take Exit 19/Lynn Valley Road and follow it to Mountain Highway. Turn left onto Mountain Highway. You can also exit the Trans-Canada Highway onto Mountain Highway directly at Exit 21. Follow this road until it ends at the junction of Mountain Highway and Borthwick Road. You'll need to find somewhere to park along Mountain Highway as no parking area is provided.

Sources of additional information: Contact the North Shore Mountain Biking Association by email to lau@wedge.com.

Notes on the trail: From the trailhead, pass the yellow gate and begin the climb up the wide double-track of the access road. The gradient is moderately uphill all the way, beginning right from the trailhead. Although there is a sign prohibiting mountain biking, this is one of the most popular rides in the area. As long as you stay on the main road, you need not worry about jurisdiction or trespassing. Continue past two large water tanks at the 0.5-km (0.3-mile) point, and round the first switchback to the left at kilometre 1 (mile 0.6). Be sure to count the switchbacks as you climb. Many of the single-track trails leaving the access road use the number of switchbacks as reference points. The trail turns sharply to the right at the 1.7-km (1.02-mile) mark. Switchback three turns left at 2.6 km (1.5 miles), switchback four counters at 3 km (1.8 miles), and number five cranks left at 3.4 km (2.04 miles). This fifth switchback is an important reference because the most well-known single-track trails of this network drop down to the left between the fifth and sixth switchbacks. Make sure you check on the current status of these trails before dropping down. They all finish on the Baden Powell trail, which is closed to bikes, and you will not want to risk a citation.

This next stretch has numerous trails dropping sharply to the left and at kilometre 4.6 (mile 2.75), until the right turn of switchback six leaves most of them behind at kilometre 5.35 (mile 3.2). At this point you've climbed 380 m (1,246 feet), and the gradient actually increases toward switchback seven at kilometre 6.3 (mile 3.8) and elevation 780 m (2,558 feet). Beyond this final switchback, the trail climbs more gradually, eventually moving out of the trees to provide an excellent view toward Burrard Inlet and the city of Vancouver. Turn around at the NO TRESPASSING sign at kilometre 9.4 (mile 5.64) and elevation 880 m (2,886 feet). Return to your car at kilometre 18.8 (mile 11.28).

RIDE 9 · Kirkwood's Seventh Secret and Leopard Trails

AT A GLANCE

Length/configuration: 1.3 km (0.78 mile) point-to-point trail. However, you'll need to climb 6.2 km (3.72 miles) along the Grouse Mountain Access Road to reach the trailhead

Aerobic difficulty: The most challenging part of this trail is getting to it. The climb up the access road involves a climb of 460 m (1,509 feet)

Technical difficulty: This is an extreme trail for solid expert riders only

Scenery: Forget about it. On this trail your only focus is keeping your wheels down and your body upright. It is dark and foreboding, but magic for those able to do it

Special comments: This ride has been badly damaged over the years by riders locking their brakes and increasing the level of erosion. This ride is only for very accomplished, technical riders

Okay, so you've had a bad week. Your boss is on your back and your car just broke down. There's nothing like a solid beating from a hard trail to make you forget these trivialities, and this is just the trail to provide it. Short but sweet, it offers a cornucopia of drops, rocks, roots, and bruises. Although it is a point-to-point trail, it can only be accessed by creating a loop with Ride 8, the Mountain Highway Trail. The actual length varies depending on which junctions you choose and whether or not you link this trail with others that seem to appear spontaneously out of the undergrowth. The basic ride includes a 6.2-km (3.72-mile) climb up the Mountain Highway, followed by 1.3 km (0.78 mile) of challenge along Seventh Secret and Leopard Trails. This leaves you with 3.4 km (2.04 mile) of downhill runout back to the car.

Ross Kirkwood is the best-known name in mountain biking along the west coast. Through his efforts, many new trails have been created and all riders owe him a debt of gratitude.

General location: North Vancouver along Mountain Highway.

Elevation change: From the trailhead along the Grouse Mountain Access Road, the trail drops 120 m (394 feet) in just 0.6 km (0.36 mile). The lower section, along the Leopard Trail, remains fairly level but extremely challenging.

Season: This ride is possible over most of the year, but it should be avoided during wet weather. The addition of rain to this trail increases the erosion and counteracts the actions of local cycle clubs that have been working on repairing many sections of the trail.

Services: All services are available in North Vancouver.

Hazards: This trail set the standard for radical riding when it was first constructed. Its main attraction is that it provides the entire spectrum of obstacles, from sheer root drops to heavy ruts to slickrock slides. Don't even think of heading out on this trail unless you are a solid, expert rider. One of the consequences of this ride's popularity has been the increasing problem of novices with locked brakes causing erosion. There are other trails on which to hone your skills before attempting this ride.

Rescue index: This is a very famous ride, so it sees a fair bit of traffic. If an accident occurs and you don't find a rider along the Seventh Secret Trail, head out to the main access road, where you will probably encounter other riders. In a worst-case scenario, ride the road down to the trailhead. This is a residential area, so you will be able to get help easily.

Land status: The status is a mixture of private land and city park. It is currently under much dispute as mountain biking is becoming more organized. With riders being charged for illegal rides, local bike clubs are trying to work with the Parks Department to ensure access and reduce the impact on the existing trail systems.

Maps: The NTS 1:50,000 topographic map is 82 G/6 North Vancouver.

RIDE 9 · Kirkwood's Seventh and Leopard Trails

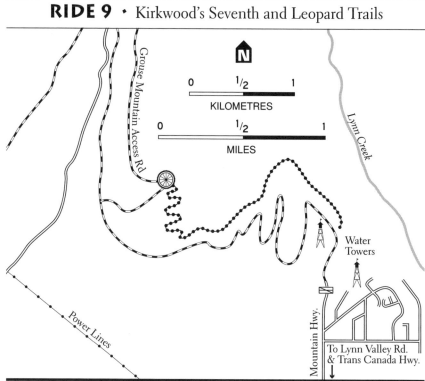

Finding the trail: If you are coming from Vancouver on the Trans-Canada Highway, take Exit 19/Lynn Valley Road and follow it to Mountain Highway. Turn left onto Mountain Highway. You can also exit the Trans-Canada Highway onto Mountain Highway directly at Exit 21. Follow this road until it ends at the junction of Mountain Highway and Borthwick Road. You'll need to find somewhere to park along Mountain Highway as no parking area is provided. Grind your way up the access road for 6.2 km (3.72 miles) until you see a trail drop off to the right just before the seventh switchback. Take this trail.

Sources of additional information: I was unable to find any additional sources of information.

Notes on the trail: From the trailhead at kilometre 6.2 (mile 3.72) of the Grouse Mountain Access Road, the trail drops down immediately, and the smooth of the access road is traded in for roots, rocks, sheer vertical drops, and numerous other obstacles for which this trail has become famous (or infamous, depending on your skill level). Although it is short, it will test your skills like few other trails. After dropping 120 m (394 feet) in only 0.6 km (0.36 mile), the trail makes a sharp switchback to the left and parallels the road for a short distance. At this point, it becomes the Leopard Trail, which stays above the road and exits at the fifth switchback at approximately kilometre 1.3 (mile 0.78).

Kirkwood's Seventh Secret is infamous for sharp root drops and extreme obstacles.

If you're not completely beaten at this point, rather than taking the road, stay on the trail as it becomes the Crinkim Crankum Trail. Follow it to Cedar Trail and finish with Roadside Attraction. This final ride spits you out onto the access road again at the water towers. This series of trails adds an additional 2.8 km (1.7 miles) to the ride, and drops you 200 m (656 feet) before rejoining the road. The trails are difficult to distinguish at times and should only be attempted by riders familiar with the area. The knowledge that the road is always to your right helps lend an element of safety to the route finding.

RIDE 10 · Seymour Demonstration Forest—Twin Bridges Loop

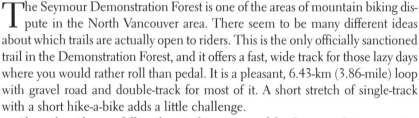

AT A GLANCE

Length/configuration: 6.43-km (3.86-mile) loop

Aerobic difficulty: Quite easy with little change in elevation

Technical difficulty: With the exception of the short hike-a-bike up the Baden Powell Trail, the ride is on wide access road and double-track

Scenery: The views along the Seymour River are quite pleasant

Special comments: This is an easy ride, but it has a short hike-a-bike section adding some technical challenge

The Seymour Demonstration Forest is one of the areas of mountain biking dispute in the North Vancouver area. There seem to be many different ideas about which trails are actually open to riders. This is the only officially sanctioned trail in the Demonstration Forest, and it offers a fast, wide track for those lazy days where you would rather roll than pedal. It is a pleasant, 6.43-km (3.86-mile) loop with gravel road and double-track for most of it. A short stretch of single-track with a short hike-a-bike adds a little challenge.

Along the ride, you follow the winding course of the Seymour River, creating a wide circle around this critical watershed.

General location: In the city of North Vancouver at the north end of Riverside Drive.

Elevation change: This trail has moderate elevation change. From the trailhead on Riverside Drive, at 60 m (197 feet), the trail drops briefly to the river and then climbs sharply to join Lillooet Road at approximately 160 m (525 ft). It then climbs gradually to the Seymour Demonstration Forest Headquarters at approximately 200 m (656 feet). The rest of the trail is in the downhill direction back to your car.

Season: Year-round.

Services: All services are available in North Vancouver.

Hazards: The only difficult section of this ride is the short stretch from the trailhead to the junction with Lillooet Road. After dropping to the river, you have a short uphill hike-a-bike and then rough single-track until you meet the road. From this point on it is wide, smooth fire road and double-track.

RIDE 10 · Seymour Demonstration Forest/Twin Bridges Loop

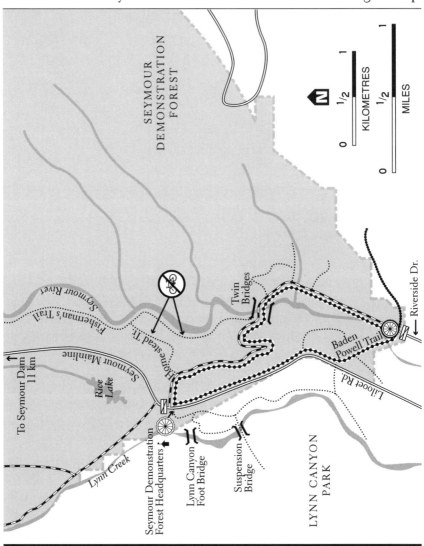

Rescue index: In case of emergency, you can call 911, or for the Royal Canadian Mounted Police call (604) 988-4111. The GVRD can be contacted in an emergency during office hours (8 a.m. to 4 p.m. Monday through Friday) at (604) 432-6286. After hours, the GVRD emergency number is (604) 444-8401.

Land status: Seymour Demonstration Forest managed by the Greater Vancouver Regional District.

Maps: The NTS 1:50,000 topographic map for this route is 92 G/6 North Vancouver; however, the route is not indicated on this map. The best map is the one produced by the GVRD on their Seymour Demonstration Forest brochure. It can be ordered from them directly.

Finding the trail: Take the Trans-Canada Highway into North Vancouver. Immediately after crossing over the Second Narrows bridge, take Exit 23B/Dollarton Highway. Follow this to Riverside Drive (the second left), and then stay on Riverside Drive until it ends at the trailhead. Park along Riverside Drive.

Sources of additional information: You can call the Greater Vancouver Regional District (GVRD) at (604) 432-6286, or check their Web site at www.gvrd.bc.ca. Their mailing address is:

GVRD
4330 Kingsway
Burnaby, B.C. V5H 4G8

Notes on the trail: From the trailhead along Riverside Drive, a trail drops down immediately to the left toward the Seymour River. After dropping to the river, you'll need to hike your bike up a very steep set of stairs, after which a rough single-track bounces you toward Lillooet Road. Turn right on Lillooet Road and follow this to the Seymour Demonstration Forest Headquarters. You should arrive at the headquarters at approximately kilometre 2.6 (mile 1.56). As you pass the headquarters, cross the Seymour Mainline Road and begin the Twin Bridges Trail. At kilometre 2.68 (mile 1.6), stay straight at the junction with Homestead Trail. Although some books recommend Homestead as a mountain bike ride, it is officially closed to all cyclists.

This wide double-track drops from the administration complex to the bridge at kilometre 2.77 (mile 1.66). The twin bridges are actually a single bridge today, with an old cable car to one side. The trail continues on the other side of the bridge. Continue on this trail, ignoring any junctions until you meet your car again at Riverside Drive at kilometre 6.43 (mile 3.86).

RIDE 11 · Cypress Mountain—Old Access Road

This 21.3-km (13.2-mile) loop entails a long grind up the paved access road to Cypress Mountain Ski Hill, followed by a wonderful double-track descent down the old access road. The climb up the paved road offers superb views of Vancouver's harbour and the city of Vancouver. Once you leave the pavement and begin the sharp descent down the double-track of the old access road, you'll enjoy a fast, bouncing drop with few breaks in the gradient. It's a great run with some technical, loose rock sections.

General location: City of West Vancouver.

Elevation change: From the trailhead at 220 m (722 feet), climb 700 m (2,296 feet) up Cypress Bowl Road to the start of the old access road at an elevation of 920 m (3,018 feet). From this point, it's all downhill.

Season: You'll want to ride this trail when it is dry. Because the trail ends at Cypress Bowl Ski Hill, you definitely want to avoid winter. It is usually rideable from March to November.

Services: All services are available in West Vancouver.

Hazards: Although this former access road is a double-track, it has deteriorated over the years. At kilometre 15.3 (mile 9.5), a culvert has partially eroded, allowing quick ejections if you're not careful. Also, the trail has numerous stretches of loose boulders, along with some rutting and loose surfaces.

Rescue index: In an emergency call 911. However, the trail is not overly busy, so you may need to return to the trailhead before you encounter anyone to help you. Be prepared to take care of yourself.

Land status: The lower section of the trail falls within British Properties land and is subject to future development. Signs at the trailhead indicate that you

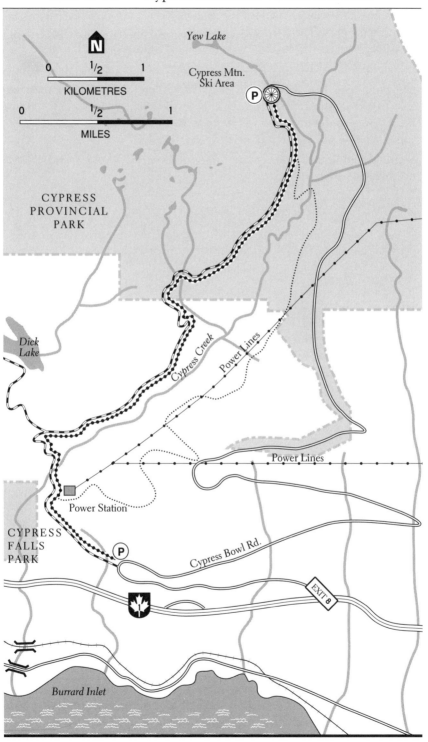

must be willing to accept all responsibility while traversing their land. The upper section is within Cypress Provincial Park.

Maps: The NTS 1:50,000 topographic map for this area is 92 G/6 North Vancouver.

Finding the trail: Take the Trans-Canada Highway into West Vancouver to Exit 8/Cypress Bowl Road Ski Area. Turn right and follow this road until it makes the first sharp switchback. At this corner, a road will radiate out to the left; park near the entrance to this road. You will begin by riding up the access road to Cypress Mountain and will later return on this road.

Sources of additional information: You can contact Cypress Provincial Park at the following address:

B.C. Parks
District Manager
1610 Mount Seymour Rd.
North Vancouver, B.C., V7G-1L3
(604) 924-2200
fax (604) 924-2244

Notes on the trail: The Cypress Bowl Road climbs unrelentingly toward the summit at 920 m (3,018 feet). Along the way, sign posts let you know how close you are to reaching this elevation goal. At kilometre 11.1 (mile 6.7) stay left as a gravel road forks off to the right. Shortly after this junction, you will reach the ski hill. Follow the road around the day lodge and toward the far end of the parking lot. The trailhead is at kilometre 13.5 (mile 8.4) and is indicated by a yellow gate. Pass through the gate, and begin dropping right away on a good, wide, loose gravel road. Shortly after two sharp switchbacks, stay right at the unsigned junction with the BLT Trail at kilometre 14.1 (mile 8.74). This is the only junction on the upper part of the trail. The trail narrows to a rough double-track after this junction. Slow down at kilometre 15 (mile 9.3), as a culvert crossing the trail has partially eroded out at the 15.3 km (mile 9.5) point and could easily send you over your handlebars if you are not prepared. Beyond this point, the scenery opens up for a short distance, offering clear views across the valley toward some of the maintenance buildings along the BLT Trail. After crossing a small creek at kilometre 16.3 (mile 10.1), the trail begins to drop in earnest. The drop remains steep for most of the remainder of the ride. The surface is uneven, with loose boulders and rocks, but is generally good riding. Two sharp switchbacks at kilometre 17.1 (mile 10.6) take you into the trees, and the remainder of the trail offers little in terms of panoramic views.

The trail widens and comes out on the corner of a sharp switchback on a gravel access road for British Properties at kilometre 19.35 (mile 12.0). Stay to the left at this junction and left again at a junction at kilometre 19.9 (mile 12.3). Cross over Cypress Creek on a high-quality bridge and through a gate at kilometre 20.1 (mile 12.5). Follow this road past several buildings, under the hydro wires, returning to your vehicle at kilometre 21.3 (mile 13.2).

RIDE 12 · BLT Trail

AT A GLANCE

Length/configuration: 23.15-km (13.89-mile) loop using Cypress Bowl Road

Aerobic difficulty: The ride includes a very challenging uphill climb of 700 m (2,296 feet) over 13.5 km (8.4 miles)

Technical difficulty: Once you begin the downhill stretch, it is fast and technical with lots of loose rock sections

Scenery: There are some excellent views toward the ocean

Special comments: This technical downhill double-track is a popular access for much of the local Cypress Mountain single-track

BLT Trail is a great loop combining a slow grind up the Cypress Bowl Road followed by a winding, technical double-track that brings you back to your car in 23.15 km (13.89 miles). Along the way, there are some excellent views south, toward the ocean. Although there are lots of junctions along the way, most of them are fairly obvious. Be sure to bring a topographic map with you in case you get disoriented.

This ride also forms the main access trail for much of the Cypress Mountain single-track, including Rides 13 through 15 in this book. This makes it popular with riders in both the uphill and downhill direction.

General location: In the city of West Vancouver.

Elevation change: From the trailhead at 220 m (722 feet), climb 700 m (2,296 feet) up Cypress Bowl Road to the start of the old access road at an elevation of 920 m (3,018 feet). From this point, it's all downhill.

Season: You'll want to ride this trail when it is dry. Because the trail ends at Cypress Bowl Ski Hill, you definitely want to avoid winter. It is usually rideable from March to November.

Services: All services are available in West Vancouver.

Hazards: Although this is a double-track former access road, it has deteriorated over the years. The trail has numerous stretches of loose boulders and some rutting and loose surfaces.

Rescue index: In an emergency call 911. The trail is not overly busy, so you may need to return to the trailhead before you encounter anyone to help you. Be prepared to take care of yourself.

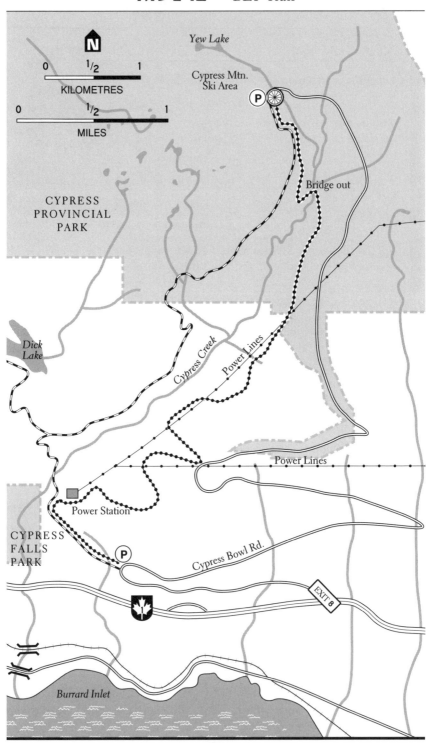

The author grinds his way up the loose surface of the BLT Trail.

Land status: The lower section of the trail falls within British Properties land and is subject to future development. Signs at the trailhead indicate that you must be willing to accept all responsibility while traversing their land. The upper section is within Cypress Provincial Park.

Maps: The NTS 1:50,000 topographic map for this area is 92 G/6 North Vancouver.

Finding the trail: Take the Trans-Canada Highway into West Vancouver to Exit 8/Cypress Bowl Road Ski Area. Turn right and follow this road until it makes the first sharp switchback. At this corner, a road will radiate out to the left. Park near the entrance to this road. You will begin by riding up the access road to Cypress Mountain and will later return on this road.

Sources of additional information: You can contact Cypress Provincial Park at the following address:

B.C. Parks
District Manager
1610 Mount Seymour Rd.
North Vancouver, B.C., V7G-1L3
(604) 924-2200
(604) 924-2244 fax

The bridge over Cypress Creek has washed out on BLT Trail, requiring a narrow board balance or a shallow ford.

Notes on the trail: The Cypress Bowl Road climbs unrelentingly toward the summit at 920 m (3,018 feet). Along the way, signposts let you know how far you are toward reaching this elevation goal. At kilometre 11.1 (mile 6.7) stay left as a gravel road forks off to the right. Shortly after this junction, you will reach the ski hill. Follow the road around the day lodge and toward the far end of the parking lot. The trailhead is at kilometre 13.5 (mile 8.4) and is indicated by a yellow gate. Pass through the gate, and begin dropping right away on a good, wide, loose gravel road. Shortly after two sharp switchbacks, stay left at the unsigned junction with the BLT Trail at kilometre 14.1 (mile 8.74).

BLT immediately begins dropping along loose, wide double-track. Stay straight as a rough trail climbs up to the right at kilometre 14.34 (mile 8.6), and be cautious as you bounce over several loose rock sections on the next stretch. The trail drops down to the river at 15.1 km (mile 9.05), but the bridge has been washed away. Riders have created a makeshift crossing on some boards and logs, but it may be very wobbly. From the ford, you climb up slightly, and then the trail descends, eventually reaching the power lines. While the trail does continue beyond the power lines, you'll see a gate that just takes you to the maintenance yard. Rather than pass the gate, go right and drop down a very steep hill that will turn left (away from the power lines), then make a wide circle, eventually returning you to the wires. Pass under them again, drop down for a short distance, and then veer left, crossing the lines again. You get a brief view of the ocean, but the lower part is obscured by Scotch broom, alder, and salmonberry.

At kilometre 19.08 (mile 11.45), after going through a large gate, take a hard right down a steep, rocky descent. While another trail continues straight, it merely interesects Cypress Bowl Road in a very short distance. The BLT trail winds under the wires, and at kilometre 20.05 (mile 12.03), the main transmission line joins a second set of wires coming in from the left (east). Along the next stretch, several single-tracks branch off to the right and left. Ignore them and stay on the wide double-track. You join the power lines again at kilometre 21.35 (mile 12.8) and soon wind your way around the left side of the power station before joining pavement at a yellow gate at kilometre 21.85 (mile 13.11). Go left on the pavement and follow this to your vehicle at kilometre 23.15 (mile 13.89).

RIDE 13 · Upper Sex Boy

AT A GLANCE

Length/configuration: 0.76-km (0.46-mile) point-to-point from trailhead to junction with Fern Trail. If you link Upper and Lower Sex Boy you can make a 1.72-km (1.03-mile) point-to-point ride. Most riders will use the BLT Trail as an access to make a 5-km (3-mile) loop

Aerobic difficulty: The climb to the trailhead is uphill all the way, but once you begin the main descent of Upper Sex Boy, it becomes a technical rather than an aerobic challenge

Technical difficulty: Extremely difficult with sharp drops and dangerous obstacles. For expert riders only

Scenery: This trail drops fast and hard. It has few views, and you have no time to enjoy them

Special comments: This is a trail for very technically proficient riders looking for a steep downhill with lots of vertical drops

Upper Sex Boy is one of these trails for days when you simply want to challenge the elements. It is short, unrelenting, and dark, but it may be just the prescription for getting rid of frustration. It is very short—only 0.76 km point-to-point for the upper section—but most riders will link up with Lower Sex Boy to add another 0.96 km (0.57 mile) to the ride. This is a point-to-point ride, so you will need to either shuttle vehicles or use BLT Trail as an access for a 5-km (3-mile) loop.

Expect sharp drops, root jumps, and endless technical challenges. In less

RIDE 13 • Upper Sex Boy

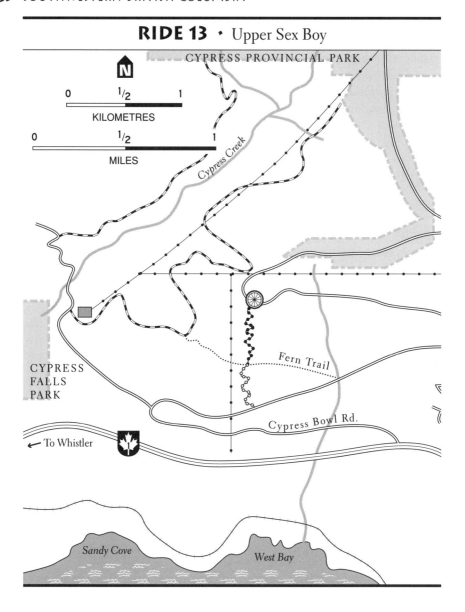

than a kilometre, the trail drops 145 m (470 feet). For those riders with the ability to ride it, this trail offers a great adrenaline rush.

General location: North Vancouver along the Cypress Bowl Road.

Elevation change: The trail drops 145 m (470 feet) from the trailhead to its junction with Fern Trail. The trail plummets straight down with little break.

Season: The trail is rideable most of the year but is best avoided during wet weather to reduce erosion and trail damage.

Services: All services are available in North Vancouver.

Hazards: You name it. This trail has sheer vertical faces, root and rock drops, ledges, deep ruts, and lots of immovable objects for collisions.

Rescue index: Because it is close to residential areas, as well as the Cypress Bowl Road, it is not difficult to find assistance. The trail is not busy, though, so don't expect to run into many other riders en route.

Land status: Most of the land falls within British Properties' land and is subject to future development. Signs at the BLT trailhead indicate that you must be willing to accept all responsibility while traversing their land.

Maps: The NTS 1:50,000 topographic map for this trail is 92 G/6 North Vancouver. The trail is not marked on the map, though, so the best map may be the one included in this guidebook.

Finding the trail: Take the Trans-Canada Highway into West Vancouver to Exit 8/Cypress Bowl Road Ski Area. Turn right and follow this road until it makes the first sharp switchback. If you are planning to use BLT Trail as an access point, park here. Otherwise, continue up Cypress Bowl Road for an additional 6.3 km (3.8 miles) until the third switchback. Behind the concrete barriers, Upper Sex Boy drops sharply.At this corner, a road will radiate out to the left. Park near the entrance to this road.

Sources of additional information: You can contact Cypress Provincial Park at the following address:

B.C. Parks
District Manager
1610 Mount Seymour Rd.
North Vancouver, B.C., V7G-1L3
(604) 924-2200
fax (604) 924-2244

Notes on the trail: As you drop off Cypress Bowl Road, the trail begins with a steep drop down a narrow gully. After bottoming out, climb over some volcanic rock and the trail begins its winding descent. Soon, you'll drop 1.5 m (5 feet) off a lava boulder, and the trail begins to plummet. The first 0.5 km (0.3 mile) is solid, sharp downhill. At this point, you'll drop off another slickrock boulder, taking you into a series of root and rock drops. The drop moderates for a short while at kilometre 0.63 (mile 0.4). Enjoy the break, because it doesn't last. After another sharp drop at 0.68 km (mile 0.4), you are back in the thick of it. Immediately beyond this drop, you bounce your way off an old cedar log. To the right, using smaller logs, previous riders have made a rough ramp, or you can simply take the airborne route to the left. Finally, the trail spits you out on the Fern Trail at kilometre 0.76 (mile 0.46). If you are planning on doing Lower Sex Boy, turn right onto Fern Trail and look for a trail dropping down to the left after approximately 50 m (55 yards).

RIDE 14 · Lower Sex Boy

AT A GLANCE

Length/configuration: 0.9-km (0.55-mile) point-to-point; by linking Upper Sex Boy, you can create a 1.72-km (1.03-mile) point-to-point plummet

Aerobic difficulty: This trail is straight down. There is little aerobic challenge

Technical difficulty: The trail drops 120 m (394 feet) in 0.9 km (0.55 mile). The gradient is extremely steep and offers a constant supply of sharp vertical drops, root gullies, and big trees

Scenery: The focus of this trail is not on scenery but technical challenge. It stays within the trees at all times

Special comments: Don't even think about riding this trail unless you are *very* comfortable with sheer vertical drops. Not only is the trail steep, but most of the elevation loss is in the form of sudden drops off ledges and logs

L ower Sex Boy is a place for expert riders to hone their techniques. It is short—only 0.9 km (0.55 miles) long; has several access options; and loses 120 m (394 feet) in less than a kilometre (0.6 mile). The obstacles are constant, with little chance to recover from one drop before you find yourself negotiating the next. For riders that enjoy sheer, radical riding, this trail may be short, but it sure is sweet.

General location: West Vancouver, along Cypress Bowl Road.

Elevation change: The trail drops from a starting elevation of 400 m (1,312 feet) to Cypress Bowl Road at 280 m (918 feet). This 120-m (394-foot) drop is accomplished in only 0.9 km (0.55 mile).

Season: It is rideable most of the year but may get snow during December and January. With the steep gradient, it is best avoided during wet weather to reduce the potential for erosion.

Services: All services are available in West Vancouver.

Hazards: Everything imaginable. The trail plummets off sharp rock and log ledges, and it has hairpin turns and an endless collection of roots, loose rocks, and large trees.

Rescue index: Cypress Bowl Road is well traveled, and cars can usually be flagged down. Also, the trail is not far from the Westmount residential area where help can be accessed.

RIDE 14 · Lower Sex Boy

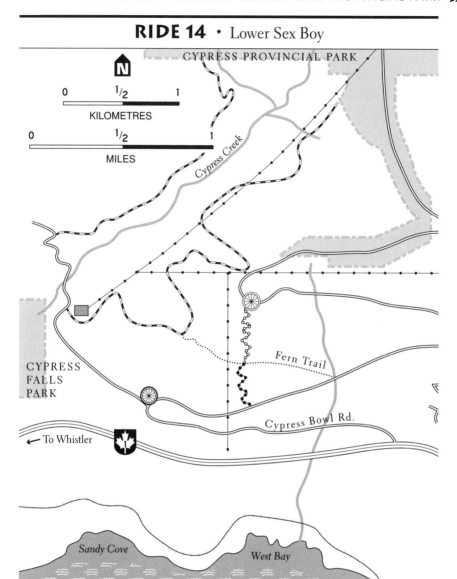

Land status: Most of the land falls within British Properties' land and is subject to future development. Signs at the trailhead indicate that you must be willing to accept all responsibility while traversing their land.

Maps: The NTS 1:50,000 topographic map for this trail is 92 G/6 North Vancouver, but the trail is not marked on any map.

Finding the trail: Take the Trans-Canada Highway into West Vancouver to Exit 8/Cypress Bowl Road Ski Area. Turn right and follow this road until it makes the first sharp switchback. At this corner, a road will radiate out to the left. Park near the entrance to this road. If you decide to access the trail via BLT and Fern Trails, follow the routing of Ride 16 to its intersection with Lower Sex Boy. Otherwise, you can use the description for Upper Sex Boy as an access point.

Sources of additional information: You can contact Cypress Provincial Park at the following address:

B.C. Parks
District Manager
1610 Mount Seymour Rd.
North Vancouver, B.C., V7G-1L3
(604) 924-2200
(604) 924-2244 fax

Notes on the trail: From Fern Trail junction, Lower Sex Boy wastes no time testing your worthiness. Starting with a tight series of root drops as it winds to the right, it climbs over a small boulder and then continues straight on. So much for the warm-up. From here the obstacles become unrelenting as you bounce and bump your way over numerous vertical drops, hairpin turns, and gullies. At this point, the trail winds to the left and begins a short, moderate section. This ends with a drop off a downed tree trunk into a serious root drop mixed with some volcanic rock. The trail settles into a routine of constant drops mixed with sheer vertical until its junction with the road at kilometre 0.91 (mile 0.55).

RIDE 15 · Fern Trail via BLT

AT A GLANCE

Length/configuration: 1.75-km (1.05-mile) point-to-point. However, to access the trail from BLT, you will need to add on 2.4 km (1.44 miles). A loop starting on BLT, traversing Fern Trail, and returning to the car along Cypress Bowl Road totals 6.15 km (3.7 miles)

Aerobic difficulty: Moderately difficult. The climb up BLT is steady, but Fern Trail is a gradual drop in elevation

Technical difficulty: BLT has rocky sections with some tricky uphill sections. Fern Trail includes a small creek crossing and numerous low deadfalls that you'll need to crawl under and over

Scenery: Although forested, some of the patches of salal and ferns are quite picturesque

Special comments: This trail offers an easy exit from Upper Sex Boy and access to Lower Sex Boy. Combined with BLT it offers a nice, intermediate-level loop

RIDE 15 • Fern Trail via BLT

Fern Trail is a wooded trail passing through some picturesque stretches of fern and salal. At times on the 1.75-km (1.05-mile) trail, you may find yourself battling the growth of plants as the forest slowly tries to reclaim the trail. As a loop with BLT and the Cypress Bowl Road, it provides a pleasant 6.15-km (3.7-mile) loop of moderate difficulty. This is a great ride for building strength and technical skill. Although not overly difficult, it has sufficient technical challenges that intermediate riders will find it a pleasant challenge.

General location: North Vancouver along Cypress Bowl Road.

Fern Trail offers a pleasant, technical roll through a dense undergrowth of ferns.

Elevation change: The trail climbs from the Cypress Bowl Road trailhead at 210 m (689 feet) to its junction with Fern Trail at 425 m (1,394 feet). Fern Trail drops 105 m (344 feet) en route to Cypress Bowl Road.

Season: This trail is rideable most of the year, but may get snowbound during December or January. It is best avoided in wet weather.

Services: All services available in North Vancouver.

Hazards: With the dense undergrowth of salal and fern, it's a good trail for choosing tights rather than shorts. Along the way, there are numerous downed logs and a few loose rock stretches. Generally though, the trail is of moderate difficulty.

Rescue index: Although you may encounter other riders along BLT Trail, once you turn off onto Fern Trail, you are pretty much on your own. Cypress Bowl Road is a busy road and usually help may be contacted by flagging down vehicles.

Land status: Most of the land falls within British Properties land and is subject to future development. Signs at the trailhead indicate that you must be willing to accept all responsibility while traversing their land.

Maps: The NTS 1:50,000 topographic map for this trail is 92 G/6 North Vancouver; however, this trail is not marked on any maps.

Finding the trail: Take the Trans-Canada Highway into West Vancouver to Exit 8/Cypress Bowl Road Ski Area. Turn right, and follow this road until it makes the first sharp switchback. At this corner, a road will radiate out to the left. Park near the entrance to this road. This is the trailhead for the BLT Trail.

After climbing BLT for 2.4 km (1.44 miles), look for a faint trail branching off to the right. To find it, look for the signed junction of the Roach-Hit Trail, after which you'll climb a steep hill toward Fern Trail. The junction is poorly marked. There is a small pile of rocks placed atop a larger, fern-covered rock, and a nearby alder has the letter M carved into it.

Sources of additional information: You can contact Cypress Provincial Park at the following address:

B.C. Parks
District Manager
1610 Mount Seymour Rd.
North Vancouver, B.C., V7G-1L3
(604) 924-2200
fax (604) 924-2244

Notes on the trail: From the poorly marked trailhead at kilometre 2.4 (mile 1.44) of the BLT Trail, Fern Trail heads through some dense forest and crosses over a patch of volcanic rock before beginning a short, rocky climb at kilometre 2.72 (mile 1.63). In wet conditions, the climb is followed by a muddy, boot-sucking stretch. Beyond this point, it becomes more interesting with a descent to a tiny creek crossing followed by a short, technical climb. Loose rocks and roots will challenge novices to keep rear tires from spinning out. At kilometre 3.3 (mile 2), Lower Sex Boy drops down to the right. This is an expert trail, best reserved for cyclists with experience in sheer vertical drops. Moments later, you'll pass another trail junction, this time with Upper Sex Boy dropping in from above. Beyond these trails, Fern Trail earns its name as the understory becomes dominated with a wonderful collection of tall ferns. At times, you almost have to push your way through the dense growth.

Beyond the ferns, at kilometre 3.6 (mile 2.14), the trail drops down a narrow, rutted slope. Midway down the hill, a large alder log blocks the path, so you'll need to clamber over the top. Beyond the log, the downhill becomes more technical with many grapefruit-sized rocks and gully slides. This descent reaches the Cypress Bowl Road at kilometre 4.14 (mile 2.5). Turn right and roll your way back to the car at kilometre 6.15 (mile 3.7).

RIDE 16 · Stupid Grouse

AT A GLANCE

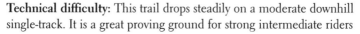

Length/configuration: 0.94-km (0.59-mile) point-to-point; a 2.13-km (1.3-mile) loop is possible using the Panorama Climb

Aerobic difficulty: Easy. This is a downhill run, so there is little aerobic challenge

Technical difficulty: This trail drops steadily on a moderate downhill single-track. It is a great proving ground for strong intermediate riders

Scenery: The best views are along the drive up to the trailhead along Cypress Bowl Road

Special comments: This is another well-known ride that has become popular for its rideable technical challenge. It is not off-the-scale difficult like much of the north shore

Stupid Grouse is a great intermediate-level technical ride. This 0.94-km (0.59-mile) single-track drops you down from the second switchback on Cypress Bowl Road along a winding single-track through a dense, mossy forest. Although the trail is technical, it is rideable by solid intermediate cyclists as long as they are comfortable with short verticals. Another nice thing about this ride is the mossy carpet through the trees. It takes away some of the dire consequences of error present on so many north shore rides. Though the metre-thick trees won't move far, at least the ground is a little softer.

As the trail approaches the creek, it becomes more technical before finally opening up into a red alder forest with some immature red cedar. From the terminus at the top of Folkstone Way, you have the option of returning partway up the Grouse and then following the wide gravel of the Panorama Climb back up to the trailhead. If you're not sufficiently cooked, consider heading back down for another run.

General location: The city of West Vancouver.

Elevation change: The trail drops 168 m (551 feet) from the trailhead at 430 m (1,410 feet) to its junction with No Stairs Allowed.

Season: Although rideable year-round, save this trail for dry weather to avoid increased erosion along its narrow course.

Services: All services are available in the city of West Vancouver.

Hazards: Most of the hazards on this trail are rideable. They consist of log and root drops along with some rutting caused by riders locking their brakes.

RIDE 16 · Stupid Grouse

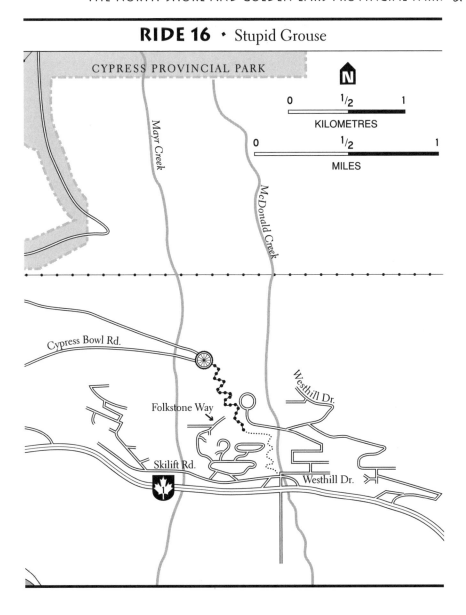

Although it is an expert ride, the surface is soft, and the consequences are less dire than riding in rocky locales like Whistler.

Rescue index: Because this trail runs through a residential area, it is not difficult to find help. It is also a very popular ride, so other cyclists may also be able to offer help.

Land status: Most of the land falls within British Properties' land and is subject to future development. Signs at the trailhead indicate that you must be willing to accept all responsibility while traversing their land.

Maps: The NTS 1:50,000 topographic map for this trail is 92 G/6 North Vancouver; however, the trail is not marked on any map.

Finding the trail: Take the Trans-Canada Highway into West Vancouver to Exit 8/Cypress Bowl Road Ski Area. Turn right and follow this road 3.7 km (2.2 miles) to the second major switchback. Park on the gravel along the inside of the switchback. The trail begins as the concrete barriers end at the upper end of the curve. Go around the barrier, take the right-hand junction, and begin dropping.

Sources of additional information: I was unable to find any additional sources of information.

Notes on the trail: From the parking lot, ride around the upper terminus of the concrete barriers placed around the outside corner of the switchback. As you round the concrete, stay to the right at an immediate junction and begin descending beneath the large rocks used to build the highway switchback. Stay straight as a trail veers to the left almost immediately. Stupid Grouse is the second left-hand junction. At kilometre 0.1 (mile 0.06), turn left on a rutted, gravel trail. This trail is a technical roller coaster of rideable obstacles composed primarily of log and root drops. As the trail winds above the river, it becomes more technical before breaking out of the forest into a more open alder forest with an understory of immature cedar trees. As you get closer to the river, the trail widens and almost becomes a double-track with a margin of salmonberry. Stay left at a junction at kilometre 0.6 (mile 0.36) and right at another junction at 0.84 km (mile 0.5). The trail finally dumps out into civilization at kilometre 0.94 (mile 0.59) at the top of Folkstone Way. At this point, you can continue on No Stairs Allowed, or you can backtrack for 0.3 km (0.18 mile) and take a wide double-track known as the Panorama Climb, which will return you to the beginning of Stupid Grouse for another run in just 1.09 km (0.65 mile).

RIDE 17 · No Stairs Allowed

AT A GLANCE

Length/configuration: 0.77-km (0.46-mile) point-to-point. A 2-km (1.2-mile) loop is possible by riding Skilift Road and Folkstone Way back to your vehicle

Aerobic difficulty: The trail is downhill all the way, but you need to climb 102 m (335 feet) to get back to your vehicle, so save yourself a Power Bar

Technical difficulty: This is a challenging downhill with numerous short drops and a steep gradient. It is rated for strong intermediate or expert riders

Scenery: The trail begins with great views of Lion's Gate Bridge and Vancouver, but the remainder of the trail is wooded

Special comments: This is a fun ride nestled within developed land. It is a great place to hone your skills as you become more proficient with obstacle-ridden downhills. It is also more open, often within alder forest, than many of the wet north shore rides

Unlike Stupid Grouse, where most of the ride feels like you are in true wilderness, this trail is urban all the way. Despite this fact, it is a wonderful 0.77-km (0.46-mile) point-to-point downhill roller coaster. A 2-km (1.2-mile) loop is possible using Skilift Road and Folkstone Way. Although No Stairs Allowed has lots of tight turns and small obstacles, it offers intermediate riders a chance to hone their skills. This is an enjoyable ride, perfect for an after-work roll.

General location: West Vancouver.

Elevation change: The trail drops 102 m (335 feet) from the trailhead (262 m/859 feet) to the junction with Skilift Road.

Season: Year-round.

Services: All services are available in West Vancouver.

Hazards: The trail drops sharply with numerous small log drops and tight turns. The challenge comes largely from the gradient, as the obstacles are generally rideable. It is still a challenging ride, though, and you should be confident with technical drops before trying this trail.

Rescue index: Because this trail rides right past numerous backyards, you are never far from help.

Land status: Most of the land falls within British Properties land and is subject to future development. Signs at the trailhead indicate that you must be willing to accept all responsibility while traversing their land.

RIDE 17 · No Stairs Allowed

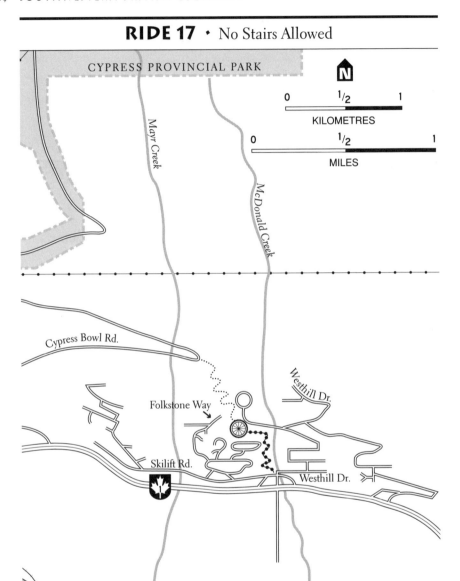

Maps: The NTS 1:50,000 topographic map for this trail is 92 G/6 North Vancouver; however, this trail is not marked on any map.

Finding the trail: Take the Trans-Canada Highway into West Vancouver to Exit 10/Westhill Drive. Stay straight over the exit to join Skilift Road. Take the first right turn onto Folkstone Way and follow it to its upper terminus, just past Constantine Place. Keep in mind that things are changing rapidly due to construction, but the trailhead heads off to the right of an orange fenced-off culvert. You can also link this trail with Stupid Grouse (Ride 16).

Sources of additional information: I was unable to find any additional sources of information.

Notes on the trail: From the trailhead, drop sharply as the trail becomes a narrow single-track. The trail parallels an orange fence with a sign indicating COVENANT AREA BOUNDARY. DO NOT REMOVE FENCE, OR DISTURB VEGETATION BEYOND THIS POINT. After a short, wet section, the trail traverses a narrow hump dropping off to both sides. After a sharp right turn, it bounces over several small log drops and then follows the fence line very closely. As it traverses the fence, it makes two short, sharp drops before finally crossing the creek on a high-quality bridge. After the bridge, bounce over a few log jumps, and the trail begins to pass through the backyards along Westhill Drive. Be careful of blackberry branches trolling for flesh as you ride past. At kilometre 0.4 (mile 0.24), a concrete bench allows a peaceful break before the trail makes a tight series of corkscrew turns. As the sound of the road begins to dominate, you finally reach pavement at kilometre 0.77 (mile 0.46) at the corner of Westhill Drive and Skilift Road. Turn right on Skilift Road, right again at Folkstone Way, and climb back to your vehicle.

RIDE 18 · Golden Ears Park—Alouette Mountain Fire Access Road

AT A GLANCE

Length/configuration: 23-km (13.8-mile) out-and-back, including 11.5 km (6.9 miles) to the terminus before backtracking along the same route

Aerobic difficulty: The trail climbs 450 m (1,476 feet) in 11.5 km (6.9 miles) and requires strong lungs and legs

Technical difficulty: The trail has a smooth, wide surface, making this an ideal trail for fit riders looking to gain some elevation

Scenery: Although mostly treed, the trail offers a pleasant ride through large stands of Douglas fir, alder, and vine maple

Special comments: This is an ideal combination ride. By riding to the Beautiful Lake Junction and then parking your bike, you can hike to this pleasant mountain pond surrounded by virgin stands of mountain hemlock and yellow cedar

The trail winds its way for 11.5 km (6.9 miles) upward along the slopes of Alouette Mountain, rarely breaking through the trees but offering a pleasant uphill roll along a high-quality fire road followed by a fast-paced downhill return route. The trail meanders its way through a forest of western red cedar, Douglas fir, and red alder with an understory of vine maple, thimbleberry, salmonberry, elder, and goatsbeard. This second growth towers over the stumps of the ancient old growth trees logged in the 1930s. Some of the stumps are more than a metre in diametre! Many still show the notches hacked into their stumps by lumberjacks so many years ago. A notch was used to support a small platform on which the logger would stand while cutting through the main trunk. In wet spots hidden beneath the second growth, skunk cabbage offers a pungent aroma, and devil's club threatens from the periphery. The trail also forms part of an outdoor laboratory for the University of British Columbia. There is a presently a study on the effects of limited thinning on the local population of northern flying squirrels.

General location: Golden Ears Provincial Park.

Elevation change: The trail climbs steadily from Mike Lake at 260 m (853 feet). It finally deteriorates after the Beautiful Lake Junction at approximately 710 m (2,329 feet).

Season: Due to the elevation gain, save this trail for good weather. It is rideable much of the year, but during the winter months it may be snowbound near the summit.

Services: All services are available in Maple Ridge.

Hazards: This is a wide, smooth fire road. There are few dangers other than the occasional loose rock and downed tree.

Rescue index: Golden Ears Park, and in particular, Mike Lake, are quite popular. Often, there will be people fly-fishing its waters for the occasional nibble. If the parking lot is empty, head out to the main road, where you will probably be able to find assistance. From a phone you can contact the Ridge Meadows Royal Canadian Mounted Police (RCMP) at the following address:

Ridge Meadows RCMP
11900 Haney Place
Haney, B.C. V2X-8R9
911

Ridge Meadows Hospital
11666 Laity St.
Haney, B.C. V2X-5A3
(604) 463-4111

Land status: British Columbia Provincial Park.

Maps: The NTS 1:50,000 topographic map for this trail is 92 G/7 Port Coquitlam. Another good map is the park map produced by Golden Ears Park. It is available by contacting the park directly.

Finding the trail: Take the Trans-Canada Highway east from Vancouver to Exit 44/Pitt Meadows/Maple Ridge. As you exit, stay in the right lane, which will fork off. Follow the Trans-Canada Highway east to Exit 44/Port Coquitlam/Pitt to the right to provide access to Mary Hill Bypass. It almost looks as if you are heading back onto the highway, but fear not; this is the correct route. As the exit forks, go left onto United Boulevard North/Pitt Meadows/Maple Ridge. Go straight at the

RIDE 18 · Golden Ears Park–Alouette Mountain Fire Access Road

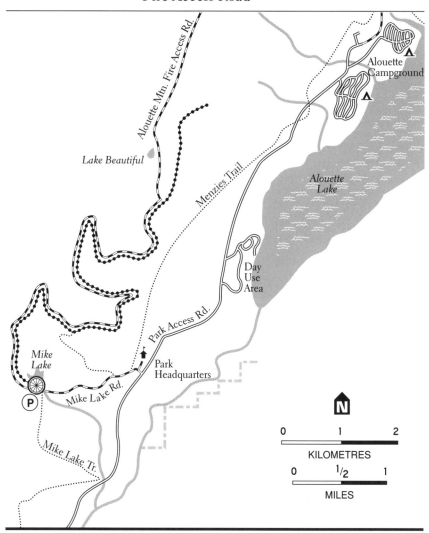

first set of lights onto the Mary Hill Bypass (Highway 7B east). Follow this route as it winds along, getting into the right lane for the junction with Lougheed Highway (Highway 7 east). Follow Lougheed Highway over the bridge until you reach Dewdney Trunk Road for the second time. You want to ignore the first turnoff for the Dewdney Trunk Road shortly after crossing the Pitt River Bridge. Instead, follow Lougheed Highway for 6.4 km (3.8 miles) and turn left when it crosses the Dewdney Trunk Road for a second time. Roll along for 6.2 km (3.72 miles) or 11 sets of lights, finally turning left onto 232 Street. Turn right onto

Fern Creek at a three-way stop and follow the signs to Golden Ears Park for 2.5 km (1.5 miles) as Fern Creek winds its way toward the main entrance. Follow the main route and the signs for the park as numerous small roads join in from the left and right. Turn left at the sign indicating PARK ADMINISTRATION AND MIKE LAKE after traveling 9 km (5.4 miles) along Fern Creek The signs are quite rustic and easily missed, but the road turns left at the bright FIRE HAZARD sign. Stay left at the junction with the gravel of Mike Lake Road, and bump your way for 2 km (1.2 miles) to the main parking lot for the Alouette Mountain Fire Access Road.

Sources of additional information: Contact the park directly at:

Golden Ears Provincial Park
Box 7000
Maple Ridge, B.C., V2X 7G3
(604) 463-3513
(604) 463-6193 fax

or contact the Lower Mainland District Office at:

1610 Mt. Seymour Rd.
North Vancouver, B.C., V7G 1L3
(604) 924-2200
(604) 924-2244 fax

Notes on the trail: This high-quality double-track climbs almost constantly, but at a very pleasant gradient. Stay straight at all major junctions, and wind your way through a pleasant forest landscape. There is a gate across the road at kilometre 5 (mile 3). Beyond the gate, at an elevation of 370 m (1,202 feet), the trail continues. A rough trail (Switchback Trail) drops to the right just beyond the gate. This offers a wonderful alternate exit for more advanced riders on the way down. Beyond the gate, the character of the trail remains the same—wide and smooth with a consistent uphill bias. By the 8-km (4.8-mile) mark, the trail slowly begins to show the effects of reduced traffic. Grass begins to invade the middle of the trail, albeit in small amounts, and the trail becomes narrower as the surrounding forest begins to encroach on the old track. At this point, the impact is subtle, and the occasional bleeding heart flower offers sympathy for cyclists beginning to run out of steam. Soon after the trail crosses the remains of an old cedar log at kilometre 11.5 (mile 6.9), the trail toward Beautiful Lake branches off to the left. Like many of the previous junctions, it is marked only by a sign indicating ALOUETTE MOUNTAIN, as is the main trail. Beyond this, the track quickly deteriorates; most riders will choose to turn around at this point. Return to the car at kilometre 23 (mile 13.8).

RIDE 19 · Golden Ears Park—Alouette Mountain/
Switchback/Eric Dunning Loop

AT A GLANCE

Length/configuration: 8.75-km (5.25-mile) loop

Aerobic difficulty: The trail begins with a moderate climb of 135 m (443 feet) over 5 km (3 miles), followed by a pleasant downhill

Technical difficulty: This is an intermediate ride with a 5-km (3-mile) climb followed by a moderate descent along the Switchback and Eric Dunning Trails

Scenery: This is principally a woodland trail

Special comments: This is a great place to play—a slow, steady uphill with a roller-coaster descent

This trail is so much fun that I could do it over and over. It incorporates parts of the Alouette Mountain Fire Access Trail and then drops down on the Switchback Trail, followed by the Eric Dunning Trail. A short road roll brings you back to your car at kilometre 8.75 (mile 5.25). The descent down Switchback and Eric Dunning Trails is steep and steady, but it presents one of the best opportunities I have seen for riders looking to improve their skills at negotiating steep switchbacks and other sudden obstacles. Although challenging, it is passable by most solid intermediate riders. Be prepared for a bruise or two if you don't make a corner, but once you've done it once, you may find yourself doing it again and again.

General location: Golden Ears Provincial Park.

Elevation change: The trail climbs up the Alouette Mountain Fire Access Road from the trailhead at 175 m (569 feet) to its junction with the Switchback Trail at 310 m (1,007 feet). Then it drops unrelentingly back to the Mike Lake Road.

Season: This trail is rideable all year, but save it for good weather to reduce erosion on the Switchback Trail.

Services: All services are available in Maple Ridge.

Hazards: The Switchback Trail and Eric Dunning Trails are chock-full of challenges and obstacles. They begin with a series of steep switchbacks, and the pace rarely slows. What makes this trail unique is that the challenge level is perfect for intermediate riders wanting to stretch their legs and develop the skills neces-

RIDE 19 · Golden Ears Park–Alouette Mountain/ Switchback/Eric Dunning Loop

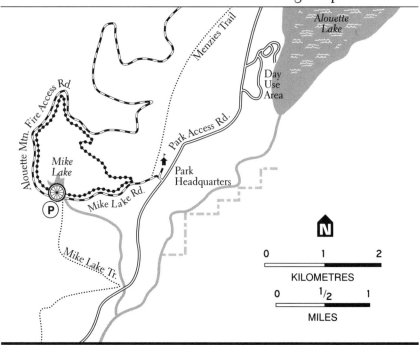

sary for negotiating switchbacks and steep descents. With this terrain come the usual dangers, the most obvious of which is an over-the-handlebar launch.

Rescue index: This loop never strays far from the main road access to Golden Ears Park, so help is usually close at hand. The park headquarters is at the beginning of the Mike Lake Road, and the Eric Dunning Trail meets the Mike Lake Road not far from these buildings.

Land status: British Columbia Provincial Park.

Maps: The NTS 1:50,000 topographic map for this trail is 92 G/7 Port Coquitlam. Another good map is the park map produced by Golden Ears Park. It is available by contacting the park directly.

Finding the trail: Take the Trans-Canada Highway east from Vancouver to Exit 44/Pitt Meadows/Maple Ridge. As you exit, stay in the right lane, which will fork off. Follow the Trans-Canada Highway east to Exit 44/Port Coquitlam/Pitt to the right to provide access to Mary Hill Bypass. It almost looks like you are heading back onto the highway, but fear not; this is the correct route. As the exit forks, go left onto United Boulevard North/Pitt Meadows/Maple Ridge. Go straight at the first set of lights onto the Mary Hill Bypass (Highway 7B east). Follow this route as it winds along, getting into the right lane for the junction with Lougheed Highway (Highway 7 east) at kilometre 7.9 (mile 4.74). Follow Lougheed Highway over the bridge until you reach Dewdney Trunk Road for the second

The sharp corners of Switchback Trail offer a great slalom course of rideable turns.

time. Ignore the option for Dewdney Trunk Road shortly after crossing the Pitt River Bridge. Instead, follow Lougheed Highway for 6.4 km (3.8 miles) and turn left onto the second option for the Dewdney Trunk Road. Roll along for 6.2 km (3.72 miles) or 11 sets of lights, finally turning left onto 232 Street. Turn right onto Fern Creek at a three-way stop and follow the signs to Golden Ears Park for 2.5 km (1.5 miles) as Fern Creek winds its way toward the main entrance. As numerous small roads join in from the left and right, simply follow the main route and the signs for the park. Turn left at the sign indicating the PARK ADMINI-STRATION AND MIKE LAKE after traveling 9 km (5.4 miles) along Fern Creek. The signs are quite rustic and easily missed, so the road turns left at the bright FIRE HAZARD sign. Stay left at the junction with the gravel of Mike Lake Road and bump your way for 2 km (1.2 miles) to the main parking lot for the Alouette Mountain Fire Access Road.

Sources of additional information: Contact the park directly at:

Golden Ears Provincial Park
Box 7000
Maple Ridge, B.C., V2X 7G3
(604) 463-3513
(604) 463-6193 fax

or contact the Lower Mainland District Office at:

> 1610 Mt. Seymour Rd.
> North Vancouver, B.C., V7G 1L3
> (604) 924-2200
> (604) 924-2244 fax

Notes on the trail: The trail climbs from the Mike Lake Parking Lot along the smooth gradient of the Alouette Mountain Fire Access Road. There is a gate across the road at kilometre 5 (mile 3). Beyond the gate at an elevation of 370 m (1,202 feet), the Switchback Trail drops to the right. It begins suddenly with a switchback to the right, followed by several more. This trail is challenging, with a seemingly unending supply of sudden obstacles, but it's more fun than a barrel of monkeys. At kilometre 5.65 (mile 3.4) there is a series of three log obstacles built to the right of the trail. These are wonderful practice spots for climbing small log pyramids and descending sudden (but small) drops. The Switchback Trail becomes the Eric Dunning Trail at kilometre 5.66 (mile 3.4) as the trail turns sharply to the left on a switchback. The trail ends all too quickly with a sudden descent to the Mike Lake Road at kilometre 7.1 (mile 4.25). Turn right and roll your way to the parking lot at kilometre 8.75 (mile 5.25).

RIDE 20 · Golden Ears Park—Menzies Trail

AT A GLANCE

Length/configuration: 9.5-km (5.7-mile) point-to-point; you can create an 18.3-km (11-mile) loop using the park access roads

Aerobic difficulty: Moderate elevation gains as the trail rolls along the lower slopes of Alouette Mountain and Evans Peak

Technical difficulty: A nice, rolling single-track that will challenge novices, but it is passable by riders of even moderate ability

Scenery: There is an excellent view toward Alouette Lake

Special comments: This pleasant ride avoids assaulting the slope like so many rides; rather, it follows the contour lines, making for a nice, rolling single-track

This pleasant 18.3-km (11-mile) loop uses a combination of rolling single-track, wide double-track, and pavement to create a pleasant afternoon ride for solid intermediate cyclists. There are some areas with washouts, downed

RIDE 20 · Golden Ears Park–Menzies Trail

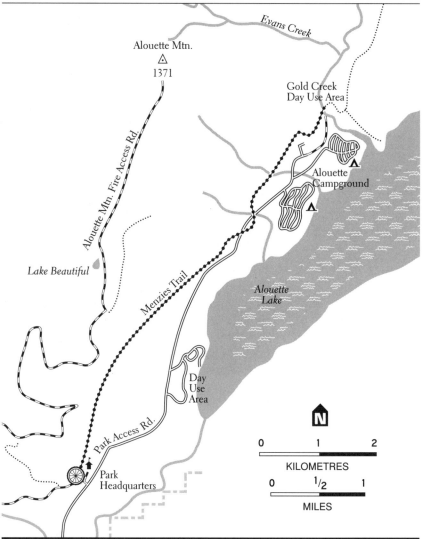

trees, and other challenges to negotiate, but even beginning riders willing to push through these stretches should enjoy this ride. Although the ride is mostly treed, there is a view, complete with picnic benches, toward Alouette Lake at the 2-km (1.2-mile) point.

Along the way, keep your eyes peeled for orange triangles nailed to trees that indicate the distance covered. Also, the trail is rimmed with red alder. A moldy interpretive sign at kilometre 2.85 (mile 1.7) indicates that the sap of this tree turns red when exposed to the air (this made it convenient for local natives to use as a dye for their baskets). Several pieces of metal, remnants of the area's hey-

While Menzies Trail climbs through the coastal rainforest, this pleasant waterfall bubbles down the hillside.

day as a logging mecca, are passed en route. In particular is a large metal wheel approximately 1 m (3.28 feet) in diametre at kilometre 3.5 (mile 2.1).

General location: Golden Ears Provincial Park.

Elevation change: The trail rolls along at 150–200 m (492–656 feet) elevation, finally cresting at a lookout at 224 m (735 feet). The gradient is neither difficult nor unrelenting; the trail traverses the lower slopes of Alouette Mountain and Evans Peak.

Season: Year-round.

Services: All services are available in Maple Ridge.

Hazards: Although the trail has only minimal elevation gain, there are numerous technical washouts crossing it. These are mixed with periodic horse-churned puddles and lots of rideable stream crossings. Most of the fords are less than a metre (a foot or two) wide and easily passable. This may vary slightly during high water. One huge washout left a massive debris flow that briefly closed the north end of the trail in 1998.

Rescue index: Because the trail is rarely far from the main park access road, help is generally not far away. The south trailhead is very near the park headquarters, and the trail crosses the main road twice. The north trailhead is at the Gold Creek parking lot, also an area where help can usually be found.

Land status: British Columbia Provincial Park.

Maps: The NTS 1:50,000 topographic map for this trail is 92 G/7 Port Coquitlam and 92 G/8 Stave Lake. Another good map is the park map produced by Golden Ears Park. It is available by contacting the park directly.

Finding the trail: Take the Trans-Canada Highway east from Vancouver to Exit 44/Pitt Meadows/Maple Ridge. As you exit, stay in the right lane, which will fork off. Follow the Trans-Canada Highway east to Exit 44/Port Coquitlam/Pitt, to the right to provide access to Mary Hill Bypass. It almost looks as if you are heading back onto the highway, but fear not; this is the correct route. As the exit forks, go left onto United Boulevard North/Pitt Meadows/Maple Ridge. Go straight at the first set of lights onto the Mary Hill Bypass (Highway 7B east). Follow this route as it winds along, getting into the right lane for the junction with Lougheed Highway (Highway 7 east) at kilometre 7.9 (mile 4.74). Follow Lougheed Highway over the bridge until you reach Dewdney Trunk Road for the second time. Ignore the option for Dewdney Trunk Road shortly after crossing the Pitt River Bridge. Instead, follow Lougheed Highway for 6.4 km (3.8 miles) and turn left onto the second option for the Dewdney Trunk Road. Roll along for 6.2 km (3.72 miles) or 11 sets of lights, finally turning left onto 232 Street. Turn right onto Fern Creek at a three-way stop and follow the signs to Golden Ears Park for 2.5 km (1.5 miles) as Fern Creek winds its way toward the main entrance. As numerous small roads join in from the left and right, simply follow the main route and the signs for the park. Turn left at the sign indicating the PARK ADMINISTRATION AND MIKE LAKE after traveling 9 km (5.4 miles) along Fern Creek. The signs are quite rustic and easily missed, so the road turns left at the bright FIRE HAZARD sign. Stay left at the junction with the gravel of Mike Lake Road and bump your way for 0.35 km (0.2 mile) to a small pullout on the left of the gravel road. Park here and roll your way back toward the junction with the Park Administration road. Menzies Trail climbs upward just before this junction.

Sources of additional information: Contact the park directly at:

Golden Ears Provincial Park
Box 7000
Maple Ridge, B.C., V2X 7G3
(604) 463-3513
fax (604) 463-6193

or contact the Lower Mainland District Office at:

1610 Mt. Seymour Road
North Vancouver, B.C., V7G 1L3
(604) 924-2200
fax (604) 924-2244

Notes on the trail: From the trailhead, follow Mike Lake Road to the right for 0.35 km (0.2 mile) and go left up the signed trail for Menzies Trail. The trail passes a small waterfall at kilometre 1.34 (mile 4.4). A small wooden pipeline extends from the falls. After cresting a mini-summit at kilometre 1.43 (mile 0.86), the trail drops sharply for 0.2 km (0.12 mile). Stay to the left at the junction with Lookout Trail at kilometre 1.8 (mile 1.1). Following this signed junction, the trail makes its final climb toward the lookout at kilometre 2 (mile 1.2). Take a break at the view point (although the view is slightly obscured by trees) and enjoy the two park benches placed there for your enjoyment. You do get something of a view of Alouette Lake and the surrounding summits. The trail begins dropping immediately beyond the view point, and at kilometre 2.31 (mile 1.4) the Loop Trail (no bikes) drops off to the right. As you pass distance marker 3 at kilometre 3.44 (mile 2.06), the trail passes through several horse-churned puddles. You may get wet feet if the trail is not reasonably dry. At the 5-km mark (mile 3), the trail meets the junction with the Alouette Valley Trail. At this **T** intersection, climb left. Riders looking to cut this ride short can exit here. The trail rolls (with an uphill bias) until it crosses a small bridge at kilometre 5.63 (mile 3.4). Cross the road at kilometre 6.45 (mile 3.9) and continue along the trail on the opposite side. Go left, ignoring the trail to the right, as the trail parallels the road for a short distance before turning to the right and heading into the forest. The trail crosses the road again at kilometre 7 (mile 4.2).

As the trail climbs from this junction, it soon crosses a small stream at kilometre 7.2 (mile 4.3). A major washout and debris flow at kilometre 7.83 (mile 4.7) has been repaired, but it may require some vigilance through some of the rocky sections. At the junction with West Canyon Trail at kilometre 8.7 (mile 5.2), turn right and stay on Menzies Trail. This junction is followed by an almost immediate left as Menzies branches off sharply from West Canyon Trail. At kilometre 9.35 (mile 5.6), the trail drops to the highway along several wide switchbacks, reaching pavement at kilometre 9.5 (mile 5.7). Turn right to return to your vehicle, or go left to cross the bridge to the Gold Creek Day Use Area. Turning right, follow the gravel until kilometre 11.4 (mile 6.85), where the pavement offers a smooth surface for most of the remainder of the ride. Turn right at the junction for the park headquarters at kilometre 17.82 (mile 10.7). Turn left almost immediately onto the gravel and meet your vehicle at kilometre 18.3 (mile 11).

RIDE 21 · Golden Ears Park—Mike Lake Trail

AT A GLANCE

Length/configuration: 11.66-km (7-mile) loop using the park access road

Aerobic difficulty: The climb to the trail summit involves rising 70 m (230 feet) in just 2 km (1.2 miles). Beyond this, the ride is mostly downhill

Technical difficulty: Numerous steps and runoff channels make the trail a technical challenge best reserved for intermediate riders

Scenery: While Mike Lake is quite picturesque, the remainder of the trail remains in the trees

Special comments: If you don't mind yielding to the horses on this trail, the steps create a nice place for intermediate riders to practice their ups and downs

The Mike Lake Trail offers a combination of road riding and bouncing descent down a long equestrian staircase. The 11.66-km (7-mile) loop includes only 5.6 km (3.4 miles) of trail, with the remainder along good-quality gravel and paved road. This is not a trail for riders looking for grand views, but it's a great place to practice dropping down and climbing up wide stairs. It's not often that riders are given such a good place to practice the bump and balance that stairs provide.

General location: Golden Ears Provincial Park.

Elevation change: From the trailhead at 125 m (410 feet), the trail climbs to a maximum elevation of 215 m (705 feet) before dropping to the Main Corral at 50 m (164 feet).

Season: Year-round.

Services: All services are available in Maple Ridge.

Hazards: Because this trail was designed to offer horses easy access between Mike Lake and the horse corrals, it has several design elements that make it a challenge for cyclists. First, there are runoff channels dug across the trail, which will test your ability to bunny-hop. Also, there is a long set of wooden steps to help the horses climb up and down the route. These are rideable, but may trip up beginners. Also, because this is bear country, be sure to check for recent bear sightings and make lots of noise as you go.

Rescue index: This trail remains close to civilization, so you are only a short walk in either direction to help. At the north end, Mike Lake is popular with day users and picnickers, and the corrals at the south end are also well used.

RIDE 21 • Golden Ears Park–Mike Lake Trail

Land status: British Columbia Provincial Park.

Maps: The NTS 1:50,000 topographic maps for this trail are 92 G/7 Port Coquitlam and 92 G/2 New Westminster. The simplest map is produced by Golden Ears Provincial Park. It is available by contacting the park directly.

Finding the trail: Take the Trans-Canada Highway east from Vancouver to Exit 44/Pitt Meadows/Maple Ridge. As you exit, stay in the right-hand lane, which will fork off. Follow the Trans-Canada Highway east to Exit 44/Port Coquitlam/Pitt, staying to the right to provide access to Mary Hill Bypass. It almost looks like you are heading back onto the highway, but fear not; this is the correct route. As the exit forks, go left onto United Boulevard North/Pitt Meadows/Maple Ridge. Go straight at the first set of lights onto the Mary Hill Bypass (Highway 7B east). Follow this route as it winds along, getting into the right lane for the junction with Lougheed Highway (Highway 7 east) at kilometre 7.9 (mile 4.74). Follow Lougheed Highway over the bridge until you reach Dewdney Trunk Road for the second time. Ignore the option for Dewdney Trunk Road shortly after crossing the Pitt River bridge. Instead, follow Lougheed Highway for 6.4 km (3.8 miles) and turn left onto the second option for Dewdney Trunk Road. Roll along for 6.2 km (3.72 miles) or 11 sets of lights, finally turning left onto 232 Street. Turn right onto Fern Creek at a three-way stop and follow the signs to Golden Ears Park for 2.5 km (1.5 miles) as Fern Creek winds its way toward the main entrance. As

Mike Lake forms the trailhead for numerous rides within Golden Ears Park, and it's also a great place to cast a line.

numerous small roads join in from the left and right, simply follow the main route and the signs for the park. Turn left into the Main Corral after traveling 4.7 km (2.8 miles). This is the trailhead.

Sources of additional information: Contact the park directly at:

Golden Ears Provincial Park
Box 7000
Maple Ridge, B.C., V2X 7G3
(604) 463-3513
(604) 463-6193 fax

or contact the Lower Mainland District Office at:

1610 Mt. Seymour Rd.
North Vancouver, B.C., V7G 1L3
(604) 924-2200
(604) 924-2244 fax

Notes on the trail: From the main corral, head out to the highway and turn left. Drop your head and roll along the pavement for 4.3 km (2.6 miles), where you will turn left at a sign indicating the ADMINISTRATION BUILDING/MIKE'S LAKE.

Turn left again almost immediately onto the gravel of the Mike's Lake Access Road. Just before the main parking lot for Mike's Lake at kilometre 6.06 (mile 3.64), Mike's Lake Trail exits to the left. It is a wide gravel trail just before the main parking lot. The only sign indicates a horse crossing. To the right, the Lakeside Trail drops. This trail is closed to bikes, but using it as a landmark can help ensure that you are on the correct trail.

The trail begins by climbing through dense, second-growth forest. The old stumps, logged in the 1920s, have also since been burned. The trail climbs for the first 2 km until it crests at 320 m (1,050 feet). The final climb to this crest and much of the following descent is interspersed with runoff channels crossing the trail. They are composed of two thin logs placed with a channel between them. This is a good place to practice that bunny-hop that you've been working on. Otherwise your back wheel hits the depression with a thud. The runoff channels are followed by a series of wooden steps designed for horses. These are rideable by experienced cyclists, but beginners will want to walk their bike down. Once you are down the steps, the trail drops steadily until kilometre 9.45 (mile 5.67). Shortly after this point, the trail crosses under a set of power lines. Beyond the wires, stay right at the next junction. Periodic orange distance markers on this trail count the distance down (in kilometres) to the main park road. The trail climbs after this junction until the 1-km (0.6-mile) marker. After this, it begins to drop until kilometre 11.25 (mile 6.76) where you turn left at the **T** intersection with Maple Ridge Trail. Stay straight at the junction for Alouette Lake Trail. Finish at the corral parking lot at kilometre 11.66 (mile 7).

RIDE 22 · Golden Ears Park—East Canyon Trail

AT A GLANCE

Length/configuration: 11.4-km (6.8-mile) out-and-back trail (5.7 km [3.4 miles] each way). There are lots of options for strong riders to extend these distances

Aerobic difficulty: The trail climbs 150 m (492 feet) over the first 4 km (2.4 miles) and must reclaim much of it on the trip out

Technical difficulty: The trail begins as a wide double-track, slowly constricting until it becomes a bumpy, technical single-track

Scenery: The scenery is beautiful, especially as you approach the river

Special comments: This is a trail with multiple personalities. It's a great ride for beginners looking for more challenge. When it gets too difficult, simply turn back. Strong riders will enjoy the bumpy, technical track near the north end of the ride

RIDE 22 · Golden Ears Park–East Canyon Trail

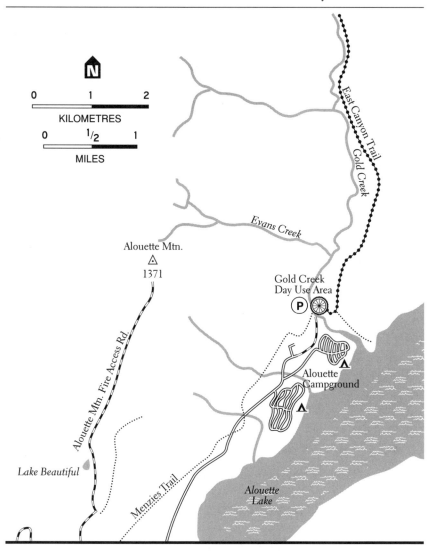

The East Canyon Trail is one of those trails that allow you some high-gear riding along with an increasingly technical single-track. The main trail is an 11.4-km (6.8-mile) out-and-back with options for extending the ride. The only limits are your kidneys and your lungs. The trail finally peters out after about 7 km (4.2 miles).

The trail begins within a dark Douglas fir forest mixed with western red cedar, red alder, and vine maple. This is interspersed with some more open cottonwood and salmonberry. It also sports some of the most luxurious ferns imaginable. Keep your eyes open for the blue flash of the Steller's jay and the white of

The East Canyon Trail slowly deteriorated before becoming a technical bounce.

the wild lily of the valley and foam flower. Hiker's Beach, at kilometre 5.7 (mile 3.4), forms a natural turnaround point.

General location: Golden Ears Provincial Park.

Elevation change: The trail climbs 150 m (492 feet) over the first 4 km (2.4 miles), only to drop 120 m (394 feet) to the river. This elevation is regained on the trip out.

Season: This ride is clear for most of the year with the exception of the occasional snowfall during December and January.

Services: All services are available in Maple Ridge.

Hazards: This trail has increasingly prevalent obstacles as the odometre climbs. This will do one of two things. It will either discourage the tender or challenge keener bikers. In British Columbia, any chance you have to hone your skills is welcome, and this is a perfect opportunity. The gradient, once you join the river, is minimal, and the obstacles gradually increase. Keep in mind, though, that this is a wilderness trail, and the further you bounce your way along, the fewer riders of similar constitution you will encounter. Prepare accordingly.

Rescue index: This is a wilderness trail with all the trimmings. Once you leave the trailhead, you quickly leave civilization behind. You will probably have to return almost all the way to the parking lot before being able to get assistance. Once you make it back, though, the Gold Creek Campground has staff and pay phones to make finding help a simple task.

Land status: B.C. Provincial Park.

Maps: The NTS 1:50,000 topographic map for this trail is 92 G/8 Stave Lake. Another good map is the Park map produced by Golden Ears Park. It is available by contacting the park directly.

Finding the trail: Take the Trans-Canada Highway east from Vancouver to Exit 44/Pitt Meadows/Maple Ridge. As you take the exit, stay in the right-hand lane, which will fork off. Follow the Trans-Canada Highway east to Exit 44/Port Coquitlam/Pitt, to the right to provide access to Mary Hill Bypass. It almost looks like you are heading back onto the highway, but fear not; this is the correct route. As the exit forks, go left onto United Boulevard North/Pitt Meadows/Maple Ridge. Go straight at the first set of lights onto Mary Hill Bypass (Highway 7B east). Follow this route as it winds along, getting into the right lane for the junction with Lougheed Highway (Highway 7 east) at kilometre 7.9 (mile 4.74). Follow Lougheed Highway over the bridge until you reach Dewdney Trunk Road for the second time. Ignore the option for Dewdney Trunk Road shortly after crossing the Pitt River Bridge. Instead, follow Lougheed Highway for 6.4 km (3.8 miles) and turn left onto the second option for Dewdney Trunk Road. Roll along for 6.2 km (3.72 miles) or 11 sets of lights, finally turning left onto 232 Street. Turn right onto Fern Creek at a three-way stop and follow the signs to Golden Ears Park for 2.5 km (1.5 miles) as Fern Creek winds its way toward the main entrance. As numerous small roads join in from the left and right, simply follow the main route and the signs for the park. Drive the main road, staying left for 13.2 km (8 miles) to the Gold Creek Day Use Area, which is easily found by following the main park road to its terminus. The last several kilometres are on good gravel. From the parking lot, the trail begins at a yellow metal gate across a gravel road.

Sources of additional information: Contact the park directly at:

Golden Ears Provincial Park
Box 7000
Maple Ridge, B.C., V2X 7G3
(604) 463-3513
(604) 463-6193 fax

or contact the Lower Mainland District Office at:

1610 Mt. Seymour Road
North Vancouver, B.C., V7G 1L3
(604) 924-2200
(604) 924-2244 fax

Notes on the trail: From your vehicle, ride past a yellow gate located to the right of the main entrance to the parking lot. A sign near the gate reads WEL-COME TO B.C. PARKS. This wide double-track climbs from the trailhead to a junction at kilometre 0.25 (mile 0.15), where you will turn left onto East Canyon Trail. Prepare to climb right away as East Canyon begins its principle ascent. Pass through a gate at kilometre 2.58 (mile 1.55)—the gate was propped open when I researched the trail. From this gate, the trail climbs sharply until it passes a primitive bridge composed of two rough-cut western red cedar logs. At any signs of spur trails, remain on the main trail, as this is the correct route. The trail finally crests the summit of the main climb at kilometre 3.45 (mile 2.1). Enjoy the rapid descent to the banks of the river after this unremarkable summit. You will pay for it on the return trip, when you must regain this elevation (although it is well worth it). When I rode the trail, heavy machinery was cutting a new trail to the right at kilometre 4.7 (mile 2.8), and another trail joined in from the left. Stay straight at this point. As the trail begins to follow the shoreline of Gold Creek, it gradually deteriorates as plants like salmonberry begin to reclaim the trail. Prepare yourself for the remainder of the trail to become gradually rougher as the double-track narrows to a rough single-track. The roots seem to leap out at you, and the ruts grow by the kilometre. Riders looking to hone their root-bouncing skills will persevere. The vast majority of riders seem to do an about-face as the trail begins to bounce beyond Hiker's Beach at kilometre 5.7 (mile 3.4). This small, sandy beach offers a sunny respite to the increasingly hostile nature of the trail. Strong riders can continue for a few more kilometres. Although there are a few rough spur trails, the main route is easy to distinguish. Every half-kilometre is marked by an orange diamond with the distance indicated. Also, an occasional horseshoe symbol may be spotted.

FRASER VALLEY

As you leave the mouth of the Fraser River behind and continue to move inland, you begin to get a better idea of the wealth of British Columbia's natural resources. Following the winding course of the Fraser, you'll notice huge log booms floating in its wide channel. These logs will eventually make their way to local mills. The time they spend in the river will slowly debark them and keep the wood from cracking.

As you move further inland, the river offers another legacy to residents lucky enough to live on its shores. Over thousands of years it has deposited a rich soil, which supports thriving agriculture today. Mile after mile of farmland takes advantage of this gift from the river. As you enter communities like Abbotsford and Chilliwack, the landscape becomes dominated by these farms.

Some of these communities are now growing very rapidly as urban life begins to radiate out of the hub of Vancouver, Burnaby, and New Westminster. Slowly, farmland is being subdivided and transformed into a suburban residential landscape. With this rush to development, many previous mountain bike networks have also disappeared. Despite this rapid change, there are still many excellent areas worth checking out.

Along the winding Fraser, many wide dikes originally built for flood protection today offer pleasant, flat biking options for the entire family. Trails like the De Boville Slough, the Old Poco Trail, and the Matsqui Trail take advantage of the winding course of the Fraser and its tributaries.

For more of a challenge, you can check out the Woodland Walk Trail on Burke Mountain. The future of the many rides on Burke Mountain are presently in limbo as the area has recently been designated as a provincial park. The status of mountain biking had not yet been determined as of this writing.

History buffs will enjoy riding the old rail bed of the Hayward Lake Railway. This winding trail follows the former bed of this turn-of-the-century railway. Many of the old trestles still stand defiantly above the waves of Hayward Lake.

Finally, the Vedder Mountain area above Chilliwack offers numerous trail options. It rises above the farmland to offer many potential areas to explore, most of which utilize former logging access roads. The views along the main logging road are spectacular.

RIDE 23 · De Boville Slough/Pitt River Dike

AT A GLANCE

Length/configuration: Out-and-back ride taking you 10.75 km (6.45 miles) before returning along the same route, for a total of 21.5 km (12.9 miles)

Aerobic difficulty: The trail is flat, perfect for a leisurely ride

Technical difficulty: The gradient is easy; the trail is wide and smooth for the entire length

Scenery: This trail passes through a birder's paradise with eagles and herons galore

Special comments: This is a great after-work roll, especially for riders equipped with binoculars and bird guides. After all, it's not always about cycling

This 21.5-km (12.9-mile) out-and-back trail takes you through the Minnekhada Regional Park, along the De Boville Slough, and finally finishes at the Pitt River Wildlife Sanctuary. Along the way, its wide, flat surface passes marshland and river channels, offering an endless supply of bird life, particularly bald eagles and great blue herons. This ride is perfect for those days when you want to just slowly meander, taking in the scenery and the bird life en route. Leave your heart rate monitor at home; bring your binoculars instead. This ride is flat, but it offers a terrific spectrum of attractions, from riverside log booms to protected wildlife sanctuaries.

General location: Within the city of Port Coquitlam.

Elevation change: Virtually none.

Season: Year-round.

Services: All services are available in Port Coquitlam.

Hazards: With its location along the slough, the trail may have clouds of small midges flying around. I had to wear sunglasses sometimes to keep the midges out of my eyes. Other than this minor annoyance, there is little to be concerned about.

Rescue index: This is a very popular trail, and as such, help is rarely far away.

Land status: The trail runs through several jurisdictions, including the city of Coquitlam Dyking District and Minnekhada Regional Park operated by the Greater Vancouver Regional District.

RIDE 23 · De Bouville Slough/Pitt River Dike

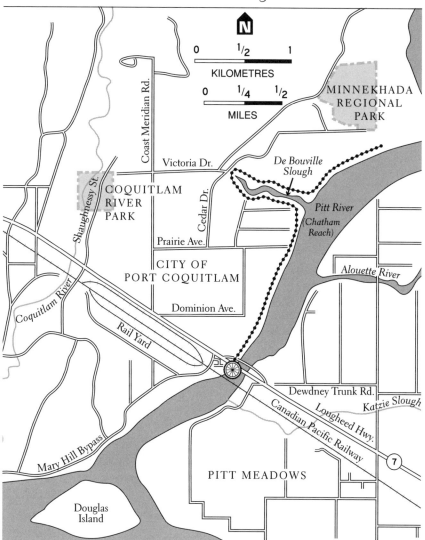

Maps: The principle NTS 1:50,000 topographic map for this trail is 92 G/7 Port Coquitlam, though the trailhead (but little else) is found on 92 G/2 New Westminster.

Finding the trail: Take the Trans-Canada Highway east from Vancouver to Exit 44/Pitt Meadows/Maple Ridge. As you take the exit, stay in the right lane, which will fork to the right to provide access to Mary Hill Bypass. As the exit forks, go left onto United Boulevard North/Pitt Meadows/Maple Ridge. Go straight at the first set of lights onto Mary Hill Bypass (Highway 7B east). Follow this route as it winds along, turning right onto Holland Avenue. At the four-way stop turn right, and then left onto Kingsway—there is a sign indicating Poco Trail Cycle Trail. As you come up to the docks, turn right into the parking lot.

Sources of additional information: I was unable to find any additional sources of information.

Notes on the trail: The trail begins on pavement, crossing under the twin bridges of the Lougheed Highway. The pavement ends shortly, and the trail joins the slough as you pass through a gate. Roll along the trail as it parallels the log booms of the Pitt River. At kilometre 3.9 (mile 2.33), the trail turns left to begin its circumnavigation of the De Boville Slough. The inlet plays host to the Pitt River Boat Club. At kilometre 4.3 (mile 2.6), a sign indicates that trucks share the trail between 11 a.m. and 3 p.m. Monday to Friday. Go through a gate at kilometre 6 (mile 3.6), cross the bridge, and rejoin the trail on the other side of the slough. This side of the slough passes through Minnekhada Regional Park and rolls through a beautiful marshland. The trail passes some agricultural land at kilometre 7.85 (mile 4.7) and rejoins the Pitt River at kilometre 8.17 (mile 4.9). Pass through a gate at 10.05 kilometres (6 miles). There is a sign indicating COQUITLAM DYKING DISTRICT, PRIVATE PROPERTY, ENTER AT OWN RISK. This is the main trail, through, so continue beyond this gate. The trail becomes paved for a short distance at kilometre 10.12 (mile 6.1) and passes through the Pitt River Wildlife Sanctuary. The trail dead-ends within the sanctuary at kilometre 10.76 (mile 6.46). Turn around and retrace your path back to your vehicle at kilometre 21.5 (mile 12.9).

RIDE 24 · Old Poco Trail

AT A GLANCE

FRASER VALLEY

Length/configuration: 15.4-km (9.25-mile) point-to-point. You'll either need to ride this as a 30.8-km (18.5-mile) out-and-back trail or arrange for a vehicle to pick you up at one of the many access points along the route

Aerobic difficulty: This is a very easy ride

Technical difficulty: There are a few stretches with loose rocks and roots, but most of the trail is easily rideable by the whole family

Scenery: The trail has numerous views along the river with ample opportunities for watching some herons and eagles. Pritchett Falls also makes for a picturesque final destination

Special comments: This wide double-track makes for a wonderful diversion on hot, sunny days when you are looking for a wooded ride that's great for the whole family. Following the meandering course of the Coquitlam River, it winds for 15.4 km (9.25 miles) before ending at a quiet waterfall

The Old Poco Trail offers a quiet roll along a meandering stream to a pleasant waterfall, all hidden from the invasion of development right at its doorstep. You can ride a straight 15.4-km (9.25-mile) point-to-point ride, or turn around and make it an out-and-back, maximizing the distance, but the length of the ride can be varied by using any of several public road access points.

As you ride, take the time to enjoy the gurgle of the stream, the chance to see salmon spawning in quiet tributaries, and the sounds of birds. It's sometimes difficult to believe that civilization is just past a thin canopy of cottonwood. For Coquitlam locals, this ride is an oasis, offering an escape from the pressures of everyday life. On hot summer days, the almost constant shade allows a welcome relief from the beating sun.

As you approach the upper reaches of the river, you will need to follow some public roads for a short distance. Beyond this short stretch, the trail takes on a rougher character, becoming a single-track with numerous roots and some moderate obstacles. They are not overly difficult and only persist for the last 3 km (1.8 miles). The trail is worth the extra effort—Pritchett Falls is a beautiful spot to relax and enjoy the sound of running water. While not a raging waterfall, its delicate ribbon of runoff seems to calm even the most jaded city dweller.

General location: City of Coquitlam.

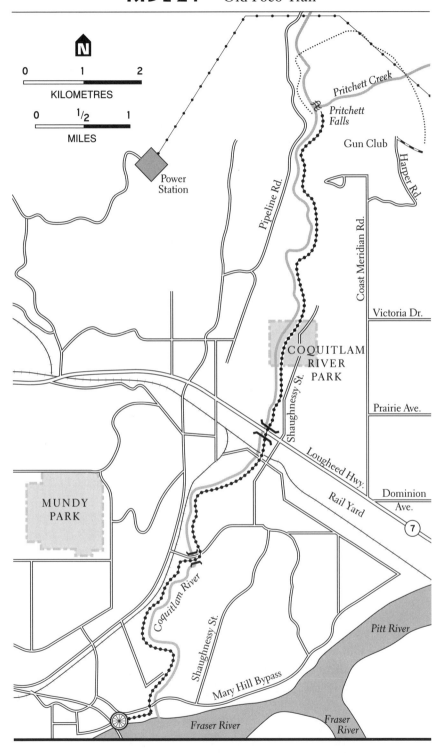

N

0   1   2
KILOMETRES

0   1/2   1
MILES

Power
Station

Pipeline Rd.

Pritchett Creek

Pritchett
Falls

Gun Club

Harper Rd.

Coast Meridian Rd.

Victoria Dr.

COQUITLAM
RIVER
PARK

Prairie Ave.

Shaughnessy St.

Lougheed Hwy.

Rail Yard

Dominion
Ave.

7

MUNDY
PARK

Coquitlam River

Shaughnessy St.

Mary Hill Bypass

Pitt River

Fraser River

Fraser
River

The Old Poco Trail is perfect when you are looking for a lazy roll along the winding course of the Coquitlam River.

Elevation change: The trail rises gradually from sea level at the trailhead to 240 metres (787 feet) at Pritchett Falls. The climb is gradual, almost unnoticeable.

Season: Year-round.

Services: All services are available in Coquitlam.

Hazards: Watch out for seemingly harmless blackberry branches overhanging the trail. The razor-sharp thorns will quickly remove chunks of flesh. When I rode the trail, I took a wrong turn, and the trail suddenly closed off into a solid wall of blackberry. It was like being attacked by a cougar.

Because the trail passes through a residential area, there will be many families and children on the trail, so remember to take it slow and yield to other users.

Rescue index: Because this trail runs through an ever-expanding area of residential development, help is rarely far away.

Land status: City of Coquitlam.

Maps: The NTS 1:50,000 topographic maps for this trail are 92 G/2 New Westminster and 92 G/7 Port Coquitlam.

Finding the trail: From Vancouver, take the Trans-Canada Highway east toward Coquitlam, to Exit 44/Mary Hill Bypass. From this exit, stay to the right, turning right onto United Boulevard, and then left immediately at Burbidge Street, circling around the Intermodal Services yard for the Canadian Pacific Railway. Stay to the left as the road circles around the Coca Cola plant toward Macquabeak Park. As you drive toward the far end of the parking lot, there is a paved route that lets you get right under the Port Mann Bridge to park.

Sources of additional information: I was unable to find any additional sources of information.

Notes on the trail: As you begin the ride by rolling beneath the Port Mann Bridge, stay sharply to the right, toward the river, and look for a yellow gate and sign stating: COQUITLAM RIVER WILDLIFE MANAGEMENT AREA. The trail begins as a wide double-track through stands of black cottonwood, red alder, blue elder, and thimbleberry. The trail begins by paralleling the noisy course of the Mary Hill Bypass. At kilometre 0.81 (mile 0.49), stay under the bridge as the Coquitlam River enters from the left. For the first part of the ride, you will stay on the west side of the river. After passing through a red metal gate, it winds along an access road before passing through another gate, this time painted yellow.

At kilometre 2 (mile 1.2), you roll your way past Colony Farm, an important wildlife preserve. Keep your eyes out for plentiful great blue herons and bald eagles. Looking across the river at the housing developments in Coquitlam, it's not hard to imagine how critical such preserves are to local wildlife and bird populations. At the 2.5-km (1.5-mile) mark, the trail leaves the river bank to cross under a set of power lines. The trail then joins the river again, winding along the shoreline until crossing under the power lines again at kilometre 4.24 (mile 2.55). Numerous small bridges cross over small runoff channels, adding a little excitement to the ride.

The next section of trail narrows and becomes slightly overgrown. At kilometre 5.16 (mile 3.1), however, you meet a bridge crossing Pitt River Road signed RED BRIDGE. Cross over the bridge, and the trail continues on the opposite side. The character changes instantly as the winding single-track becomes a wide, buffed double-track. Because the trail runs through dense residential areas, lots of side trails join in from the right. In most cases, just stay with the river and you won't go wrong. After passing a ball diamond at kilometre 7 (mile 4.2), the trail parallels a gravel alley and eventually goes through a gate at kilometre 7.6 (mile 4.56).

At kilometre 8 (mile 4.8), the trail passes under the double-tracks of the Canadian Pacific Railway. You'll want to dismount because the ceiling is quite low. After rolling past picturesque Lyons Park, you'll cross under another set of bridges, this time the two lanes of Lougheed Highway. Dismount again, and the trail continues on the other side. Beyond the underpasses, the trail crosses a small gravel clearing. When you enter the open area, cross to the other side and follow the left margin until you find a paved double-track trail continuing. When you see a high-quality bridge crossing the river at kilometre 9.5 (mile 5.7), avoid the temptation to cross and remain on the right bank by riding under the bridge crossing.

The river is an important spawning area for salmon, and a display at kilometre 11.2 (mile 6.7) describes work that has been done to help improve the spawning grounds along the Coquitlam River. Just past this display, the trail heads out to David Avenue. Because the trail is blocked by private property at this point, you'll need to follow David Avenue and turn left on Shaughnessy Street. At the end of Shaughnessy Street, the trail begins again at kilometre 12.39 (mile 7.43).

The trail takes gets wilder at this point. After passing a sign that indicates CAUTION ON MAINTAINED TRAIL AHEAD, the trail becomes a narrow single-track with lots of mud holes, roots, and more challenging sections. After a few minutes, you'll cross a log pyramid followed by a narrow bridge made of logs placed side by side lengthwise. Finally, at kilometre 15.4 (mile 9.25), you reach Pritchett Falls.

RIDE 25 · Woodland Walk to Coquitlam River Loop

AT A GLANCE

Length/configuration: 19-km (11.4-mile) loop using public roadways. For locals with two vehicles, it can be done as a shorter point-to-point ride, avoiding 7.2 km (4.3 miles) of road cycling

Aerobic difficulty: The challenge on this ride is the climb up to the main trailhead. Beyond this, the grade is downhill. If you have sufficient technical skill to do this ride, you'll probably have the aerobic gumption to get there

Technical difficulty: This is an expert ride with severe drops, large root exposure, and a very steep gradient.

Scenery: The scenery along the river is beautiful; however, the challenging section of the ride is in dense west coast rain forest

Special comments: This trail forms an excellent transition between intermediate and hairball hard-core. Unlike many of the north shore rides, the trail is extremely challenging, but the consequences of mistakes are not as dire as some of the other hard-core rides in the area

Okay, you've passed some of the tests, and you want to head out onto an expert-level ride. (Remember, *expert* on the west coast is an entirely different breed.) You've lowered your seat, you've installed riser bars, and you want to

RIDE 25 · Woodland Walk to Coquitlam River Loop

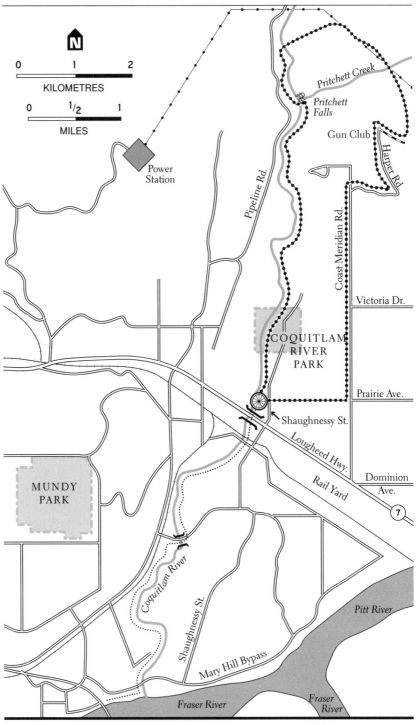

The woodland walk plummets down sheer root drops from Pinecone-Burke Provincial Park to the Coquitlam River.

go for it. This may be a good trail. It's no place for sissies, but it isn't as dire as some of the other expert rides on the coast. It is a 19-km (11.4-mile) loop ride that takes advantage of 7.2 km (4.3 miles) of public roads to create the loop. Much of the ride is beginner level with the exception of 3 km (1.8 miles) between the junction with the Woodland Walk Trail and the crossing of the Coquitlam River that are challenging. The combination makes this a nice trail for days when you want to have a hard ride but also want to catch your breath and have a good time. It mixes some difficult technical riding with some pleasant, scenic, riverside rolling.

General location: Pinecone-Burke Provincial Park.

Elevation change: From the trailhead along the Woodland Walk Trail, the trend is downhill, losing 120 m (394 feet) in approximately 1.8 km (1.1 miles).

Season: Due to the sensitive nature of this trail, be sure to wait for dry weather. It is extremely prone to erosion, and if the park staff find mountain biking to be impacting the park in a negative way, we will probably find ourselves ejected.

Services: All services are available in Coquitlam.

Hazards: This trail is an expert ride with numerous wheelie drops, exposed roots, and steep gradients. With this comes a seemingly endless number of immovable objects on which to bounce your bike (and carcass). Stay off of this trail unless you can confidently negotiate daunting rides.

Rescue index: Although the trail is popular, it is not uncommon to meet only a few riders here. Your best option in case of emergency is to continue toward the bottom of the trail and the junction with the Old Poco Trail. Once you begin following this much more popular trail, you will encounter many other trail users. You are also riding through a residential area where help is only a knock on the door away.

Land status: This trail falls primarily within the boundaries of the newly established Pinecone-Burke Provincial Park. As such, its future, along with the many other rides within the Burke Mountain area, is uncertain. It is critical that riders respect the other users of the trails and that we reduce our impact to ensure future access to this great network.

Maps: The NTS 1:50,000 topographic map for this trail is 92 G/7 Port Coquitlam.

Finding the trail: In Vancouver, take Lougheed Highway (Highway 7) east toward Coquitlam. Shortly after entering the city of Coquitlam, turn left onto Shaughnessy Street and left again on Prairie Avenue. Park at the Coquitlam River Dike.

Sources of additional information: Because this trail lies within the boundaries of the newly formed Pinecone-Burke Provincial Park, it is maintained by the British Columbia Provincial Parks Department.

Notes on the trail: From the parking area, ride east on Prairie Avenue for approximately 1.5 km (0.9 mile) and turn left on Coast Meridian Road. Climb up Coast Meridian for 3.7 km (2.2 miles) and turn right on Harper Road. Continue climbing up this road for just under 2 km (1.2 miles), staying on it as it makes a 90-degree left turn halfway. It ends at a parking lot for a local gun range. You will see a gated road climbing from the parking lot. Follow this wide double-track until you see a wide trail turning left. This is the Woodland Walk Trail. Climb this high-quality track until it joins the power lines. Keep climbing until you see a sign that reads TO COQUITLAM RIVER. This should be the 11-km (6.6-mile) point. From here the character changes dramatically. The wide double-track becomes a narrow, rutted, steep single-track that loses 120 m (394 feet) in just a few kilometres. As the trail bottoms out, stay to the left and it will bring you to a shallow ford for an easy crossing of the Coquitlam River. From this point on the trail becomes a bumpy single-track for 3 km (1.8 miles), after which it suddenly becomes a wide double-track roll back to your car at kilometre 19 (11.4 miles).

RIDE 26 · Hayward Lake Railway Trail

AT A GLANCE

Length/configuration: 5.73-km (3.44-mile) point-to-point ride, or you can make a 13.65-km (8.2-mile) loop using existing roadways

Aerobic difficulty: The trail is rolling, requiring a moderate fitness level. The road back to the trailhead includes a long uphill followed by a lengthy coast to the finish line

Technical difficulty: There are some narrow technical stretches, but the majority is beginner-level riding

Scenery: Beautiful, hugging the shores of Hayward Lake and rolling past evidence of the old railway

Special comments: This was the route of Canada's shortest incorporated railway, and many of the old trestles still stand today

For riders interested in mixing a little riding with a bit of history, the 5.73-km (3.44-mile) Hayward Railway Trail provides the perfect mix. Along the route, numerous interpretive signs help bring the history of this unique rail line back to life. While you pedal along this serene mountain lake, it's difficult to imagine the black smoke and noise that accompanied the old steam locomotives during the early part of the century. During its heyday, beginning at the turn of the century and extending into the 1940s, the trains chugged their way along this route. In 1921, the steam locomotives were replaced by electric engines, and in 1929–30 the Ruskin Dam was built, creating Hayward Lake. The construction of the dam meant the rail line had to be elevated above the high-water line, and many of these original trestles still stand today, a haunting reminder of the romantic age of train travel.

While you ride, stop periodically for a quick energy break—the trail is lined with blackberry, salmonberry, and thimbleberry. Above you, bigleaf maple, alder, and Douglas fir offer shade. Be sure to be off the trail by dusk, as the gates are locked at night.

General location: Port Coquitlam.

Elevation change: The trail is level, with only small rolling changes in elevation. If you choose to create a loop with the Dewdney Trunk Road, you will climb sharply and steadily for 5 km (3 miles) to the junction with Wilson Street at elevation 180 m (590 feet). From here, hang onto your brakes and scream your way back down to the trailhead.

RIDE 26 · Hayward Lake Railway Trail

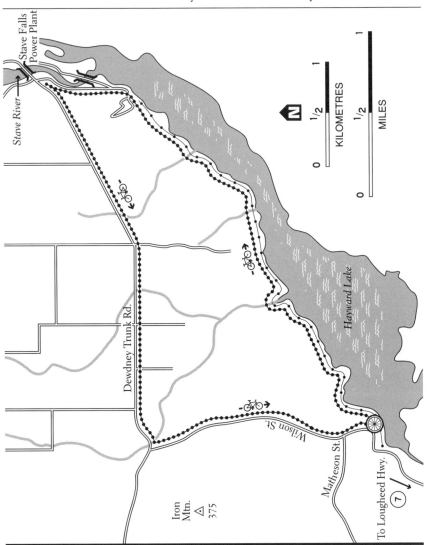

Season: Year-round.

Services: All services are available in Maple Ridge and Mission.

Hazards: While cycling the trail on a hot summer day, it may be tempting to take a quick dip in the lake to refresh yourself. As this is a hydro-generating lake, avoid swimming except in specifically designated areas. The currents from the dam can make it exceedingly dangerous to swim in the wrong place. This trail is used by many hikers. Keep your speed low to allow for rapid reaction when hikers or other cyclists appear suddenly.

Hayward Lake Railway Trail mixes a pleasant roll with some unique history.

At kilometre 2.37 (mile 1.4), a sign asks cyclists to walk their bike. Please comply with this request even though the stairwells are narrow, making it even more challenging to push your bike. While the blackberries offer a tasty treat along the ride, watch out for the occasional branch creeping onto the trail. Their sharp claws love to grab a passing biker.

Rescue index: This is a very popular trail, so help is usually available. It also has a major day-use area at each end where help can be recruited.

Land status: British Columbia Hydro Land.

Maps: The NTS 1:50,000 topographic map for this trail is 92 G/1 Mission. It offers a good look at the ride.

Finding the trail: Follow the Trans-Canada Highway east to Exit 44/Port Coquitlam/Pitt, staying to the right to provide access to Mary Hill Bypass. It almost looks like you are heading back onto the highway, but fear not; this is the correct route. As the exit forks, go left onto United Boulevard North/Pitt Meadows/Maple Ridge. Go straight at the first set of lights onto Mary Hill Bypass (Highway 7B east). Follow this route as it winds along, getting into the right lane for the junction with Lougheed Highway (Highway 7 east) at kilometre 7.9 (mile

4.74). Follow Lougheed Highway over the bridge following signs for Hayward Lake and Stavely (287 Street). You will stay on Lougheed for quite some time before turning left onto 287 Street. This road winds slightly to the right to become Wilson Street. After approximately 4 km (2.4 miles), turn right into the day-use area signed Hayward Lake Railway Trail.

Sources of additional information: I was unable to find any additional sources of information.

Notes on the trail: The trail begins just above the dam and follows the left-hand shoreline of the lake, following the route of the former railway. The first kilometre is level. Turn right at a junction at kilometre 1.14 (mile 0.7) and drop down a series of rideable steps along a boardwalk bordering the lake. After crossing a small bridge at kilometre 1.35 (mile 0.8), the trail makes a short, sharp climb. Stay straight at the junction with the Tall Tree Loop Trail at kilometre 1.66 (mile 1). You will need to dismount for a short bit as you round a corner at kilometre 2.37 (mile 1.4). The trail at this point is signed as environmentally sensitive, and cyclists are asked to walk their bikes until kilometre 2.62 (mile 1.57). At this juncture the trail winds around a small, marshy inlet. It goes up a series of steps, along a boardwalk, and over some narrow bridges. The pushing, although only for a short time, can get tricky, so be sure to take your time.

A service road joins at kilometre 5.53 (mile 3.3); stay on the main trail. Pass the junction with the Pond Trail Loop at kilometre 5.73 (mile 3.44) and roll past this small marsh as it appears on your left. For a short distance, you will have the beaver pond on your left and Hayward Lake Reservoir on your right. At this point, you can finally satisfy that urge for a swim—a small area is set aside for bathers. Beyond, the trail winds through a picnic area, past the warden's office, and then climbs sharply past the Stave Falls Power House to the junction with Dewdney Trunk Road. Turn left almost 180 degrees (do *not* go to the traffic lights), and continue climbing. Stop for an ice cream at Clark's General Store (make sure you have cash—that's all they accept). The climbing ends at kilometre 11 (mile 6.6) with the junction with Wilson Street. Turn left and enjoy a long, screaming downhill to the trailhead at kilometre 13.65 (mile 8.2).

RIDE 27 · Matsqui Trail

AT A GLANCE

Length/configuration: 8.44-km (5.1-mile) point-to-point or 16.88 km (10.2 miles) if you ride the trail and then return along the same route

Aerobic difficulty: Very flat, excellent for the whole family

Technical difficulty: Wide double-track with little challenge

Scenery: Beautiful as it winds along the river with periodic views

Special comments: A great family ride along the shores of the Fraser River

FRASER VALLEY

One of the more pleasant riverside rides along the Fraser River, the Matsqui Trail takes you on an 8.44-km (5.1-mile) point-to-point trip along the winding course of this famous river. Along the way, it winds through some of the agricultural land that borders the Fraser. Although close to civilization, this trail has a decidedly rural feel to it. Bring the kids, as there is little to slow them down on this well-designed trail. For riders looking for a little more challenge, the trail offers periodic single-track forks heading toward the river. These undesignated trails tend to bob and weave through the trees, allowing for a little diversion from the flat of the main trail.

Although the trail doesn't actually skirt the shoreline and offers only occasional views, it does benefit from the cool breezes that usually blow off the water. This makes it ideal for hot summer days. Like many coastal areas, the name *Matsqui* is a translation of a native term meaning "easy portage," possibly referring to the flat nature of the land, allowing local Halkomelem Indians an easy portage between the Fraser and nearby rivers and lakes.

General location: City of Matsqui.

Elevation change: None.

Season: Year-round.

Services: All services are available in Mission.

Hazards: This trail is wide and smooth, with few hazards.

Rescue index: This trail is quite popular, and help is rarely far away.

Land status: Matsqui Trail Regional Park.

Maps: The NTS 1:50,000 topographic map for this trail is 92 G/1 Mission.

RIDE 27 · Matsqui Trail

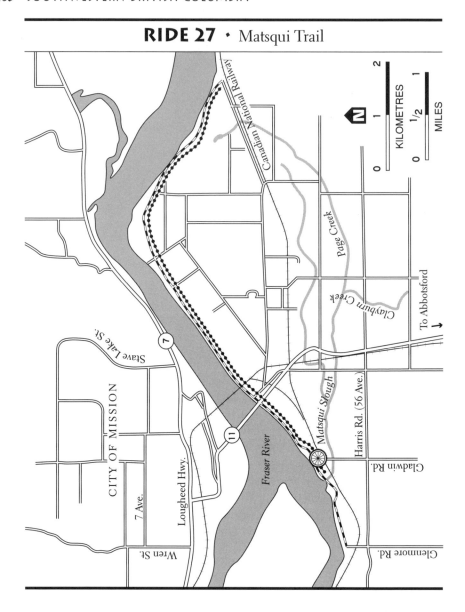

Finding the trail: Take the Trans-Canada Highway east from Vancouver to Exit 44/Pitt Meadows/Maple Ridge. As you take the exit, stay in the right-hand lane, which will fork off. Follow the Trans-Canada Highway east to Exit 44/Port Coquitlam/Pitt, staying to the right to provide access to Mary Hill Bypass. It almost looks like you are heading back onto the highway, but don't worry; this is the correct route. As the exit forks, go left onto United Boulevard North/Pitt Meadows/Maple Ridge. Go straight at the first set of lights onto Mary Hill Bypass

The wide gradient of Matsqui Trail offers a pleasant riverside roll.

(Highway 7B east). Follow this route as it winds along, getting into the right lane for the junction with Lougheed Highway (Highway 7 east) at kilometre 7.9 (mile 4.74). Follow Lougheed Highway over the bridge and continue until the Highway 11/Abbotsford Exit. Shortly after crossing the Fraser River, turn right at the first set of lights onto Harris Road. After approximately 2 km (1.2 miles), turn right onto Gladwin Road and follow this over the railway tracks. You'll see the trailhead on the right. Find a place to park along the side of the roadway, but be sure not to block access to the gate as emergency vehicles occasionally need to pass through.

Sources of additional information: For further information about Matsqui Trail, call the GVRD Parks' East Area office at (604) 530-4983, or write:

Greater Vancouver Regional District Parks Department
4330 Kingsway
Burnaby, B.C. V5H 4G8

Notes on the trail: The trail is remarkably easy to follow. Simply stay on the main gravel route as it makes its way adjacent to the Fraser River. There are several opportunities to take informal single-track trails along the river. These run parallel to the main path and eventually return to it. As the trail winds along, there are periodic road crossings through gates. At kilometre 1.37 (mile 0.82), the trail passes a picnic site beside the river and then passes under the noisy highway bridge. There is a short stretch of pavement until you join the trail again at 1.9 km (1.1 miles). By the time you pass the 4-km (2.4-mile) mark, the trail has moved further from the river and passes through agricultural land on both sides. The trail begins to move closer to the river again after kilometre 6 (mile 3.6), although the view of the water is largely obscured by cottonwood and willow trees. The trail ends at a gate at kilometre 8.44 (mile 5.1). Retrace your path to return to your vehicle at kilometre 16.88 (mile 10.2).

RIDE 28 · Vedder Mountain Ridge Trail

AT A GLANCE

Length/configuration: 17.2-km (10.3-mile) loop

Aerobic difficulty: The trail involves some steep climbing and requires strong lungs

Technical difficulty: Some of the loose rock is very challenging, making this a ride for expert riders

Scenery: Periodic views north toward the Vedder River and the lush farmland at the base of Vedder Mountain

Special comments: This is the site of a popular annual mountain bike race. The course differs from this route and is much more difficult

The Ridge Trail on Vedder Mountain combines a gradual climb up the wide gravel of the Vedder Mountain Forest Service Road with an up-and-over route to traverse a shoulder of Vedder Mountain. The 17.2-km (10.3-mile) loop provides a combination of wide, fast fire road and narrow single-track. Don't be fooled by the wide approach—the trail is at times narrow and technical and should be reserved for strong riders only. Once you leave the Forest Service road, the trail, which is mostly an old forestry road, often nar-

RIDE 28 · Vedder Mountain Ridge Trail

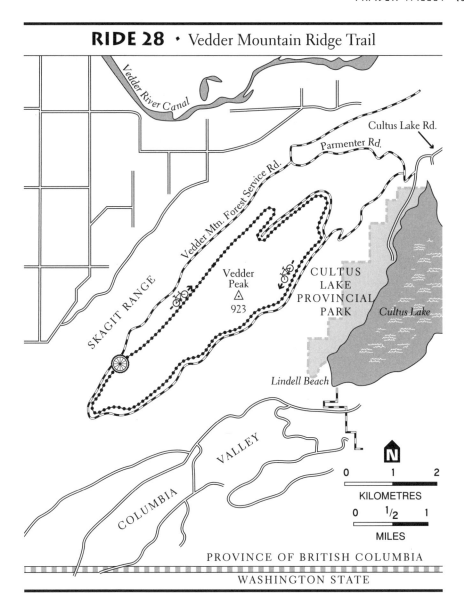

rows and becomes quite rutted in spots. Melon-sized boulders will test your balance on other sections.

The trail runs through an understory of alder, Douglas fir, elder, and thimbleberry. Tiny bleeding heart flowers seem to sympathize with your pain from some of the uphill stretches. The views of the surrounding farmland are spectacular and showcase the canals built for irrigation in the area. Keep your ears and eyes open for Steller's jays as they taunt you from the trees. Their raucous

Vedder Mountain Ridge offers a rolling technical challenge with some excellent views near the summit.

call, once you've heard it, is rarely mistaken for any other bird. Some of the old logging stumps are in excess of 1 m (3.28 feet) in diametre.

General location: South of Chilliwack.

Elevation change: From the trailhead at approximately 500 m (1,640 feet), the trail rolls past the 780 m (2,558 feet) mark before descending back to the Forest Service road.

Season: Year-round.

Services: All services are available in Chilliwack or Abbotsford.

Hazards: There are many loose rocks on downhills that could easily send a novice over the handlebars. In addition, large boulders will challenge you on some of the uphills. Periodic washouts are another hazard, and the regular occurrence of unsigned spur trails adds an additional challenge. Be sure to bring a topographic map and compass with you on this ride.

Rescue index: You probably won't encounter a large number of riders once you leave the Forest Service road. Be prepared to hoof it out to the road, and perhaps all the way to town, in the case of a breakdown. This is a wilderness ride with all of the requisite cautions.

From Vedder Mountain, snowcapped peaks contrast sharply with the lush agricultural wealth of the Fraser Valley.

Land status: British Columbia Forestry Demonstration Forest,

Maps: The NTS 1:50,000 topographic maps for this trail are 92 G/1 Mission and the western edge of 92 H/4.

Finding the trail: From Vancouver, travel east toward Chilliwack along the Trans-Canada Highway until you come to Exit 119 B, Vedder Road. Head south on Vedder Road until it crosses the Vedder River. Once across the river, stay right at the junction with Vedder Mountain Road. Follow Vedder Mountain Road for a short distance until you reach Cultus Lake Road. Turn left onto Cultus Lake Road and follow the road as it begins to climb almost immediately. Follow this road for 2.2 km (1.32 miles) and turn right onto the gravel of Parmenter Road. This road is marked by a sign for PARMENTER ROAD across the top of an upright log and two descending strips of wood forming an upside-down triangle. The gravel begins climbing immediately as you bump your way up Parmenter Road. Turn right at the first junction at 0.6 km (0.36 mile) and climb Vedder Mountain Forest Service Road. After an additional 0.6 km (0.36 mile), stay right as the Vedder Mountain Forest Service Road climbs up to the left. In 1 km (0.6 mile) take the rougher road that branches off to the left (if you don't, you will reach a locked gate). Climb on this road for 7 km (4.2 miles) until you see a rough trail joining from the left. The trail is marked by a post with a featureless white sign.

Sources of additional information: I was unable to find any additional sources of information.

Notes on the trail: The trail begins climbing almost immediately along a narrow double-track. Ignore the trail that branches to the right after you begin the climb. After kilometre 0.8 (mile 0.48) the trail drops along a rolling gradient for a short distance. Shortly after, the trail begins to close in slightly to resemble more of a wide single-track. At kilometre 1.3 (mile 0.78), the trail begins to climb steeply again, followed by a short, moderate downhill. At the bottom of the downhill, a short washout requires vigilance. A washed-out corduroy bridge at kilometre 1.9 (mile 1.14) is followed by a rather dark, foreboding stretch of forest. The western hemlocks shade the trail, making a haven for ferns and mosses in the abundance of downfall. You quickly climb out of this into an alder and willow forest followed by a short, technical downhill that brings you onto a wide side-cut along the lower slopes of Vedder Mountain. At kilometre 2.9 (mile 1.74) stay on the main trail as an overgrown trail enters from the right. There is an arrow sign indicating this. Turn right at the T intersection at kilometre 3.4 (mile 2.04) and follow the wide double-track. As you pass a communications tower at kilometre 4.7 (mile 2.8), the trail makes a sharp switchback to the right and begins climbing steeply until kilometre 5.8 (mile 3.5). A small clearing is reached at kilometre 6.2 (mile 3.7), where trails radiate to the right and left of the main trail. Stay straight at this junction. The trail climbs slightly and passes through a short section that holds water, creating a large puddle. Once through this, the trail drops for a short distance. When I rode the trail, there was some pink and green flagging tape with the words LONG RIDE on it. Stay to the left at the junction at kilometre 7.8 (mile 4.7). You meet the fire road at kilometre 8.6 (mile 5.16). Turn right on the good gravel and follow the road, continuing as it makes a sudden right at kilometre 9.8 (mile 5.9). The views to the surrounding farmland open up and escort you to the car at kilometre 17.2 (mile 10.3).

RIDE 29 · Vedder Mountain Road Ride

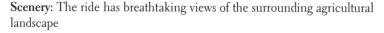

AT A GLANCE

Length/configuration: 19.9-km (11.9-mile) loop

Aerobic difficulty: A moderate uphill followed by a long descent

Technical difficulty: The trail is an easy logging road with an occasional stretch of loose rocks

Scenery: The ride has breathtaking views of the surrounding agricultural landscape

Special comments: An excellent ride for families with older children or cyclists looking for an easy ride with a little wilderness flavour

RIDE 29 · Vedder Mountain Road Ride

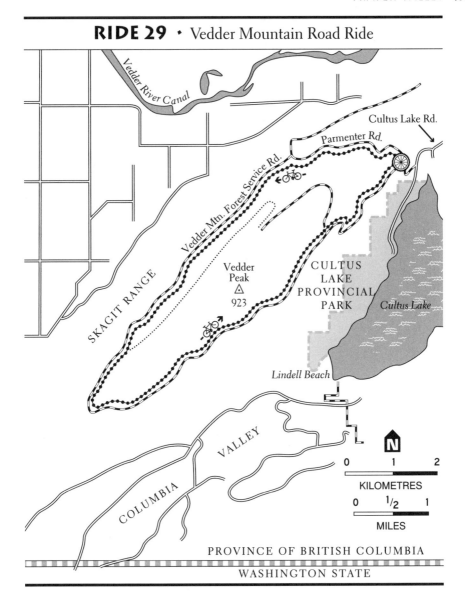

If you are looking for a ride with spectacular panoramas, along with a minimum of technical challenge, then this 19.9-km (11.9-mile) loop may just fit the bill. This wide forestry access road circumnavigates the base of Vedder Mountain, providing sweeping views of the surrounding agricultural lands. From the roadside, the views stretch north to the community of Yarrow, the Vedder Canal, and Sumas Prairie. To the north, the snow-capped peaks of the Golden Ears dominate the skyline. The area has been previously logged, with giant stumps in excess of 1 metre in diametre. The second growth of western red cedar has a lush undergrowth of thimbleberry, bleeding heart, and goatsbeard.

The view of Fraser Valley from Vedder Mountain Road.

General location: South of Chilliwack.

Elevation change: From the trailhead, at approximately 160 m (525 feet), the trail climbs gradually to almost 600 m (1,968 feet) over the course of 11 km (6.6 miles).

Season: Year-round.

Services: All services are available in Chilliwack.

Hazards: With the exception of a few loose rocks, this trail is very safe. It does have some vehicle traffic on it, so be cautious around blind corners. The final descent is moderately steep and may be loose and slightly rutted.

Rescue index: Because this road forms the primary access to Vedder Mountain, there is generally some vehicle traffic. In the odd case where you don't meet anyone, head down to the park office at Cultus Lake, near the base of Parmenter Road.

Land status: British Columbia Forestry Demonstration Forest.

Maps: The NTS 1:50,000 topographic maps for this are 92 G/1 Mission, and the western edge of 92 H/4.

Finding the trail: From Vancouver, travel east toward Chilliwack along Trans-Canada Highway until you come to Exit 119 B, Vedder Road. Head south on Vedder Road until it crosses the Vedder River. Once across the river, stay right at the junction with Vedder Mountain Road. Follow Vedder Mountain Road for a short distance until you reach Cultus Lake Road. Turn left onto Cultus Lake

Road and follow the road as it begins to climb almost immediately. Follow this road for 2.2 km (1.32 miles) and turn right onto the gravel of Parmenter Road. This road is marked by a sign for PARMENTER ROAD across the top of an upright log and two descending strips of wood forming an upside-down triangle. The gravel begins climbing immediately as you bump your way up Parmenter Road. Turn right at the first junction at 0.6 km (0.36 mile) and climb Vedder Mountain Forest Service Road. After an additional 0.6 km (0.36 mile), you'll see the Vedder Mountain Forest Service Road climb up to the left. Park near this junction.

Sources of additional information: Because this route has been chosen by the British Columbia Forest Service as a self-guided forestry tour, it is worth your time to obtain one of the brochures explaining the various stops. These offer a wealth of information on forestry and can be obtained from the British Columbia Forestry office in Rosedale, 9880 South McGrath Rd., Rosedale, B.C. V0X 1X0, phone (604) 794-2100.

Notes on the trail: The trail is generally ridden in a counterclockwise direction, so stay right at the trailhead junction (the trail returns down the steep gravel climbing from this point). In 1 km (0.6 mile) take the rougher road that branches off to the left of the main road (if you don't, you will reach a locked gate). Although it appears to be a rough gravel road when first viewed from the junction, it quickly opens up to become a wide, high-quality gravel road. A rough trail comes in from the right at kilometre 2.3 (mile 1.4). Stay straight along the main forestry road. At kilometre 2.7 (mile 1.6), the views begin to open up to the surrounding farmland. Another rough road joins in from the right at kilometre 3.2 (mile 1.9). Despite these periodic spurs, the main road is always obvious. At the 3.6-km (2.2-mile) mark, an old clear-cut to the right allows clear views of the surrounding valley. The previous ride branches off to the left at kilometre 8.4 (mile 5.04). Ignore this junction and stay on the main road; follow it as it makes a sharp left turn just 1 km (0.6 mile) beyond forestry stop 12 (15.8 km/9.5 miles). After another kilometre, you pass the terminus of Ride 28, the Vedder Mountain Ridge Trail, on your left. Beyond this, the trail begins to drop steadily, finally reaching your car at kilometre 19.9 (mile 11.94).

SEA TO SKY HIGHWAY (HIGHWAY 99)

As you leave West Vancouver and begin heading north along the Sea to Sky Highway (Highway 99), the meandering course runs along some of the most spectacular views imaginable. To the east, the open waters of Howe Sound and its numerous islands make even the most jaded Vancouverite's jaw drop. This drive is exquisite, although it is extremely winding, prone to delays from rock slides and road work, and as busy as a Los Angeles freeway. As the Sea to Sky corridor has continued to open up over the last 20 years, once quiet communities like Squamish, Whistler, and Pemberton find themselves struggling against ever grander development schemes. As developers see dollar signs, mountain bikers have seen opportunity. Over the last decade, this corridor has evolved into a premier mountain biking mecca.

Squamish, once a sleepy community built on the logging industry, has grown more slowly than Whistler to the north, but the pace of development is accelerating. Logging still plays a critical role, but this industry has now found its old trails and roads popular with mountain bikers. Squamish has become a very popular place for rock climbers, wind surfers, and mountain bikers. Rising above Squamish is the Stawamus Chief, the largest granite monolith in Canada. Its sheer face attracts a steady stream of climbers. Around Squamish, mountain bike races like the Cheakamus Challenge and the Test of Metal, along with trail networks like Crumpit Woods have brought more and more cyclists into the area. Every rider in the Squamish area owes it to themselves to grind their way up Diamondhead to Elfin Lakes, one of the few alpine areas accessible to mountain bikers. Epic rides like the Ring Creek Rip will have your lungs burning as you make your way toward the top of Bonk Hill. This is classic mountain bike country.

Beyond Squamish, the community of Whistler epitomizes rapid growth and instant fame. Only 30 years ago, it was a seven-hour ordeal to reach the tiny community of Alta Lake, as Whistler was originally known. The first paved road was laid down in 1964, and the first ski lift was installed just one year later. Whistler Mountain continued to grow, and 15 years later Blackcomb Mountain followed suit. Today, the community is known around the world for the finest skiing in North America; in fact, *Snow Country Magazine* has repeatedly designated it as the number one ski resort on the continent. Ski resorts attract large numbers of young people seeking seasonal work; over time, they began to discover the area's summer potential as well. With the growth of mountain biking, Whistler has stayed on the cutting edge. New trails seem to pop up on a continual basis, and the classic trails will test the most determined gearhead.

Numerous trail networks, such as Cut Yer Bars and Mel's Dilemma, offer convoluted fun, while high climbs like the routes over Microwave Hill and up to Black Tusk will push your endurance. Other classic rides like Shit Happens, A River Runs Through It, and Kill Me, Thrill Me offer endless diversity.

Beyond Whistler, the pace of development slows, and communities like Pemberton are only now beginning to feel the sting of the bulldozer as it begins to put more and more land under concrete. Now that Whistler's real estate has become unattainable by most mortals, locals are beginning to discover Pemberton's wonderful location. Mountain biking is also growing; loops like the Birkenhead Loop and the grind up Blowdown Creek are helping to fan the flames of mountain bike fame. This area has much to offer and will see continued expansion over the next decade.

RIDE 30 · Squamish Estuary Trails

AT A GLANCE

Length/configuration: 4-km (2.4-mile) loop

Aerobic difficulty: The trail is flat and requires little effort

Technical difficulty: A great, easy trail for the whole family

Scenery: The trail offers ever-changing views along the estuary as tide levels and weather systems change

Special comments: Bring the family and a good pair of binoculars on this easy loop

A popular ride within the town of Squamish, the estuary trails are a smooth, wide, flat series offering a pleasant diversion from the hard-core rides on the other side of town. The 4-km (2.4-mile) loop is an exercise in contrasts, varying from pristine coastal views to noisy log dumps. While you ride, listen for the clicking call of the belted kingfisher. You may see it as it flies along the water moving from one favourite vantage point to another. Watch for great blue herons and bald eagles as well. Munch on blackberries, but beware their dark

RIDE 30 · Squamish Estuary

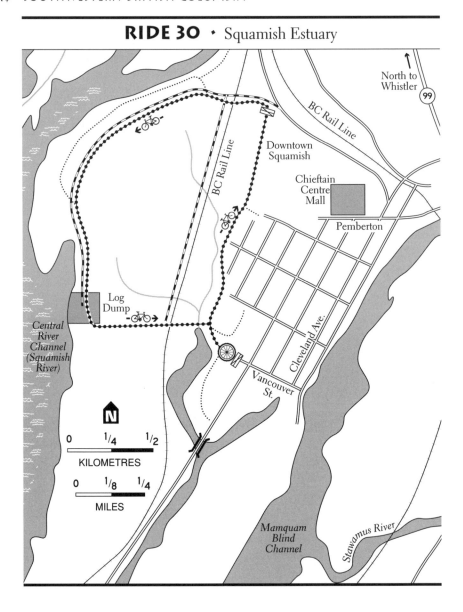

side. Their long, thorny branches grow outward, invading the trail and slashing at you as you whiz by. Within the estuary area, six glacial rivers enter the ocean. The tides rise and fall, and the character continually changes. As well as a pleasant ride, this is also a great place to park your bike to explore on foot some of the spur trails that are too soft for bikes.

As the trail enters the lumber depot, you'll need to be cautious of the heavy equipment. The blackberries are beyond this minor obstacle and well worth the

The Squamish Estuary mixes quiet coastal cycling with a busy log dump and a smorgas-bord of blackberries.

effort, so keep on going. This industrial detour also serves notice to the lack of protection of the estuary and surrounding area. As industry threatens the estuary, we risk losing this wondrous ecosystem.

General location: Within the town of Squamish.

Elevation change: None.

Season: Year-round.

Services: All services are available in Squamish.

Hazards: The sharp drop over the river can offer a sudden dismount to riders out on a simple roll if they are not paying attention. Even easy trails require vigilance. Remember as you traverse the log dump that this is a busy industrial site with large vehicles constantly buzzing about.

Rescue index: Because this trail runs right behind a busy residential area, help is rarely far away.

Land status: Community of Squamish.

Maps: The NTS 1:50,000 topographic map for this trail is 92 G/11 Squamish; however, local town maps are just as good.

Finding the trail: For the loop as described, follow Squamish's main drag, Cleveland Street, to its junction with Vancouver Street. Turn right and continue until the road ends at a gate. A small parking area is available.

Sources of additional information:

Squamish Off-Road Cycling Association
Box 793
Garibaldi Highlands, B.C., V0N 1T0
(604) 898-3519

Notes on the trail: This network of informal trails follows the estuary inland and offers a variety of views based on the tide, season, and luck. Traveling counterclockwise, the trail follows the estuary inland until it dissipates. Stay straight at a junction at kilometre 0.2 (mile 0.12), despite the more prominent, double-track nature of the adjoining trail. The trail enters the forest for a short distance, surrounded by water at high tide. After passing a housing subdivision on your right, another access trail feeds in from the right, beyond which the trail drops down sharply to a narrow bridge over the river. Stay on this trail until you reach a gate at kilometre 1.2 (mile 0.7). Turn left beyond the gate and roll your way along a gravel access road. Follow this road as it swings to the left and terminates at a log dump. This is a place full of activity as tractors scurry about with loads of logs in their caliper-like jaws. It reminds one of a giant anthill, with these heavy vehicles shuttling the logs from one pile to another. Staying vigilant, cross the entire site. At the far end, a turnaround loop swings left. Follow this for a few metres until a single-track branches to the right. Take this welcome exit and enjoy the crazy contrasts between industry and the adjacent estuary.

Along this narrow single-track, a lonely picnic bench offers a rest spot. During August, blackberries offer a tantalizing and tasty diversion. The trail crosses the tracks, after which you turn right at the final junction before returning to your vehicle at approximately 4 kilometres (2.4 miles).

RIDE 31 · Elfin Lakes (Diamondhead)

AT A GLANCE

Length/configuration: There are two options: either 25 km (15 miles) one way for a total of 50 km (30 miles) out-and-back if you decide to ride the main access road; or 10.7 km (6.42 miles) one way for a total of 21.4 km (12.8 miles) out-and-back should you decide to drive the access road and ride the trail only

Aerobic difficulty: This trail has extreme elevation gain and is suitable for experienced, fit cyclists

Technical difficulty: The trail largely follows a former access road and is wide and moderately smooth

Scenery: As you climb above the valley bottom, the views of Garibaldi Provincial Park begin to open up. They improve with elevation until you finally reach the twin gems of the Elfin Lakes

Special comments: This is a ride strong cyclists will do over and over. It mixes splendid landscape with a good, lung-burning uphill

This ride reminds one of why mountain bikes were invented in the first place—to leave the world behind and access magical locations. The climb to Elfin Lakes can be done one of two ways—hard or harder. By parking near the Squamish Valley Golf and Country Club, you can add an additional 14.3 km (8.6 miles) and 860 metres (2,821 feet) to the ride. Riders sufficiently challenged by the 21.4 km (12.8 miles) of the main trail may choose to drive this stretch and save their legs (and lungs) for the entrée. The trail offers different distances, so that both groups of riders will have accurate distances to follow.

The trail climbs steadily, and the views improve until Mount Garibaldi (2,488 m/8,162 feet) and its three glaciers (the Diamond, the Bishop, and the Lava Glaciers) dominate the northern skyline. As you crest the summit of Round Mountain, the impressive face of Mamquam Mountain (2,400 m/7,873 feet) rolls into view to the east.

The lakes are beautiful. An old backcountry ski lodge stands defiantly against the elements, although it has been closed for many years. The views to Mount Garibaldi and Mamquam Mountain are unobstructed. Take the time to properly drink in this magical location; there are few areas of such majesty so accessible to mountain bikes. Most similar alpine panoramas have long been closed to fat tires.

General location: Garibaldi Provincial Park.

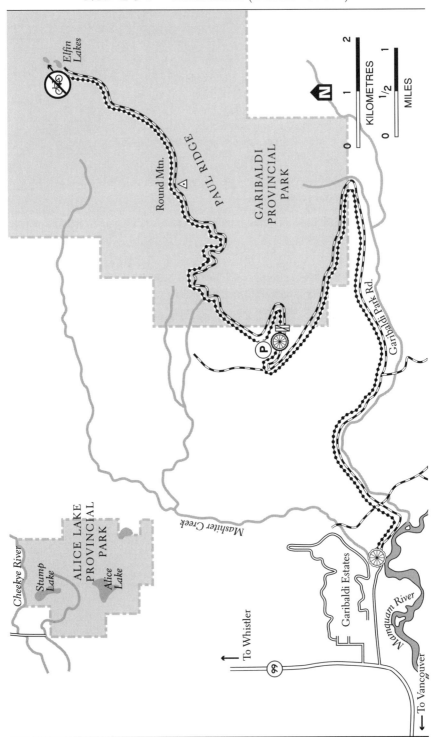

The arrival at Elfin Lake rewards cyclists with one of the premier panoramas on the West Coast.

Elevation change: From the golf course, at elevation 73 m (236 feet), the road climbs steadily, 860 m (2,821 feet) to the trailhead. After the trailhead, the climbing continues to the summit of Round Mountain at elevation 1,677 m (5,500 feet). From this summit, the trail drops to the lakes at elevation 1,479 m (4,850 feet).

Season: This is west coast high country and has heavy winter snowfalls. The best time to ride the trail is between mid-July and early September.

Services: All services are available in Squamish.

Hazards: This is a wilderness trail and must be treated with respect. Although very popular, the combination of high elevation and variable weather can cause difficulties. Also, the snow may remain on the ground well into the summer, especially in sheltered areas near the summit of Round Mountain. In the case of inclement weather, there is a shelter at the Red Heather Campground.

Rescue index: In an emergency, this trail is quite busy, and help is usually not far away. However, should you need to phone for help, the Squamish Royal Canadian Mounted Police can be reached at (604) 898-9611. British Columbia Garibaldi Provincial Park Staff are available at (604) 898-3678. The nearest pay phone is located at the golf course at the bottom of the hill; however, there is good cellular signal in the area, and cell phones are becoming a common addition to many hiker and biker daypacks. I have made many a phone call from remote summits to let my wife know of my whereabouts, even though there was no signal until I crested the peak.

Land status: The trail begins within British Columbia Crown land and finishes within Garibaldi Provincial Park.

Maps: The NTS 1:50,000 topographic maps for this trail are 92 G/11 Squamish, 92 G/14 Cheakamus River, and a tiny bit of 92 G/15 Mamquam Mountain. The best maps for the route are *Discover British Columbia's Garibaldi Region* (1:100,000), published by International Travel Maps (345 West Broadway, Vancouver, B.C., V5Y 1P8), and the Garibaldi Provincial Park Map produced by the park itself.

Finding the trail: From Squamish, travel north on the Sea to Sky Highway (Highway 99) until you see a sign indicating GARIBALDI – DIAMOND HEAD 16 KM. Turn right at the traffic lights, drive through a residential area, and pass the Squamish Valley Golf and Country Club. Gearheads will want to park as the road forks to the right and becomes gravel. This offers keen riders an additional 14.3 km (8.6 miles) of uphill climbing in, and downhill screaming out.

Mere mortals will choose to drive this winding gravel road to its terminus at the Elfin Lakes trailhead parking lot. As you climb, stay right as the Ring Creek Road North branches to the left.

Sources of additional information:

Garibaldi/Sunshine Coast District
Alice Lake Park
P.O. Box 220
Brackendale, B.C. V0N 1H0
(604) 898-3678,
(604) 898-4171 fax
email: parkinfo@prkvctoria.elp.gov.bc.ca

Squamish Off-Road Cycling Association (SORCA)
Box 793
Garibaldi Highlands, B.C., V0N 1T0
(604) 898-3519

Notes on the trail: Drop your head and grind (DYHAG, pronounced "dee-hawg") is the order of the day. The climbing along the access road is immediate and unrelenting. The road can be quite dusty in dry weather; it's amazing how many vehicles will blast past you without slowing down to reduce the dust produced. A spur trail to the right at kilometre 2 (mile 1.2) provides access to the Ring Creek Rip Trail and the various trails of the Crumpit Woods area. A further 2.8 km (1.7 miles) brings you to the junction with the Ring Creek Road North. Forking to the left, it provides access to the Powersmart and Pseudotsuga Trails (not covered in this guide). After passing several cottages, take a left junction at kilometre 7.7 (mile 4.6). A few kilometres later, your view opens up for a quick glimpse all the way to Squamish Harbour. The trailhead is only a few minutes away at kilometre 14.3 (mile 8.6).

From the Elfin Lakes parking lot, the trail continues to climb 756 m (1,260 feet) to the Red Heather Campground and Cabin. The cabin costs $10 a night and offers a panoramic slumber. Just beyond the cabin stands a two-story out-house. (You haven't really lived until you've used a two-story outhouse! In the winter, the doorway can still be completely obscured by snow.) Almost immedi-ately, a junction ushers mountain bikers to the right and hikers to the left. The main climbing is concluded 21.1 km from the road or 6.9 km from the trailhead (12.7/4.1 miles). From here, the trail drops to its terminus at the lakes. You'll reach the lakes at kilometre 25/10.7 (mile 15.0/6.4). When your spirit has been sufficiently recharged, return along the same route. Remember, you have to repay the final downhill by climbing for 3.8 km (2.3 miles). Once you crest Round Mountain again, the endless descent begins. Although the drop to the trailhead is constant, keep your speed slow to avoid obstacles on the trail and hikers and cyclists riding uphill.

RIDE 32 · Ring Creek Rip

AT A GLANCE

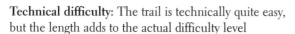

Length/configuration: 26.3-km (15.8-mile) loop

Aerobic difficulty: This trail has very challenging uphill sections requiring strong fitness levels

Technical difficulty: The trail is technically quite easy, but the length adds to the actual difficulty level

Scenery: The views north toward Garibaldi Mountain are spectacular

Special comments: This trail is a must for riders who enjoy a wilderness challenge along with some spectacular views of the surrounding peaks

The Ring Creek Rip, part of the classic Test of Metal bike race, is one of the rides that should be on the itinerary of every strong rider passing through the Squamish area. This 26.3-km (15.8-mile) loop combines a lung-burning climb, affectionately known as Bonk Hill, cresting to superb views of Mount Garibaldi (2,488 m/8,162 feet) and the surrounding Coast Mountains. Beneath you, the Mamquam River roars to alert you to its presence. Distant clear-cuts give evidence to the main economic base of the area. After crossing the Mamquam River, the trail climbs again, up Lava Flow Hill, followed by a long single-track roller coaster. This overgrown fire road traverses a prehistoric lava flow (complements of Mount Garibaldi), passes two abandoned vehicles, and eventually joins with the Garibaldi Park Road. After a few kilometres of this gravel,

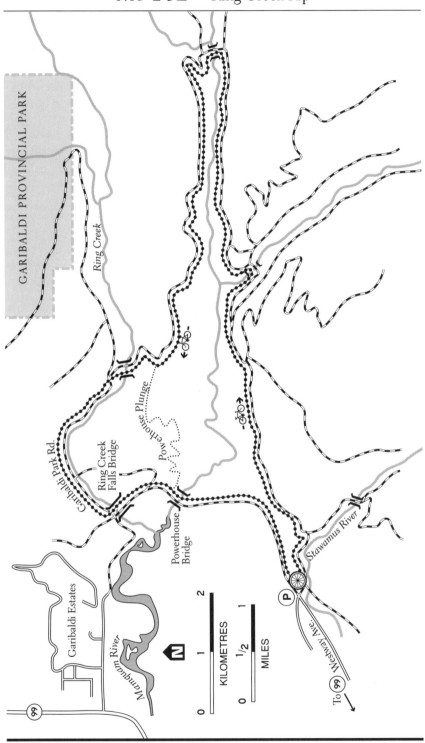

Something old and something new—Ring Creek Rip takes you past numerous old junker cars.

you head back into the woods along the Ring Creek Falls Trail, which will bring you back to your car.

Even though the route follows many active logging roads, this is a wilderness loop and must be treated with respect. The climbs are long and unrelenting, and the trail takes you far from the major highways.

General location: The trail runs along present and former logging roads adjacent to Squamish.

Elevation change: The trail climbs from a low 42 m (100 feet) to 530 m (1,740 feet) as you crest the top of Lava Flow Hill.

Season: April through September.

Services: All services are available in Squamish.

Hazards: This is a long, steady climb along a dusty logging road. The heat and humidity can be daunting on a hot day. Once you begin the descent, the trail is a smooth single-track, but there are many sudden, loose rocks with the potential for mishap. Like many British Columbia rides, you have to choke on excessive amounts of gravel when logging vehicles zoom by with little concern for your dust-filled lungs. As the trail spins rapidly downhill, it passes two old junked cars. The first, a Toyota wagon, has deposited glass on the trail as hunters have used the headlights for target practice.

Rescue index: This is a wilderness trail, and although it's a popular ride, there is every chance that you may not encounter any other cyclists en route. Bring lots of water and some food to snack on. Be prepared to be self-sufficient on this ride.

Land status: British Columbia Crown land.

Maps: The NTS 1:50,000 topographic maps for this trail are 92 G/11 Squamish and 92 G/10 Pitt River. Another good map is the *Discover British Columbia's Garibaldi Region Map* (1:100,000), published by International Travel Maps (345 West Broadway, Vancouver, B.C., V5Y 1P8).

Finding the trail: From Squamish, head south on the Sea to Sky Highway, and turn left onto Clark Drive. Follow the road as it turns sharply left, and then take the first right onto Guilford Drive. Follow this by taking the first left on Westway Avenue; continue through the residential area to a locked gate. Park near the gate.

Sources of additional information:

> Garibaldi/Sunshine Coast District
> Alice Lake Park
> P.O. Box 220
> Brackendale, B.C. V0N 1H0
> (604) 898-3678,
> (604) 898-4171 fax
> email: parkinfo@prkvctoria.elp.gov.bc.ca

> Squamish Off-Road Cycling Association (SORCA)
> Box 793
> Garibaldi Highlands, B.C., V0N 1T0
> (604) 898-3519

Notes on the trail: From the trailhead, follow the good-quality logging road past several junctions. You will pass a large stand of western hemlock trees being logged due to an infestation of hemlock mistletoe disease; the stand will be replanted with fir and cedar. At the 1-km (0.6-mile) mark, take the second left up the Mamquam Forest Service Road. Look for this turn at a **Y**-shaped junction signed MAMQUAM OPERATION. This is where the climbing begins in earnest, and you begin the lung-burning ascent of Bonk Hill. "Bonking" is a term referring to that pleasant state where your body completely shuts down, you lose all control, and you simply don't care if you live or die. The road crosses under the power line, offering some quick views to the north and northeast. The road passes numerous new logging access roads with creative names like Branch 70, Branch 50, and the always popular Branch 20. Stay on this main road as each of these tributary roads join. Bonk Hill is crested at kilometre 4.3 (mile 2.6). If you have an odometre on your bike, you can simply DYHAG (drop your head and grind) and live for this junction. The climbing doesn't end here, but it becomes more mode-rate. The views soon open up after this point. At the 5-km (3-mile) mark, you crest the main climb. This is where you're rewarded with exquisite views of Mount Garibaldi and its neighbouring peaks. At this point, you have climbed over 335 m (1,120 feet) to an elevation of 372 m (1,220 feet). Soon after this viewpoint, a road will branch off to the left at kilometre 5.7 (mile 3.4). Stay to the right at this junction as the other road drops down toward a hydro station on the river. If you happen to be riding at a time when they release the water, you will be treated to a loud, obnoxious horn that warns people to stay clear of the channel.

Beyond this point, the road drops suddenly to the right to cross a bridge just above river level. The trail drops 18 m (60 feet) to this bridge, and this loss must be regained immediately after as you climb back up to a height of 378 m (1,240 feet). Another view-filled crest is reached at the 7-km (4.2-mile) mark at elevation 439 m (1,440 feet). The trail drops down to river level at kilometre 10.6 (mile 6.4) as it crosses the river over a sturdy bridge.

Immediately after the bridge, the road swings to the right and crosses another bridge over Skookum Creek. Do *not* cross this bridge. As the road winds right, a rock-blocked route will go straight. Ride past the rocks. This signifies the beginning of the final ascent of the ride—Lava Flow Hill. Though rideable, the surface is a loose, dry gravel. As you spin your way to the summit, you will climb from river level at 400 m (1,312 feet) up to the summit at 530 m (1,740 feet). At kilometre 12 (mile 7.2), you pass a small opening in the forest. Turn sharply left onto an ancient logging road. This trail drops steadily down a wonderful roller-coaster single-track. As a marker, it passes several abandoned vehicles—a Toyota wagon at kilometre 13.7 (mile 8.2) and a Chevy Beaumont at kilometre 15 (mile 9). A major junction at kilometre 17.4 (mile 10.4) offers strong expert riders the option of continuing with the Test of Metal race route for the hair-raising descent down Powerhouse Plunge or continuing on the more sane Ring Creek Rip Trail.

The main trail turns right at the Powerhouse Plunge junction. Stay on this trail if you are not used to expert-level single-track descents. From this junction, the trail climbs up to cross Ring Creek on a log crossing and then joins with Garibaldi Park Road. Descend the road for slightly over 2 km (1.6 miles), and take the left junction down to an excellent bridge over Ring Creek Falls. This trail bottoms out at a **T** intersection. Turn right, finally crossing the high-quality Powerhouse Bridge onto a good fire road. Turn right at the junction with the chlorine building and ride the downhill back to your car at approximately kilometre 26.3 (mile 15.8).

RIDE 33 · Powerhouse Plunge Loop

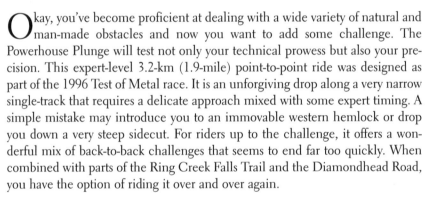

AT A GLANCE

Length/configuration: 3.2-km (1.9-mile) point-to-point

Aerobic difficulty: Because the hill is downhill, there is little challenge in terms of fitness

Technical difficulty: This is an expert ride with very challenging obstacles, root drops, tight switchbacks, and log pyramids

Scenery: This is a wooded trail more famous for its challenge than its scenery

Special comments: This trail is famous locally for its tight series of unforgiving switchbacks

Okay, you've become proficient at dealing with a wide variety of natural and man-made obstacles and now you want to add some challenge. The Powerhouse Plunge will test not only your technical prowess but also your precision. This expert-level 3.2-km (1.9-mile) point-to-point ride was designed as part of the 1996 Test of Metal race. It is an unforgiving drop along a very narrow single-track that requires a delicate approach mixed with some expert timing. A simple mistake may introduce you to an immovable western hemlock or drop you down a very steep sidecut. For riders up to the challenge, it offers a wonderful mix of back-to-back challenges that seems to end far too quickly. When combined with parts of the Ring Creek Falls Trail and the Diamondhead Road, you have the option of riding it over and over again.

General location: Adjacent to Squamish.

Elevation change: This trail drops 395 m (1,335 feet) from its junction with the Ring Creek Rip to its terminus at the Powerhouse Bridge.

Season: May through October.

Services: All services are available in Squamish.

Hazards: This is a challenging ride with log drops, roots, extremely challenging switchbacks, and just about anything else you can imagine. Although very demanding, it lacks the hard rock impacts so famous a little further north in Whistler. This makes it a good place for strong riders to test their skills.

Rescue index: If you don't encounter riders along the trail, your best bet is to either return to the Garibaldi Park Road or continue down to the residential areas of Valleycliffe.

RIDE 33 · Powerhouse Plunge Loop

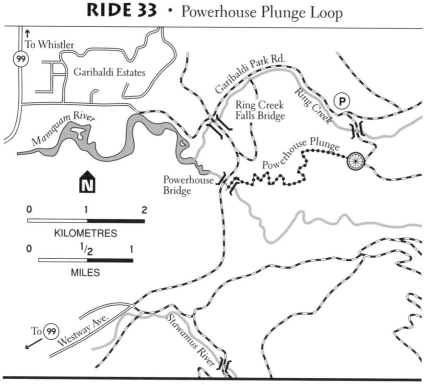

Land status: British Columbia Crown land.

Maps: The NTS 1:50,000 topographic map for this trail is 92 G/11 Squamish. The trail is not marked on any of the topographic maps available, though.

Finding the trail: This trail is generally accessed from the Ring Creek Rip Trail, but can also be accessed directly from the Garibaldi Park Road. From Squamish, travel north on the Sea to Sky Highway until you see a sign indicating GARIBAL-DI—DIAMOND HEAD 16 KM. Turn right at the traffic lights, drive through the Garibaldi Estates residential area, and pass the Squamish Valley Golf and Country Club. Approximately 6 km (3.6 miles) up this road, the Ring Creek Rip Trail branches off to the right. Following this trail for just under 1 km (0.6 mile) will bring you to the start of the Powerhouse Plunge. The trail takes off to the right as the Ring Creek Rip makes a hard left. The junction is signed.

Sources of additional information:

Squamish Off-Road Cycling Association
Box 793
Garibaldi Highlands, B.C., V0N 1T0
(604) 898-3519

Notes on the trail: Once you begin the Powerhouse Plunge, the first 1.4 km (0.84 mile) is quite pleasant and may provide a false sense of security, but then a double log jump begins the major descent. Soon you'll be traversing a narrow sidecut with a sheer drop down to your left. After a short climb, bounce your way over a log pyramid and prepare yourself for the switchbacks. The first switchback will warm you up at kilometre 2.3 (mile 1.4). The main group is still 0.2 km (0.12 mile) down the trail. When you enter the corkscrew, you'll find yourself on a tight series of narrow switchbacks with little margin for error. Experts will love the technical challenge offered by these narrow turns; novices will be terrified. The trail bottoms out all too soon at kilometre 2.9 (mile 1.75), bouncing its way through a mixed forest of western hemlock and Douglas fir. Finally, the trail ends just before the Powerhouse Bridge at kilometre 3.2 (mile 1.9). At this point you can turn right and head back toward the Garibaldi Park Road to make a loop. You may also choose to continue across the bridge and follow the road back to the Valleycliffe trailhead.

RIDE 34 · Crumpit Woods Network

AT A GLANCE

Length/configuration: Network offering loops of varying length up to approximately 10 km (6 miles)

Aerobic difficulty: Moderate elevation gain

Technical difficulty: Varies from extreme to tender depending on the routes you select

Scenery: Limited views north to Garibaldi Park and west to Squamish Harbour

Special comments: This is a great network for honing your skills

Crumpit Woods is a wondrous place where riders of all abilities can find a challenge level suited to their personal needs and wishes. Hammerheads can find huge verticals, with sheer drops down trails like the Face of Dick and The Raa. More moderate riders will enjoy the intermediate rides along Route 99 and the Lost Loop. Regardless of your ability, you will find something within this wonderful network. Distances vary depending on the route you select, but it is not difficult to make loops in excess of 10 km (6 miles) by riding up the S&M Connector, along Route 99, around the Lost Loop, and out the Far Side.

As you crest the various summits, including Five Point Hill, The Maker, Mount Crumpit, or the open slopes of the Lost Loop, views open up in all directions, making the climbing worthwhile. While you ride, you may pass a motor-

RIDE 34 · Crumpit Woods Network

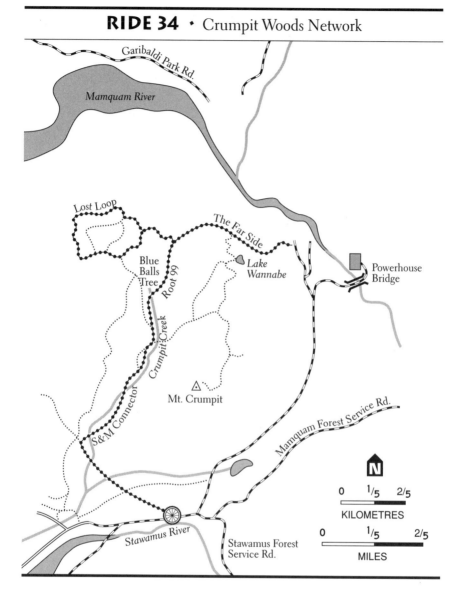

cycle or two. These specially designed trials bikes are made for negotiating the technical obstacles for which this network is known. These same riders are also responsible for much of the trail building in the Crumpit Woods area, so please be courteous.

General location: Squamish.

Elevation change: Moderate, varying from the valley bottom at 100 m (328 feet) to the top of Mount Crumpit at just over 300 m (984 feet).

Crumpit Woods covers the spectrum, from beginner rides all the way to hardball drops.

Season: Year-round.

Services: All services are available in Squamish.

Hazards: Depending on the route and line chosen, the trails may include sharp verticals, root drops, log pyramids, slickrock, and any of a long list of other dangers. Be sure to choose your route based on your ability.

Rescue index: This is a popular network close to the highway and the Valleycliffe residential area. Help is not far away.

Land status: A mixed bag of private land, Crown land, and some under municipal control.

Maps: The NTS 1:50,000 topographic map for this trail is 92 G/11 Squamish.

Finding the trail: To find the Crumpit Woods network, turn east off of the Sea to Sky Highway onto Clark Drive. Take the first right onto Guilford Drive and the next left onto Westway Avenue. Follow this until the road ends at a locked gate. Park near this gate.

Sources of additional information:

Squamish Off-Road Cycling Association
Box 793
Garibaldi Highlands, B.C. V0N 1T0
(604) 898-3519

Notes on the trail: For the purpose of this book, I chose a moderate route heading up the S&M Connector, along Route 99, around the Lost Loop, and then exiting along The Far Side. This route takes you past most of the major junctions within Crumpit Woods and allows numerous options for expert riders to vary.

From your car, follow the Mamquam Forest Service Road, staying straight as another road joins in from the right at kilometre 0.5 (mile 0.3). Shortly after this junction turn left onto a wide single-track that provides access to Crumpit Woods. As you ride along this wide trail, your second junction will be for the S&M Connector. This high-quality trail forms the major access route into the Crumpit Woods network. Expert riders may choose to continue a little further beyond this junction to climb an expert line up The Maker.

The S&M Connector follows the narrow course of an intermittent stream, Crumpit Creek. At kilometre 3 (mile 1.8) there is a bridge over the creek that is well hidden. Watch for it. In dry weather, you can simply ride through the rocky channel to one side of the bridge. Beyond the bridge, the trail passes under the power lines and at kilometre 3.3 (mile 1.98) crosses over a rough bridge. Just a single log laid down lengthwise, it can be very slippery when wet. After the bridge, at kilometre 3.9 (mile 2.34), Lacking Head Trail takes off to the left. This is simply a small side loop, and the trail crosses again at kilometre 4.1 (mile 2.46). Stay straight at this junction, continuing on S&M Connector. Another side loop branches off to the left shortly after this junction. Stay straight until you reach the Blue Balls Tree at kilometre 4.3 (mile 2.6). You can't miss it—a large tree has a wooden phallus with blue, um, appendages. This indicates the start of Route 99. Turn right onto this trail, and climb up to the junction with The Far Side Trail at approximately kilometre 4.7 (mile 2.8).

For a little fun at this point, take a left and head toward the twin loops of Lost Loop and Really Lost Loop. Once you enter the loops, though, there are numerous trail options, so be sure to keep track of your progress. When you've had sufficient fun, either head back to The Far Side or exit from the south side of Lost Loop back down S&M Connector. This option also allows expert riders access to Meet Yer Maker and, for extreme riders, a short, vicious series of rock steps called Face of Dick.

Returning to The Far Side, continue past the previous junction with Route 99 and follow this trail as it traverses the lower slopes of Five Point Hill. After bouncing over a log pyramid, a trail to the right marks the beginning of Five Point Hill North. This offers expert riders an impressive view followed by two expert rides dropping down the south side of Five Point Hill toward Lacking Head Trail.

If you continue past this junction, you'll meet the road after 0.9 km (0.54 mile). Stay to the right at each junction and return to your car in a further 3.2 km (1.9 miles).

RIDE 35 · Whistler Mountain Bike Park

AT A GLANCE

Length/configuration: If you take advantage of the chairlift, the trails max out at around 1 km (0.6 mile). Distances can be varied by playing on the upper loops before descending toward the valley bottom

Aerobic difficulty: This ride is accessible by chairlift, but hardy souls can ascend approximately 320 m (1,050 feet) for each downhill run

Technical difficulty: This great network of trails varies between fall-line drops to rolling access roads. There is something for everybody

Scenery: The views toward the village and the surrounding peaks are spectacular along this unobstructed network

Special comments: This is one of those rare networks with chairlift access for mountain bikes

This network of trails offers a great place for novices and experts alike. The well-designed labyrinth of trails provide some steep drops down the fall line, along with some more rolling descents for novices. By using the chairlift to access the park, you can get a lot of vertical in a short time. This has the added benefit of raising your skill level at an increased pace. The more downhills you have under your belt, the better you will be at negotiating the challenges they entail.

General location: Whistler.

Elevation change: From the village at 680 m (2,230 feet), routes crest at approximately 1,000 m (3,280 feet).

Season: April through September.

Services: All services are available in Whistler.

Hazards: Expect anything. The trails include sudden drops, logs, roots, chutes, and numerous other obstacles.

RIDE 35 · Whistler Mountain Bike Park

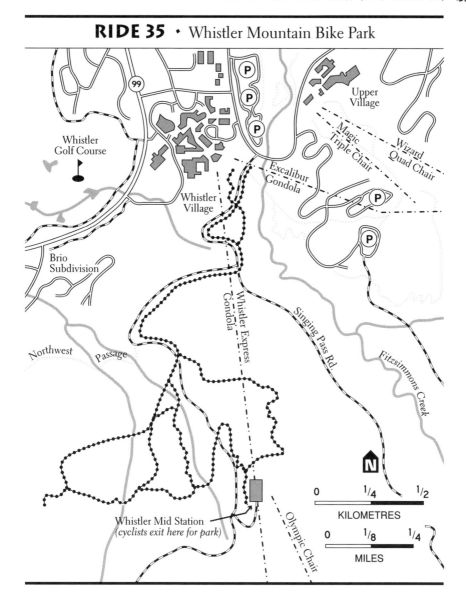

Rescue index: You are never far from civilization while riding this network. If need be, mountain bike park staff can offer assistance.

Land status: Private land.

Maps: The NTS topographic map for this trail is 92 J/2 Whistler, but the very best map for the Whistler area is the *Whistler Area Mountain Biking & Recreation Map* produced by TerraPro GPS Surveys Ltd. (Box 1016, Whistler, B.C. V0N 1B0 or bikemap@whistler.net). The map is available from most local bike shops in Whistler.

Finding the trail: The network begins within the village, at the base of the Whistler Express Gondola. To access the village, simply turn off of Highway 99 and follow signs for the village.

Sources of additional information:

Whistler Off-Road Cycling Association
Box 3500-31
Whistler, B.C. V0N 1B0
(604) 938-9893

Notes on the trail: This network is a work in progress, with numerous loops offering a variety to downhill drops with the option of using the chairlift for the uphill portion. It was closed at the time the author was researching the book, so check with the ski hill for current maps.

RIDE 36 · Cut Yer Bars

AT A GLANCE

Length/configuration: Varies depending on which routes you choose

Aerobic difficulty: Moderate

Technical difficulty: This is a great place to play, often in just a few places. Trials riders will enjoy the potential to pick a few lines and work them

Scenery: This network remains within the trees, offering little in the way of views

Special comments: Like Mel's Dilemma, this is a network where you are surrounded on every side by civilization, so go, play, and when you've had enough, make a quick exit

Cut Yer Bars represents an intermediate to expert network with numerous trails, each with special challenges, all contained within Highway 99 to the east and Lorimar Road and Tapley's Farm to the south and west. To the north, the power lines mark the boundary. Within this narrow corridor, lots of trails offer all manner of challenges, from stiff wheelie drops to log obstacles to tight lines and narrow chutes. Go, enjoy, and tell your friends!

General location: Whistler.

Elevation change: The landscape is rolling with a maximum of just over 60 m (197 feet) within the entire network.

RIDE 36 • Cut Yer Bars

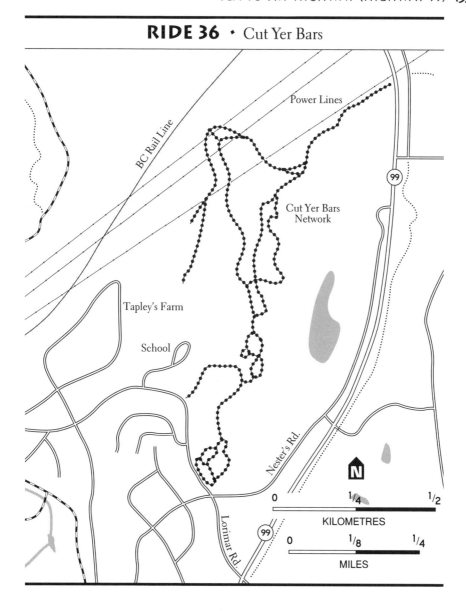

Season: April to October.

Services: All services are available in Whistler.

Hazards: Expect anything. The trails include sudden drops, logs, roots, chutes, and numerous other obstacles.

Rescue index: You are never far from civilization while riding this network. If need be, you can quickly access help from the south end of the network.

Land status: Undeveloped private land.

The Cut Yer Bars Network beckons you back time and again to challenge its numerous technical lines.

Maps: The NTS 1:50,000 topographic map for this trail is 92 J/2 Whistler, but the best map for the Whistler area is the *Whistler Area Mountain Biking & Recreation Map* produced by TerraPro GPS Surveys Ltd. (Box 1016, Whistler, B.C. V0N 1B0 or bikemap@whistler.net). The map is available from most local bike shops in Whistler.

Finding the trail: From the village, head north on Highway 99 and then turn left on Lorimar Road. Follow Lorimar Road to its junction with Nester's Road. The trail network drops off to the right just beyond this junction.

Sources of additional information:

Whistler Off-Road Cycling Association
Box 3500-31
Whistler, B.C. V0N 1B0
(604) 938-9893

Notes on the trail: Pick a route, play, and then head south until you rejoin Lorimar Road. Although the network is convoluted, the many trails all trend north to south. If you reach the power lines or Highway 99, simply turn around and bounce your way to the opposite end of the network.

RIDE 37 · Kill Me, Thrill Me

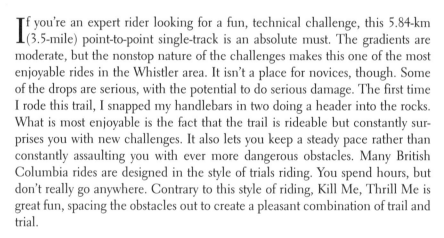

AT A GLANCE

Length/configuration: 5.84-km (3.5-mile) point-to-point; or make a 9.75-km (5.85-mile) loop using Highway 99

Aerobic difficulty: Although there is limited climbing, the climbs are technical and challenging

Technical difficulty: This is a solid expert ride

Scenery: Occasional views across the valley toward Phalanx Peak and Parkhurst Mountain within Garibaldi Provincial Park

Special comments: This trail offers the best of Whistler single-track

---

If you're an expert rider looking for a fun, technical challenge, this 5.84-km (3.5-mile) point-to-point single-track is an absolute must. The gradients are moderate, but the nonstop nature of the challenges makes this one of the most enjoyable rides in the Whistler area. It isn't a place for novices, though. Some of the drops are serious, with the potential to do serious damage. The first time I rode this trail, I snapped my handlebars in two doing a header into the rocks. What is most enjoyable is the fact that the trail is rideable but constantly surprises you with new challenges. It also lets you keep a steady pace rather than constantly assaulting you with ever more dangerous obstacles. Many British Columbia rides are designed in the style of trials riding. You spend hours, but don't really go anywhere. Contrary to this style of riding, Kill Me, Thrill Me is great fun, spacing the obstacles out to create a pleasant combination of trail and trial.

General location: Whistler.

Elevation change: From the trailhead at 645 m (2,116 feet) the trail climbs to its maximum elevation (685 m/2,247 feet) as it passes the helipad. From here the trail rolls up and down, varying between 660 m (2,165 feet) and 590 m (1,935 feet).

Season: April to October.

Services: All services are available in Whistler.

Hazards: This trail is for expert riders and includes root drops, log pyramids, narrow bridges, corduroy descents, and lots of variations in terrain. The most challenging sections are the short scree drop past the helipad and the slickrock beneath the power lines. Most of the other challenges involve sudden obstacles that require finesse and skill. You need to be ready for just about anything.

RIDE 37 · Kill Me, Thrill Me

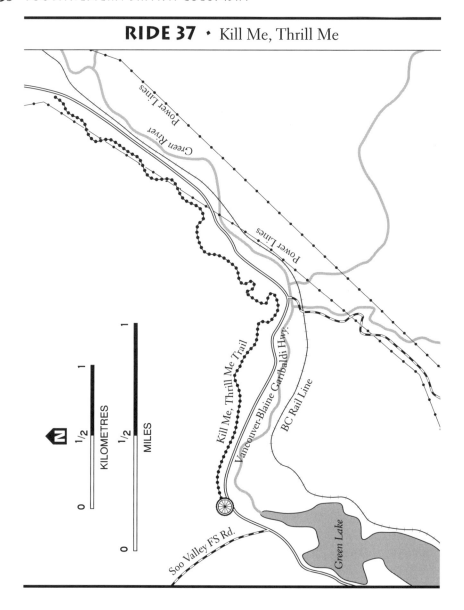

Rescue index: The trail provides several potential exits in the case of emergency. Once you exit, you should be able to flag down a vehicle along Highway 99. This road is always busy. You may also encounter other cyclists along this popular trail.

Land status: Mixture of private and Crown land.

Maps: The NTS 1:50,000 topographic map for this trail is 92 J/2 Whistler, but the best map for the Whistler area is the *Whistler Area Mountain Biking & Recreation Map* produced by TerraPro GPS Surveys Ltd. (Box 1016, Whistler,

After a rolling introduction, Kill Me, Thrill Me heads vertical with a sheer slickrock drop down the power lines.

B.C. V0N 1B0 or bikemap@whistler.net). The map is available from most local bike shops in Whistler.

Finding the trail: From Whistler, head north on Highway 99 and continue to the north end of Green Lake. As the highway makes a sweeping right turn, concrete barriers have been placed along the outside of the corner. You'll notice a trail heading into the woods on the end of the barriers closest to Whistler. There is a sign and a rating—Double Black Diamond.

Sources of additional information:

Whistler Off-Road Cycling Association
Box 3500-31
Whistler, B.C. V0N 1B0
(604) 938-9893

Notes on the trail: Almost right away, the technical challenges begin with a pair of log pyramids. This sets the tone for a trail that is designed to test your technical prowess and push your limits. The first stretch of trail is technical but easily rideable as it begins to climb above the highway. You'll want to keep up your speed to power over some of the roots and other obstacles. At kilometre 0.35 (mile 0.2), the trail makes a hard left to cross a creek over two small bridges. Beyond this, the trail moves onto a narrow sidecut followed by a short, steep, rocky, rooted drop. A number of logs have been placed to help reduce erosion on this descent. The climbing begins again at kilometre 0.9 (mile 0.55) and moderates after crossing another small bridge. At kilometre 1 (mile 0.6), the trail crosses two bridges over an intermittent stream that is usually dry by midsummer.

After these two bridges, the trail makes a hard left and begins climbing to circumnavigate the upcoming helicopter pad. Finally, at kilometre 1.29 (mile 0.77) and elevation 685 m (2,247 feet), the trail turns right and begins to drop slightly as you pass the helipad. As it descends, it drops down a technical, loose rock scree slope. The trail heads back into the woods at the base of this slope; soon after, the trail comes into a gravel opening and a gravel road climbs up from the highway beneath and to the right. Stay straight, as the trail continues straight across, just past a white pole.

The trail becomes darker now, winding through a dark hemlock and fir forest with a carpet of needles. Several log pyramids offer a place to play in the shade. The first is followed by a larger pyramid, which in turn is succeeded by a series of steps that cross over a log and then drop down. The trail opens up as you climb onto a short stretch of lava rock at kilometre 2.16 (mile 1.3). Drop off the slickrock onto a stretch of log corduroy and roots. The sound of the highway rumbles as you traverse the hillside above the pavement. Head into darker forest at kilometre 2.25 (mile 1.35), and wind your way through a carpet of cedar and hemlock needles. After a short, sharp climb, the trail descends and winds to the right to parallel a small stream. As you cross the bridge over the creek, there is an abandoned Berkeley oven, complete with pots, a china cup, and cutlery. The door has been used to form part of the landing for the bridge.

Beyond the creek, the trend is uphill. Stay to the right as a trail joins from the left at kilometre 3 (mile 1.8). The climb tops out on an narrow sidecut above the highway. You can feel the exposure as you traverse this narrow ledge with the highway far below. A new road has been cut up from the right, meeting the trail. Ignore it and stay on the main route. Beyond this point, bounce your way down a corduroy drop followed by a log ramp over a notched cedar log. Climb through a sandy, smooth stretch before heading into a mixed forest of cedar, hemlock, and thimbleberry. The climbing finally ends as the power lines appear on your right and you climb your way onto the slickrock. This is the most challenging section of trail—the route drops right down the lava rock. It's a great place for enders, and nonexperts will want to walk this stretch. Pass under the transmission tower and continue the technical descent until your next bridged creek crossing at kilometre 4.15 (mile 2.5). You've now dropped 70 m (230 feet) down the slickrock, and the drop becomes more moderate.

After a large root drop, the trail heads into the woods and becomes a technical, wooded ride. Following another log pyramid, the trail heads back to the wires and begins to double back on itself. At kilometre 4.75 (mile 2.85), the trail makes another hard left and regains its westerly direction, above the highway again. Return to the cutline beneath the power lines at kilometre 4.9 (mile 2.9). After crossing a small bridge, you climb above the power lines and finally leave them behind.

The trail emerges on a narrow sidecut above the highway at kilometre 5.17 (mile 3.1). Although a flimsy railing protects you, it doesn't provide much more than psychological comfort. Following another log obstacle, the trail begins to drop and widens out to become a good-quality double-track. The descent is fast and furious until it makes a hard right to join the highway at kilometre 5.84 (mile 3.5). Turn right and return to your car at kilometre 9.75 (mile 5.85).

RIDE 38 · Shit Happens

AT A GLANCE

Length/configuration: 4.96-km (2.98-mile) point-to-point, or make an 8.44-km (5.06-mile) loop using Highway 99

Aerobic difficulty: This is a rolling trail requiring strong fitness levels

Technical difficulty: An expert-level ride with numerous obstacles, drops, and chutes

Scenery: The views are limited, but you are offered a wonderful panorama south all the way to Black Tusk

Special comments: Of Whistler's expert rides, this is one of the most enjoyable

Shit happens! We've all said it, and this 4.96-km (2.98-mile) point-to-point ride proves it. It's a roller coaster where anything is possible. This expert ride combines moderate changes in elevation with an endless supply of challenging obstacles, not to mention a paintball course forcing you to run the gauntlet. If that doesn't deter you, you'll find one of the most enjoyable expert rides in Whistler. Though the challenge is stiff, the trail remains largely rideable. Most of the obstacles can be negotiated with a little perseverance and courage, and the gradient allows you to maintain a little speed along the way.

The ride passes two tiny lakes offering a picturesque reflection of the surrounding peaks, and then it rewards you with an excellent panorama to the south; Black Tusk, with its volcanic tooth, dominates much of the skyline. Whistler is famous for its challenging single-track, and rides like this one, along with Kill Me, Thrill Me, represent some of the best Whistler has to offer.

RIDE 38 · Shit Happens

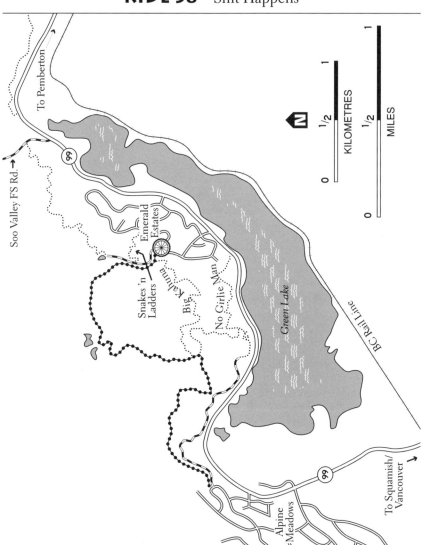

General location: Whistler.

Elevation change: From the trailhead at approximately 695 m (2,280 feet), the trail initially climbs to 765 m (2,509 feet) as it passes two small lakes. Then it drops steadily to approximately 680 m (2,230 feet) before making the final ascent to 715 m (2,345 feet). The remainder of the ride is downhill to the terminus at 685 m (2,247 feet).

Season: April through October.

Shit Happens mixes a roller coaster of roots and sudden drops with periodic views toward Alta Lake.

Services: All services are available in Whistler.

Hazards: This expert-level ride contains many obstacles, some appearing with little or no notice. You must be prepared for slippery log crossings, sudden drops, root and rock challenges, and just about anything else that might pop up. This doesn't even mention the fact that this ride goes through a paintball battle zone.

Rescue index: Though this is a popular trail, you may not encounter other riders along its length. It begins and ends at residential areas, so you should be able to get help if needed.

Land status: Mixture of private and Crown land.

Maps: The NTS 1:50,000 topographic map for this trail is 92 J/2 Whistler, but the best map for the Whistler area is the *Whistler Area Mountain Biking & Recreation Map* produced by TerraPro GPS Surveys Ltd. (Box 1016, Whistler, B.C. V0N 1B0 or bikemap@whistler.net). The map is available from most local bike shops in Whistler.

Finding the trail: From the traffic lights at Alpine Way, head north on Highway 99 and turn left into Emerald Estates. Climb straight up Autumn Drive, and turn right onto Emerald Drive. The trailhead is a gravel road branching to the left as Emerald Drive makes a right turn.

Sources of additional information:

Whistler Off-Road Cycling Association
Box 3500-31
Whistler, B.C. V0N 1B0
(604) 938-9893

Notes on the trail: From the trailhead, climb the access road for Whistler's water supply along the wide gravel. Shit Happens forks off to the left at kilometre 0.37 (mile 0.22). The trail begins as a good-quality single-track that climbs right away. The first obstacle occurs at kilometre 0.57 (mile 0.34), where a cedar log has been packed with smaller logs to make a rideable crossing. The climbing remains steady, with periodic log obstacles. At kilometre 0.86 (mile 0.52), the trail becomes much rockier but remains rideable. A log crossing the trail at an oblique angle at kilometre 1.21 (mile 0.73) has a notch cut across to allow crossing. However, the angle, when combined with a wet trail, allows your back wheel to slide out, so be cautious. Beyond this, the character of the trail soon changes as it makes a sharp right and begins to climb on a loose, rooted carpet. You crest the high elevation point of the trail shortly after you begin traversing two picturesque ponds at kilometre 1.42 (mile 0.85). As the trail switches back to the left and climbs above the ponds, you climb a soft carpet of needles complicated by some large roots. The elevation maxes out at kilometre 1.76 (mile 1.06) at 765 m (2,509 feet). This is followed by the start of a solid downhill trend mixed with a long supply of obstacles to challenge your abilities.

At kilometre 2.65 (mile 1.6), the Big Kahuna Trail climbs up to the left. This is a very serious expert ride that literally plummets you back down to Emerald Estates along a series of treacherous obstacles. To continue on Shit Happens, stay to the right and ignore this junction. Another double-black trail, No Girlie Man, takes off to the left 100 m (328 feet) beyond Big Kahuna. Again, stay to the right at this junction. After you leave these trails behind, the trail begins to drop sharply but remains rideable. As you continue to descend, bouncing your way over log and root drops, the sound of the highway becomes louder. The trail makes a sharp right at kilometre 3.2 (mile 1.9) and begins to leave the road behind again.

As the trail enters a dark stretch of hemlock, dogwood, bunchberry, and maple, you'll cross over a slippery log bridge. It is just a single log placed lengthwise and covered with a thin coat of algae in wet weather. The gradient changes to uphill beyond this bridge. This is the final uphill grind as you climb toward an excellent view of the local peaks and the jagged tooth of Black Tusk. From here, you head back into the woods and traverse a deep ravine down to your right. Beyond this point, the trail begins dropping again down a very technical stretch that will find novices pushing their limits. At kilometre 3.76 (mile 2.26), you'll see rope and flagging tape along with a DANGER AREA sign. This indicates the beginning of the paintball zone. A local company sells paintball war games and this is the battle zone. Continue riding, but remain vigilant; if you find yourself in a battle zone, be sure to make your presence known. If you get hit, well then, the trail lives up to its name.

You leave the paintball zone at kilometre 4.05 (mile 2.43). A wet, marshy section follows the paintball zone. Two wet bridges take you through the mush. You may need to explore a little—the trail has become quite braided from riders looking for ways through the wet. As the trail begins to dry out, you'll cross another bridge at kilometre 4.27 (mile 2.56). After this, the trail joins a wide double-track bringing you toward the Alpine Meadows housing development. Stay straight on this wide track until you meet civilization at kilometre 4.96 (mile 2.98).

Stay to the left on the pavement as you arrive at the road, and left again on Meadow Lane. Turn left on the highway and return to your vehicle at kilometre 8.44 (mile 5.06).

RIDE 39 · Section 102

AT A GLANCE

Length/configuration: 3.06-km (1.84-mile) point-to-point or 5.95-km (3.57-mile) loop using Highway 99

Aerobic difficulty: Though the climbing is not extreme, it is very challenging and requires a strong fitness level

Technical difficulty: This is a very challenging trail for expert riders only

Scenery: There is one picturesque viewpoint en route that brings Green Lake and the snowcapped peaks of Garibaldi Provincial Park into view

Special comments: One of Whistler's most challenging expert rides

---

This 3.06-km (1.84-mile) point-to-point trail is reserved for riders looking to master the very best of Whistler's expert single-track. If it were any more difficult it would earn a double-black rating. For riders up to the task, it makes a great way to extend the length of Kill Me, Thrill Me. Together, they make a 9.54-km (5.72-mile) point-to-point ride or a 16.07-km (9.64-mile) loop using Highway 99 for the return.

The scenery is spectacular, but you rarely have an opportunity to view it. There is only one main viewpoint; after enjoying the view of Green Lake and

RIDE 39 · Section 102

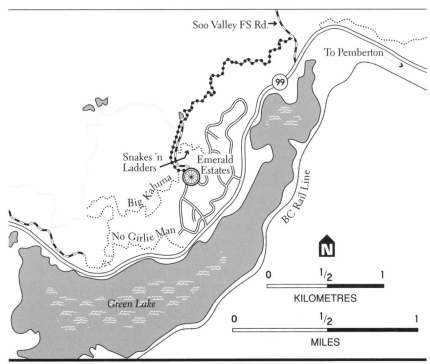

the mountains to the south, you'll be too busy keeping your wheels down and your body up to think about it. Even moderate expert riders will find themselves pushing much of this trail, so save it for when you are cleaning rides like Shit Happens, Mel's Dilemma, and Lower Sproat. Once you gain a sufficient comfort level, you'll even look forward to the teeter totter that marks the terminus of the ride.

General location: Whistler.

Elevation change: From the trailhead at 680 m (2,230 feet), the trail climbs steadily to approximately 780 m (2,558 feet). The remainder of the trail is rolling downhill to the terminus on the Soo Valley Road at elevation 620 m (2,034 feet).

Season: April through October.

Services: All services are available in Whistler.

Hazards: Expect anything, as this trail throws lofty wheelie drops, huge logs, roots, rocks, narrow chutes, and even some man-made obstacles at you. The teeter totter at the end of the trail adds one last challenge before civilization.

Rescue index: This extremely challenging trail is also quite popular. I passed numerous riders when I was out, and you may be able to find help if necessary. Be sure your tool kit is complete as this trail has many ways to trash your body and your bike.

Land status: Mixture of private and Crown land.

Section 102 offers endless challenge. Minutes after this photo, one of these riders blew out a rear derailleur.

Maps: The NTS 1:50,000 topographic map for this trail is 92 J/2 Whistler, but the best map for the Whistler area is the *Whistler Area Mountain Biking & Recreation Map* produced by TerraPro GPS Surveys Ltd. (Box 1016, Whistler, B.C. V0N 1B0 or bikemap@whistler.net). The map is available from most local bike shops in Whistler.

Finding the trail: From the traffic lights at Alpine Way, head north on Highway 99 and turn left into Emerald Estates. Climb straight up Autumn Drive, and turn right onto Emerald Drive. The trailhead is a gravel road branching to the left as Emerald Drive makes a right turn.

Sources of additional information:

Whistler Off-Road Cycling Association
Box 3500-31
Whistler, B.C. V0N 1B0
(604) 938-9893

Notes on the trail: As you ride up the good gravel of Whistler's water supply, ignore Shit Happens Trail radiating to the left and Snakes 'n Ladders to the right.

Stay straight until you reach the drinking water reservoir at kilometre 0.63 (mile 0.38). The trail begins on the far side of the reservoir, so follow the chain-link fence around the water supply. As you round the opposite side, bounce your way over a large cedar log, then take a right turn into the bush, leaving the water behind. Immediately the trail becomes a tricky, technical uphill climb. When I did the ride, another cyclist blew out his derailleur within the first 100 m (328 feet) of the trail. Make sure your toolkit is complete before continuing.

As you climb, the trail crests two large lava boulders, the second of which gives you a great view of Green Lake and the snow-capped peaks to the south. Be sure to go left off this viewpoint at kilometre 1.09 (mile 0.65) to avoid the ravine beyond the viewpoint. Following the sheer drop off this lava rock, you will need to climb over another boulder, followed by a sharp drop. The climbing begins immediately, rising up a very technical ascent. Once you crest this lava boulder, you have the option of a 2-m (6.56-foot) wheelie drop or a more reasonable switchback to the right. After a left turn, the climbing resumes. Although rideable, nonexperts (who really should not be here at all) will find themselves pushing. At kilometre 1.55 (mile 0.93), the trail makes four sharp switchbacks, beginning to the right and bringing you into a badly rooted section. Tiny, sinuous roots seem to grab at your bike, and the larger roots attempt to either stop your front tire or cause your rear one to spin out. This next section is so root-bound that it almost becomes a hike-a-bike. As you pass a small, marshy pool covered in yellow pond lilies, the trail continues its uphill trend. At kilometre 2 (mile 1.2), the trail makes a spaghetti switchback, almost backtracking to crest the lava rock. The trail then spits you into a narrow, rooted gully and over a downed log. Soon you'll meet another obstacle: a large log with two small logs, creating a pyramid. What you may not see is that they drop you into a sharp downhill on the opposite side, so be prepared. After you cross a small log at kilometre 2.3 (mile 1.4), you'll drop into a brake-lock gully and over an even larger log before the trail levels out for a short distance. At kilometre 2.42 (mile 1.45), skid your way down the slickrock over two wheelie drops. This next stretch is very challenging, with large rocks and sudden drops. You know you are nearing the end of the trail when you are faced with a narrow, suspended bridge 1.5 m (5 feet) high with an equally narrow ramp down the far side. Less gutsy riders simply circumnavigate the bridge, but the call to ride is difficult to resist. After keeping a precise line on the bridge, you begin the final descent toward the road. Just before you reach gravel, there is one more challenge: a long teeter totter. Again, you can portage around it, but the easiest line is up and over. Beyond this, meet the road at kilometre 3.06 (mile 1.84). Turn right, and right again at the highway at kilometre 3.33 (mile 2). Return to your vehicle in Emerald Estates at kilometre 5.55 (mile 3.33).

RIDE 40 · Lower Sproat

AT A GLANCE

Length/configuration: 3.04-km (1.82-mile) point-to-point

Aerobic difficulty: There is only moderate climbing, with few very challenging slopes

Technical difficulty: This is a moderate trail, suitable for intermediate riders

Scenery: Periodic views of Alpha, Nita, and Alta Lakes

Special comments: Best ridden as described, from north to south

This popular ride is a great place for intermediate riders to take in some of Whistler's famous fat-tire landscape. It includes a stiff climb from the trailhead, but then becomes an intermediate-level, 3.04-km (1.82-mile) point-to-point with some great views south toward Nita and Alta Lakes and the snow-capped peaks beyond.

The climbing is more moderate if you ride from north to south; this also allows expert riders to switch from Lower Sproat to the expert drop of Danimal for a little excitement before reaching the pavement. The trails in the Alta Lake area can be linked together in many ways to create extended rides or loops of varying ability.

General location: Whistler.

Elevation change: From the north trailhead, Lower Sproat climbs from 780 m (2,558 feet) for 1.32 km (0.79 mile) to a maximum elevation of approximately 870 m (2,854 feet). After a moderately level stretch, the final 0.45 km (0.27 mile) drops straight down the fall line from 755 m (2,476 feet) to the south trailhead at approximately 655 m (2,148 feet).

Season: April through October.

Services: All services are available in Whistler.

Hazards: This challenging ride includes a stiff climb from the trailhead and another steep drop to the terminus. The remainder of the trail provides a mixed bag of solid surface interspersed with badly eroded stretches. You'll need to be ready for sudden changes in character along this ride.

Rescue index: This popular trail begins and ends in residential areas, so help is rarely far away. On quiet days, you may need to continue to either the north or south trailheads before you are able to find assistance.

RIDE 40 · Lower Sproat

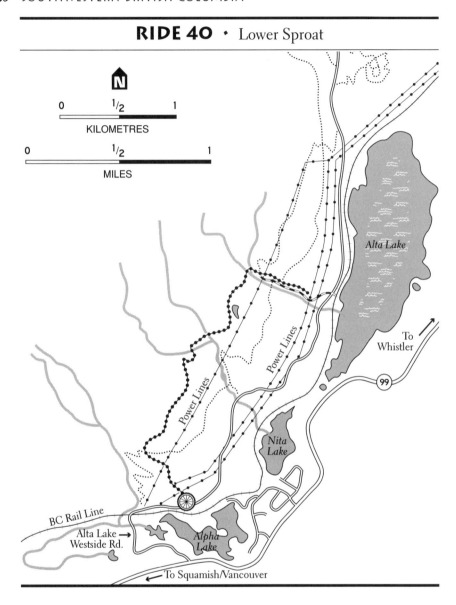

Land status: Mixture of private and Crown land.

Maps: The NTS 1:50,000 topographic maps for this trail are 92 J/3 Brandywine Falls and 92 J/2 Whistler, but the best map for the Whistler area is the *Whistler Area Mountain Biking & Recreation Map* produced by TerraPro GPS Surveys Ltd. (Box 1016, Whistler, B.C. V0N 1B0 or bikemap@whistler.net). The map is available from most local bike shops in Whistler.

Finding the trail: From Highway 99, take the Alta Lake Westside Road. Follow this road for 4.9 km (2.59 miles) until you see a gravel road climbing to the left.

Lower Sproat passes this picturesque marsh shortly before rejoining civilization.

It is located just after passing a sign indicating NEIGHBOURHOOD SPEED CON-TROL and just before the first speed bump. Park along the road and climb this gravel. From the road, pedal your way up the access road for just over 1 km (0.6 mile). Pass the junction for Danimal Trail, your first major left junction, and continue climbing until the next left. The trailhead appears just after several satellite dishes come into view to your right. Turn left onto a wide double-track.

Sources of additional information:

Whistler Off-Road Cycling Association
Box 3500-31
Whistler, B.C. V0N 1B0
(604) 938-9893

Notes on the trail: The trail continues to climb, crossing a culverted stream at kilometre 0.23 (mile 0.14). The wide double-track climbs toward Stubs Lake at kilometre 0.47 (mile 0.28) and elevation 810 m (2,659 feet). This picturesque pond is covered with pond lilies and cattails. Beyond the lake, the trail narrows into a wide single-track and continues climbing. From the lake, cross a small stream and begin bouncing your way up a rougher single-track. As you climb toward the 880-m (2,886-foot) mark at kilometre 1.32 (mile 0.79), the trail begins descending. Views down toward Nita Lake and the Alta Lake Road open up as you traverse a small ridge at kilometre 1.46 (mile 0.88). Beyond this, the trail follows the lower slopes of Sproat Mountain and passes a small knoll to the left at kilometre 1.75 (mile 1.05). The descent is quite steady here, making a sharp S-turn at kilometre 2.05 (mile 1.23), and is beginning to get somewhat rutted and rocky. Pass the junction with Danimal Trail at kilometre 2.38 (mile 1.43) and begin the final descent toward the road at kilometre 3.04 (mile 1.82).

RIDE 41 · Beaver Pass Trail

AT A GLANCE

Length/configuration: 2.75-km (1.65-mile) point-to-point

Aerobic difficulty: This trail has a stiff, short climb followed by moderate changes in elevation

Technical difficulty: The trail begins as an intermediate ride, but it becomes a solid expert ride at the north end

Scenery: The views are spectacular to the southeast toward Alta Lake and the distant Fitzsimmons and Spearhead Ranges. The village of Whistler is also visible

Special comments: This is a good ride for sunny days with a camera, but make sure your skill level is up to it

Oh, what a rare experience—an expert ride with a view! So many of the expert-level rides in British Columbia are heavily treed rain forests with little to look at. Beaver Pass offers a constantly changing panorama along its 2.75-km (1.65-mile) point-to-point course. This doesn't mean you'll have a lot of opportunity to enjoy it. Once you find yourself on the expert stretch, your eyes had better be on the trail and your focus on choosing your line. The magic is in finding a sunny location to sit, relax, and drink in the panorama before gritting your teeth for the descent.

To the east, the peaks of the Spearhead Range dominate the skyline, along with the slopes of Blackcomb Mountain Ski Resort. To the southeast, you can see all the way to the microwave tower on Black Tusk. Beneath you, the placid waters of Alta Lake remind you of the rewards waiting for you at the bottom. There's nothing like a cool swim after a hot ride.

RIDE 41 · Beaver Pass Trail

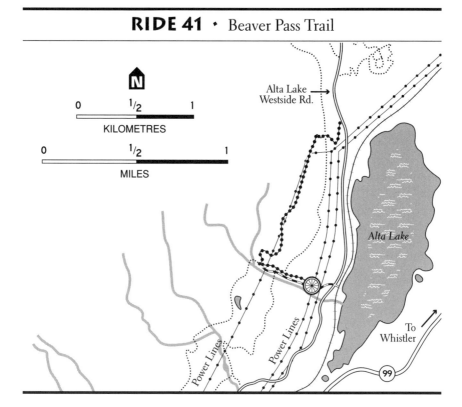

Once you're ready, trade in the summit for the expert-level downhill back to the road. This ride is *not* to be taken lightly—the gradient and the hard rock surroundings increase the potential consequences of a fall. When you reach the road, Alta Lake will be waiting.

General location: Whistler.

Elevation change: From the roadside, the trail climbs 120 m (394 feet) to the beginning of Beaver Pass. By the time you meet the trail, you have already completed the majority of the uphill climbing. An additional 60 m (197 feet) await you as you make your way to the summit viewpoint. The remainder of the ride is downhill, finally spitting you back out on the Alta Lake Road.

Season: April through October.

Services: All services are available in Whistler.

Hazards: This trail begins deceptively with a moderate climb and improving views. Once you pass the viewpoint, though, the character changes, and it becomes a serious expert ride. It drops sharply through a rugged, rocky landscape; the consequences of a fall here can be dire. Be sure to ride with a buddy and be prepared for a technical, expert-level descent replete with narrow chutes, rock ledges, and tight switchbacks.

Rescue index: Because the ride begins and ends along Alta Lake Road, there is always help to be found at either end of the ride. Don't count on meeting other riders en route, though, and be sure to bring your first-aid kit.

Land status: A mixture of undeveloped private and Crown land.

Maps: The NTS 1:50,000 topographic map for this trail is 92 J/2 Whistler, but the best map for the Whistler area is the *Whistler Area Mountain Biking & Recreation Map* produced by TerraPro GPS Surveys Ltd. (Box 1016, Whistler, B.C. V0N 1B0 or bikemap@whistler.net). The map is available from most local bike shops in Whistler.

Finding the trail: From the village of Whistler, head south on Highway 99. Turn right on the Alta Lake Westside Road. Follow this for 4.9 km (2.59 miles) until you see a gravel road take off to the left. Park near this junction, and ride up the wide gravel.

Sources of additional information:

> Whistler Off-Road Cycling Association
> Box 3500-31
> Whistler, B.C. V0N 1B0
> (604) 938-9893

Notes on the trail: Climb the gravel access road for approximately 0.75 km (0.45 mile). Pass the junction for Danimal Trail and then Lower Sproat, both on your left. As you pass the Lower Sproat junction, you'll notice several satellite dishes. The junction to Beaver Pass will be to your right. Take this trail as it passes under the power lines just beyond the dishes. The trail tends to follow the power lines for most of its course and begins a technical climb at kilometre 1.11 (mile 0.67). The trail crests a small summit at kilometre 1.27 (mile 0.76) and elevation 845 m (2,772 feet). The views are spectacular from this point, stretching south to the microwave stations on Black Tusk (the tusk itself is hidden) and to the glacier-capped peaks of the Spearhead Range to the east. Drop off this knoll and continue along the power lines as views of Alta Lake and Blueberry Hill begin to dominate the panorama. At kilometre 1.6 (mile 0.96), the trail begins to drop steeply down a narrow sidecut. Although this provides great views, you'll need to focus on the trail rather than the scenery. The drop grows in difficulty as it rounds several expert-level switchbacks at kilometre 1.91 (mile 1.15).

The trail bottoms out beyond these switchbacks, becoming a soft roller coaster through dense second growth. Enjoy it while it lasts, because it gets technical again almost right away, crossing a narrow, single-log bridge at kilometre 2.22 (mile 1.33) and meeting Whip Me, Snip Me at kilometre 2.25 (mile 1.35). Stay straight at this junction and continue the technical switchbacks until you meet the road at kilometre 2.89 (mile 1.73).

RIDE 42 · Whip Me, Snip Me

AT A GLANCE

Length/configuration: 2.41-km (1.45-mile) point-to-point

Aerobic difficulty: Moderate climb followed by a winding descent

Technical difficulty: An intermediate-level descent following a moderate uphill

Scenery: Limited views of Alta Lake and the Spearhead Range as the trail climbs toward the Beaver Pass access road

Special comments: A great place for intermediate riders to hone their skills

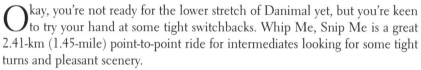

Okay, you're not ready for the lower stretch of Danimal yet, but you're keen to try your hand at some tight switchbacks. Whip Me, Snip Me is a great 2.41-km (1.45-mile) point-to-point ride for intermediates looking for some tight turns and pleasant scenery.

The trail begins with a wide access road that climbs above Alta Lake and provides a vantage point with some great views. As you climb, you'll pass the main access for Rainbow Lake. From here, the trail turns sharply downhill, paralleling the gravel road and providing a winding intermediate challenge. Watch for hikers on their way up and have fun.

General location: Whistler.

Elevation change: From Alta Lake Road, the trail climbs 60 m (197 feet) to its junction with Beaver Pass at 700 m (2,296 feet). Although it stays fairly level for a while after this junction, it eventually climbs another 80 m (262 feet) to its junction with the Rainbow Lake Trail. The remainder of the trail is a winding downhill.

Season: April through October.

Services: All services are available in Whistler.

Hazards: Though this is a great intermediate ride, it does have some tight turns bordered by immovable objects. Use caution as you work on negotiating the turns, and be on the lookout for hikers. This is a popular access trail; be sure to yield to the vibram-soled crowd.

Rescue index: The ride crosses numerous access roads and trails, so help is rarely far away. In addition, it finishes along the Alta Lake Road where vehicles and cottages are always nearby.

RIDE 42 · Whip Me, Snip Me

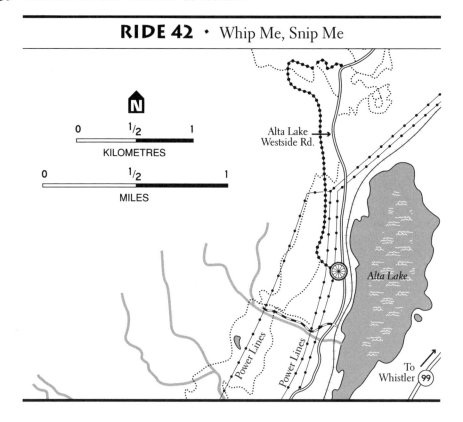

Land status: A mixture of Crown land and undeveloped private land.

Maps: The NTS 1:50,000 topographic map for this trail is 92 J/2 Whistler, but the best map for the Whistler area is the *Whistler Area Mountain Biking & Recreation Map* produced by TerraPro GPS Surveys Ltd. (Box 1016, Whistler, B.C. V0N 1B0 or bikemap@whistler.net). The map is available from most local bike shops in Whistler.

Finding the trail: From the village, head south on Highway 99 and right onto Alta Lake Westside Road. Follow this winding road for just over 5.5 km (3.3 miles). Approximately 100 m (328 feet) north of the Whistler Youth Hostel, you'll notice a gravel road climbing to the left. Park your car and ride up this road.

Sources of additional information:

> Whistler Off-Road Cycling Association
> Box 3500-31
> Whistler, B.C. V0N 1B0
> (604) 938-9893

Notes on the trail: Ride the wide fire road for approximately 0.6 km (0.36 mile) as it passes Danimal and finally the Beaver Pass Trail. Stay on the wide double-track as it passes though a forest of Douglas fir, cedar, and alder. Take in some views as the trail continues to climb gradually at the 0.84-km (0.5-mile) mark. It begins to narrow after kilometre 1.24 (mile 0.74), and the climbing increases as you cross a small bridge. The trail becomes more urban as you join the main access for the Rainbow Lake Hiking Trail at kilometre 1.63 (mile 0.98). Things get a little confusing here as you meet the gravel access road just as it makes a wide switchback. Follow the road in the downhill direction and stay straight as the gravel road drops down another switchback. Beginners may select this quick exit, but intermediate riders will want to stay straight as the trail enters the bush slightly and then begins its own switchbacking path downward. Although technical, this is an enjoyable intermediate track with numerous sharp corners.

The trail touches the road again at kilometre 2.05 (mile 1.23). As the road makes a wide switchback, the trail cuts across it and continues on the opposite side, again leaving the gravel behind. Immediately there is a trail junction, with the trail for Rainbow Falls taking off to the left. Stay straight and watch for a switchback down to the left. The trail appears to go straight at this point (2.25 km/1.35 miles), but it's obvious if you look for it. Finally, meet the road at the Rainbow Medley Trailhead at kilometre 2.41 (mile 1.45).

RIDE 43 · Danimal North

AT A GLANCE

Length/configuration: 4.79-km (2.87-mile) point-to-point with several entry and exit options

Aerobic difficulty: The trail has moderate changes in elevation and requires moderate fitness level

Technical difficulty: This is an expert ride with some challenging sections, large obstacles, and sheer drops

Scenery: Numerous views showcase the surrounding lakes and the volcanic spire of Black Tusk in the distance

Special comments: Danimal is often ridden in multiple configurations. This route describes it from the south entrance of Lower Sproat to its north trailhead

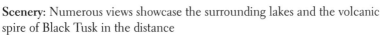

If you have done Lower Sproat and are looking for a little more challenge, simply move downhill a short distance and bounce your way down this 4.79-km (2.87-mile) point-to-point trail. In fact, the two can be easily done in succession

RIDE 43 · Danimal North

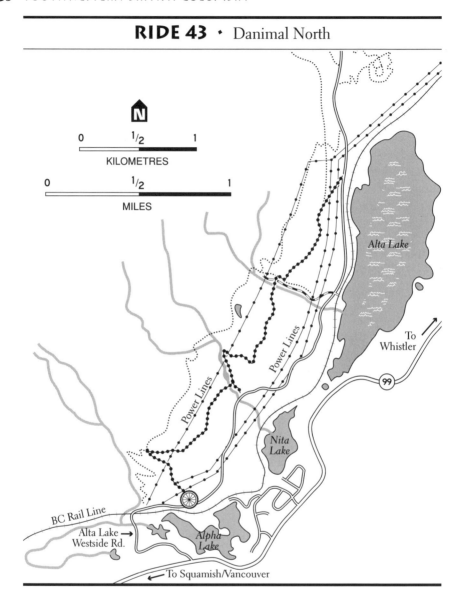

to create a loop. Begin with this ride, and when you meet the access road at kilometre 3.41 (mile 2.05), turn left and climb for 0.12 km (0.07 mile) to the junction with Lower Sproat. On your way back, you can choose to descend the final stretch of Lower Sproat or continue down the treacherous drop of Danimal South.

As you roll along your way, periodic views of the surrounding lakes and distant Black Tusk and the Spearhead Range add some magic to an already challenging ride. Depending on your fitness level and ambition, you have numerous

Preparing for the plummet: these cyclists are about to head down the sheer drop of Danimal South.

exit and entrance options as the trail passes three different access points. You can also link it with other rides like Whip Me, Snip Me or the technical descent at the north end of Beaver Pass. The options are endless, but your technical prowess better not be. This is a challenging ride, best suited for strong technical riders.

General location: Whistler.

Elevation change: From the trailhead along Alta Lake Road at 655 m (2,148 feet), climb 110 m (361 feet) to the junction with Danimal North. While rolling, the trail maxes out at 790 m (2,591 feet).

Season: April through October.

Services: All services are available in Whistler.

Hazards: The trail has plenty of large obstacles, including wheelie drops off lava rocks, large roots and logs, sections of deep rutting, and other potential challenges.

Rescue index: The trail is popular, particularly with the numerous loop options it provides, but be prepared to make your way to one of the many exits in the case of an accident. Once you are on Alta Lake Road, help will not be difficult to find.

Land status: A mixture of undeveloped private land and Crown land.

Maps: The NTS 1:50,000 topographic maps for this trail are 92 J/3 Brandywine Falls and 92 J/2 Whistler, but the best map for the Whistler area is the *Whistler Area Mountain Biking & Recreation Map* produced by TerraPro GPS Surveys Ltd. (Box 1016, Whistler, B.C. V0N 1B0 or bikemap@whistler.net). The map is available from most local bike shops in Whistler.

Finding the trail: From the village, head south on Highway 99 and turn right onto Alta Lake Westside Road. Follow this road as it crosses the tracks and then branches to access Alpha Lake. Turn right and park near this junction. Climb back onto the Alta Lake Road, crank your bars right, and the trailhead is almost immediately on your left. Take this double-track and begin climbing.

Sources of additional information:

> Whistler Off-Road Cycling Association
> Box 3500-31
> Whistler, B.C. V0N 1B0
> (604) 938-9893

Notes on the trail: Climb the Lower Sproat Trail for 0.73 km (0.44 mile) to the junction with Danimal Trail. Turn right and begin to climb toward the power lines, followed by a short, technical descent. Wind along this single-track until it makes a sharp right and then a left at kilometre 1.82 (mile 1.09) before ascending a sharp, rooted opening between some alder and cedar. The climb is challenging, but not very long. After crossing a small bridge over the creek at kilometre 1.99 (mile 1.19), a single-track drops down to the right offering an alternative entrance/exit to the ride. Turn left as the climbing continues, and the trail temporarily climbs above the power lines. The climbing ends at kilometre 2.27 (mile 1.36) as the trail turns to the right and descends back toward the transmission line.

As the trail continues to drop beyond the power lines, it turns sharply to the left at kilometre 2.44 (mile 1.46) and begins to climb a technical stretch. Climb over a large lava boulder at kilometre 2.81 (mile 1.69), and stay straight as a trail joins in from the left. The climbing soon ends and you earn a downhill stretch, crossing over a small bridge before the final drop to the access road leading to Lower Sproat and Beaver Pass Trails. Cross this road, and continue on the opposite side. After passing under a single transmission line, the trail continues to drop sharply. The descent becomes increasingly technical; at times the forest begins to encroach on the trail. Turn onto the access road at kilometre 4.54 (mile 2.72). If you want to continue on Whip Me, Snip Me, turn left at this junction and climb for 60 m (200 feet) and take the trail on the right near an abandoned car. To exit, turn right and join Alta Lake Road in approximately 0.25 km (0.15 mile).

RIDE 44 · Danimal South

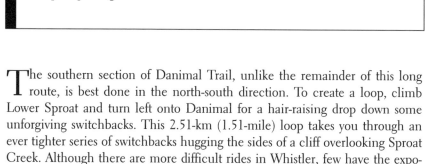

AT A GLANCE

Length/configuration: 2.51-km (1.51-mile) loop

Aerobic difficulty: Moderate climb for 0.73 km (0.44 mile), after which it is all downhill

Technical difficulty: Extreme exposure, for expert-level riders only

Scenery: A few views along the cliff bands

Special comments: This short loop allows expert riders quick access to the sharp drop along the south end of Danimal Trail

The southern section of Danimal Trail, unlike the remainder of this long route, is best done in the north-south direction. To create a loop, climb Lower Sproat and turn left onto Danimal for a hair-raising drop down some unforgiving switchbacks. This 2.51-km (1.51-mile) loop takes you through an ever tighter series of switchbacks hugging the sides of a cliff overlooking Sproat Creek. Although there are more difficult rides in Whistler, few have the exposure that is de rigueur on this ride. This ride is not for everyone, and the consequences of a fall can be dire, so save this trail for when you are cleaning other local expert rides.

General location: Whistler.

Elevation change: The trail climbs 125 m (410 feet) up the Lower Sproat Trail and then plummets just under 200 m (656 feet) on its descent back to the Alta Lake Road.

Season: April through October.

Services: All services are available in Whistler.

Hazards: This ride, with its habit of hugging the cliff edge, brings some extreme consequences in the case of a fall. The drops are sharp, sudden, and unforgiving. Expect pain.

Rescue index: On this route you are never far from Alta Lake Road, and help is generally available along this busy stretch of road.

Land status: A mixture of private and Crown land.

Maps: The NTS 1:50,000 topographic map for this trail is 92 J/3 Brandywine Falls, but the best map for the Whistler area is the *Whistler Area Mountain Biking & Recreation Map* produced by TerraPro GPS Surveys Ltd. (Box 1016,

RIDE 44 · Danimal South

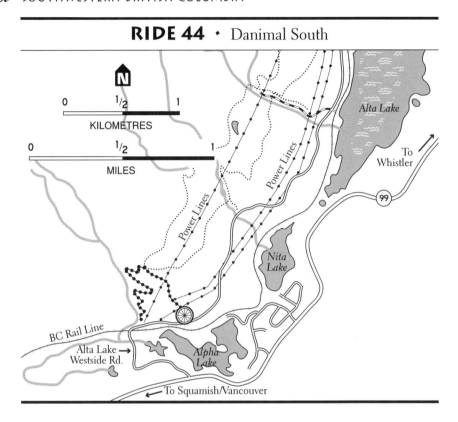

Whistler, B.C. V0N 1B0 or bikemap@whistler.net). The map is available from most local bike shops in Whistler.

Finding the trail: From the village, head south on Highway 99 and turn right onto Alta Lake Westside Road. Follow this road as it crosses the tracks and then branches to access Alpha Lake. Turn right and park near this junction. Climb back onto the Alta Lake Road, turn right, and the trailhead is almost immediately on your left. Take this double-track and begin climbing.

Sources of additional information:

Whistler Off-Road Cycling Association
Box 3500-31
Whistler, B.C. V0N 1B0
(604) 938-9893

Notes on the trail: Climb the Lower Sproat Trail for 0.73 km (0.44 mile) to the junction with Danimal Trail. Turn left onto the single-track of Danimal, and stay straight as a rougher single-track joins in from the right at kilometre 0.92 (mile 0.55). Just beyond this junction, the trail makes a hard left and begins to traverse a cliff band. After a hard right switchback, the descent begins in earnest.

Danimal Trail winds past small stands of devil's club, a well-armed plant that can easily slash your legs.

By kilometre 1.2 (mile 0.72), the trail begins to cross a steep sidecut high above Sproat Creek. Beyond this, it makes a hard left to leave the sound of the creek behind. This is countered by another hard right at kilometre 1.31 (mile 0.79), bringing the trail back toward the sound of water. As the path descends, the switchbacks gradually tighten as the trail begins dropping down the cliff at kilometre 1.87 (mile 1.12). Grit your teeth and make sure you keep the rubber down along this stretch of extreme exposure before joining with the road at kilometre 2.17 (mile 1.3). Turn right and return to your car at kilometre 2.51 (mile 1.51).

RIDE 45 · Bob's ReBob

AT A GLANCE

Length/configuration: 2.9-km (1.74-mile) fish-shaped loop

Aerobic difficulty: The climb is steady and requires a high degree of fitness

Technical difficulty: This is a very serious trail with extreme obstacles on the descent

Scenery: This ride remains largely within dense British Columbia rain forest with little in the way of views. As you crest the top of the ride, you get a brief view across the valley toward the peaks of the Spearhead Range

Special comments: Save it for a day when you feel invincible, and make sure your ability level matches your ego

This is a trail for those days when your stress level is so high you feel like you're about to burst. This 2.9-km (1.74-mile) figure-eight consists of a sharp climb followed by a bone-crushing drop back to the road, crossing the original climb. The drops are sharp and unforgiving, and even expert riders will probably gain a bruise or two on this drop.

If your skill level is up to the challenge, this trail forms an excellent afternoon outing. It also offers the option of multiple loops of the upper section before finishing the lower descent. Essentially, you ride up a sharp climb, make a hard left, and then drop straight through the underbrush to rejoin your main access. Either turn left for another loop or turn right for a short distance for access to another drop to your left. This one will eventually bring you back to the Alta Lake Road.

General location: Whistler.

Elevation change: From the trailhead at 680 m (2,230 feet), you climb steadily for 1.26 km (0.76 mile) to a maximum elevation of 815 m (2,673 feet). Beyond this, it's downhill all the way.

Season: April through October.

Services: All services are available in Whistler.

Hazards: This trail has large vertical drops, logs, roots, and every other challenge imaginable.

Rescue index: Beginning and ending along Alta Lake Road, you are rarely far from help.

Land status: A mixture of Crown land and undeveloped private land.

RIDE 45 · Bob's Rebob

Maps: The NTS 1:50,000 topographic map for this trail is 92 J/2 Whistler, but the best map for the Whistler area is the *Whistler Area Mountain Biking & Recreation Map* produced by TerraPro GPS Surveys Ltd. (Box 1016, Whistler, B.C. V0N 1B0 or bikemap@whistler.net). The map is available from most local bike shops in Whistler.

Finding the trail: From the village, head north on Highway 99 and turn left at the lights on Alpine Way. Turn left again onto Alta Lake Westside Road and wind your way until you meet the trailhead for Rainbow Medley Trail, just as Alta Lake Road crosses Twenty-One Mile Creek. Bob's ReBob climbs on the north side of the creek.

Sources of additional information:

Whistler Off-Road Cycling Association
Box 3500-31
Whistler, B.C. V0N 1B0
(604) 938-9893

Notes on the trail: From the trailhead along Alta Lake Road, the climbing begins right away as you push your way through a short tangle of roots. Beyond this, the gradient continues, but the trail widens out to become easily rideable.

While a lung-burner, the uphill section is virtually all rideable. Stay straight as rough trails fork off to the right at kilometre 0.44 (mile 0.26) and again at kilometre 0.69 (mile 0.41). Soon after passing this last junction, a rough trail comes in from the left at kilometre 0.76 (mile 0.46). You will later return on this trail as you complete the ReBob loop. For now, stay straight. At kilometre 1 (mile 0.6), the trail forks just as you pass an old log that partially blocks the trail. Stay to the left. Soon after you pass this junction, the trail begins its sharp turn to the left, preparing for the return run. Beyond the switchback, the climbing moderates to give you a chance to prepare for the sharp drop ahead of you.

As you cross a narrow sidecut at kilometre 1.23 (mile 0.74), be prepared to drop sharply down ReBob as another fork heads off to the right. With this drop at kilometre 1.26 (mile 0.76), the character instantly changes to a narrow, steep, rocky, rooted drop. This is expert-only country and should be treated with respect. As you drop, the trail rarely leaves the fall line and literally plummets over a series of greasy roots and past some stands of prickly devil's club. You finally rejoin ReBob at kilometre 1.48 (mile 0.89). Dust yourself off, and if you enjoyed that, consider heading around for another loop. Otherwise, turn right and then make a quick left at the first junction. This single-track takes no prisoners as it takes you over high wheelie drops, narrow chutes, roots, and logs until it crosses a small bridge over a stream at kilometre 1.64 (mile 0.98). Beyond the bridge the descent moderates and becomes more easily rideable. The trail joins a technical single-track at kilometre 1.71 (mile 1.03). Turn left and join Alta Lake Road at kilometre 1.92 (mile 1.16). Wind right to return to your vehicle in a little less than 1 km (0.6 mile).

RIDE 46 · A River Runs Through It

AT A GLANCE

Length/configuration: 3.32-km (1.99-mile) loop

Aerobic difficulty: The trail has little change in elevation and requires little in the way of fitness

Technical difficulty: This is a technical playground for riders looking to play on some of the obstacles or increase their ability to deal with pyramids and logs

Scenery: The trail runs through a sensitive marshland and, although forested, is quite pretty

Special comments: This trail was built by the Whistler Off-Road Cycling Association through an environmentally sensitive area. Please wait until you are a solid intermediate-level rider and only ride when the trail is dry. This will help reduce erosion on the trail

RIDE 46 · A River Runs Through It

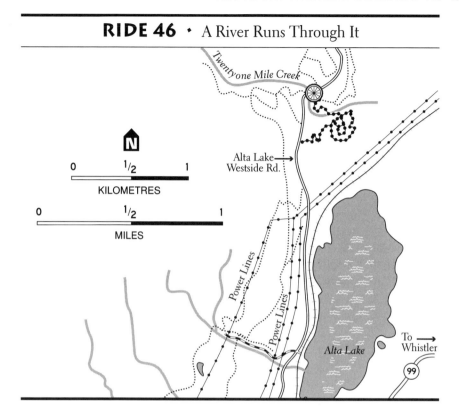

This well-designed and challenging 3.32-km (1.99-mile) loop is a wonderful place to play on a variety of obstacles with soft landings and only moderate difficulty. It was designed by the Whistler Off-Road Cycle Association and includes a teeter totter, plenty of log pyramids, a log designed to be ridden lengthwise, and one of the most challenging river crossings in the area. Though it is in a sensitive area, it has very little change in elevation, and most of the area is a carpet of moss and needles. This lack of hard surfaces, with the exception of a forest of immovable trees, allows you to relax a little, take some risks, and not worry about a mistake carrying you off the edge of a cliff. This confidence boost makes it a great place for solid intermediate riders to increase their skills. Beginners should ride elsewhere until they have more experience with negotiating pyramids and crossing downed logs. Many of the obstacles offer bypass options or, in some cases, smaller obstacles beside larger ones, again allowing you to decide the final level of difficulty.

General location: Whistler.

Elevation change: The trail is very flat with negligible change in elevation.

Season: April through October.

Services: All services are available in Whistler.

Hazards: This ride was built with challenge in mind, and obstacles such as teeter totters and log pyramids have been strategically placed. Remember, you can't always see what is on the other side of a pyramid, and some spit you into narrow chutes on the far side. Also, the crossing over Twenty-one Mile Creek is a single log, wide enough to allow strong riders to pedal, but sending those who make mistakes into the strong waters of the creek.

Rescue index: The ride starts and finishes on the Alta Lake Westside Road, so help can be accessed from either end of the trail. It is a very popular ride, so other cyclists will likely also ride past.

Land status: Crown land.

Maps: The NTS 1:50,000 topographic map for this trail is 92 J/2 Whistler, but the best map for the Whistler area is the *Whistler Area Mountain Biking & Recreation Map* produced by TerraPro GPS Surveys Ltd. (Box 1016, Whistler, B.C. V0N 1B0 or bikemap@whistler.net). The map is available from most local bike shops in Whistler.

Finding the trail: From the village, head north on Highway 99 and turn left at the lights on Alpine Way. Turn left again onto Alta Lake Westside Road, and wind your way until you meet Twenty-One Mile Creek. Just before crossing the creek, you'll see a parking lot to the left. The trailhead is shared with Bart's Dark Trail, but almost immediately you'll see a trail branching to the right. This is A River Runs Through It.

Sources of additional information:

Whistler Off-Road Cycling Association
Box 3500-31
Whistler, B.C. V0N 1B0
(604) 938-9893

Notes on the trail: The trailhead is shared with Bart's Dark Trail, but almost immediately you'll see a trail branching to the right. This is A River Runs Through It. There is a sign a little way down the trail, beyond which the trail makes a sharp right although it appears to climb over a log and continue straight. Right away, you begin a technical drop down toward the river. Numerous riders have continued toward the actual water, but the trail actually makes a hard left and finally brings you out to a greasy log over the river at kilometre 0.48 (mile 0.29). Once you make your way over the bridge (I won't tell anyone you didn't ride it), the trail passes under what resembles an old lookout tower.

As you wind past the 1-km (0.6-mile) mark, a wooden teeter totter will test your balance. Be careful if the wood is wet, though; it can get slippery. At kilometre 1.41 (mile 0.85), a downed cedar has been used as a runway for many riders, but you can bypass it and climb over a log pyramid instead. Another pyramid beyond this point looks inviting, but it spits you out into a rooted drop off that will toast nonexperts. Some board steps require a little momentum at kilometre 1.65 (mile 0.99). A bridge over a runoff channel at kilometre 2.17 (mile

1.3) offers a wet-weather alternative to simply dropping down into the streambed. Bounce your way around a log bridge that forms a banked corner at kilometre 2.39 (mile 1.43) and join the road all too soon at kilometre 2.87 (mile 1.7). Turn right onto Alta Lake Road and meet the main parking lot at kilometre 3.32 (mile 1.99).

RIDE 47 · Mel's Dilemma

AT A GLANCE

Length/configuration: This tight network of loops is designed for play rather than mileage. A point-to-point trip through the network is only 1 km (0.6 mile) or so in total. Plenty of loops allow you to play for several hours

Aerobic difficulty: Moderately challenging with a maximum climb of 60 m (197 feet) within the network

Technical difficulty: Varies from beginner to expert depending on which line you choose

Scenery: This trail system remains within the dense canopy of British Columbia rain forest. This is a place to work on technique and is thus not known for its views

Special comments: This network allows you to choose your route and play until you get tired

Mel's Dilemma, like Cut Yer Bars, is a tight network of trails allowing you to play within a confined area for as long as you please. It's not a trail system with any particular destination in mind, and the actual distance covered is not great. The network is bordered on the south by the Alta Lake Road and the east by Alpine Way and Forest Ridge Drive, so there is little potential to get lost. Just immerse yourself in the trails and when you have had enough, head down the slope and you'll eventually emerge along Alta Lake Road or at the end of Forest Ridge Drive.

General location: Whistler.

Elevation change: A maximum of 60 m (197 feet) within the network.

Season: April through October.

Services: All services are available in Whistler.

RIDE 47 · Mel's Dilemma

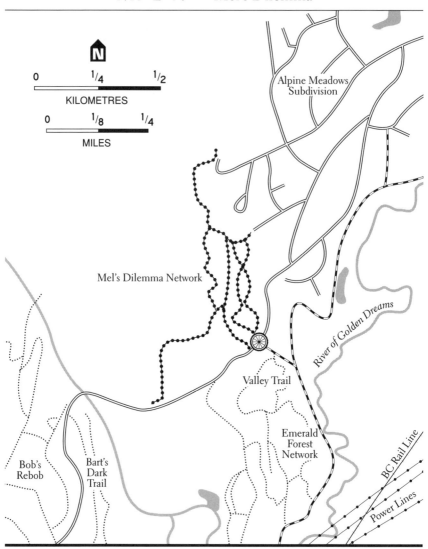

Hazards: They vary depending on which route you choose, but be ready for rocks, logs, sudden drops, and eroded chutes.

Rescue index: Because this is a tight network, bordered on the south and east by roads, you can always make a quick exit to get help.

Land status: A mixture of Crown land and undeveloped private land.

Maps: The NTS 1:50,000 topographic map for this trail is 92 J/2 Whistler, but the best map for the Whistler area is the *Whistler Area Mountain Biking &*

Recreation Map produced by TerraPro GPS Surveys Ltd. (Box 1016, Whistler, B.C. V0N 1B0 or bikemap@whistler.net). The map is available from most local bike shops in Whistler.

Finding the trail: The easiest access point is either along Alta Lake Road, just across from where the Valley Trail (coming from the village) crosses Alta Lake Road. You can also access it from the west end of Forest Ridge Drive.

Sources of additional information:

Whistler Off-Road Cycling Association
Box 3500-31
Whistler, B.C. V0N 1B0
(604) 938-9893

Notes on the trail: From the trailhead, simply take whatever junction looks good at the time. This is not a network to worry about directions, but simply to explore. New routes appear regularly, and the lines seem to change as your abilities increase. When you're sufficiently pooped, follow the lay of the land downhill and you'll eventually emerge onto the Alta Lake Road or Forest Ridge Drive.

RIDE 48 · Valley Trail

AT A GLANCE

Length/configuration: This trail winds through the valley bottom joining all the facilities and housing subdivisions around Whistler. It has many branches, with the length limited only by your timeline and energy level. Each offers a different character, with some stretches winding past pristine marshland and others traversing more urban landscapes. If you have sufficient time, you can easily ride this trail for the better part of a day

Aerobic difficulty: It is an easy, paved trail, rolling with the valley bottom

Technical difficulty: The trail is paved and easy

Scenery: The scenery is great, with the trail passing all the local lakes, through the village, along the golf course—all with great views of the surrounding landscape

Special comments: This is used largely as an access path for locals, but it makes for a wonderful family ride

A re you tired of gnarly single-track? Maybe you're simply looking for a per-fect family ride. The Valley Trail within Whistler Townsite may be exactly what the doctor ordered. This winding, convoluted trail system dissects the various areas of Whistler and offers access to just about any of the area's many subdivisions and recreation areas. Hop on the bike, drag the Burley, and simply head out and explore. Be sure to bring along a town map as the valley trail is clearly marked on most of the maps of the village. You can make quite a long excursion with this trail, so be sure to keep track of how far you have traveled — you may have to backtrack.

General location: Whistler.

Elevation change: The trail varies little in elevation. It climbs only a short distance at any given time. You will barely discern a change throughout the ride.

Season: April through October.

Services: All services are available in Whistler.

Hazards: The most dangerous part of this ride is crossing busy highways and golf courses. Watch for flying golf balls.

Rescue index: The trail rides through civilized landscapes, so help is always close at hand.

Land status: Private and municipal land.

Maps: The NTS 1:50,000 topographic maps for this trail are 92 J/3 Brandywine Falls and 92 J/2 Whistler, but the best map for the Whistler area is the *Whistler Area Mountain Biking & Recreation Map* produced by TerraPro GPS Surveys Ltd. (Box 1016, Whistler, B.C. V0N 1B0 or bikemap@whistler.net). The map is available from most local bike shops in Whistler.

Finding the trail: This trail can be accessed at numerous points throughout the community. Refer to local maps, available everywhere, for relevant access points.

Sources of additional information:

Whistler Off-Road Cycling Association
Box 3500-31
Whistler, B.C. V0N 1B0
(604) 938-9893

Notes on the trail: Beginning at the Whistler Marketplace on Lorimar Road, turn right onto Lorimar and ride toward the first set of lights at Blackcomb Way. Diagonally across the intersection, the trail winds along the road before heading into the woods at kilometre 0.5 (mile 0.3). After crossing a bridge over Fitzsimmons Creek, you enter Lost Lake Park. Continue on the gravel trail to the left of the log cabin, although the trail seems to trend right. Along the way, lots of winter cross-country skiing trails branch off the main trail. These trails can be ignored (as far as this main route is concerned). Look for posts that look like regular street signs. These are the signs that indicate the summer bike trail system.

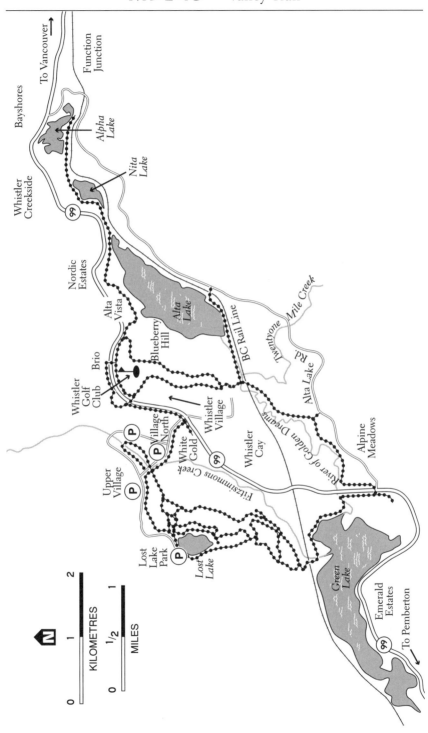

After crossing Horstman Creek, turn left, soon after crossing Blackcomb Creek. Stay straight at the junction following the crossing. Lost Lake, with its numerous access points, will now be on your left. This lake is quite small, but it's busy with swimmers and fishermen (it's stocked with rainbow trout). Beyond the first access point, the trail traverses the west shore of the lake before leaving the lake behind entirely and entering the woods. The 3-km (1.8-mile) mark brings another junction. Go left to return to the lake, or stay to the right to continue on Valley Trail. The wide gravel of this trail is a very pleasant ride. Stay right, and then left at successive junctions. Stay straight at the next junction, after which the trail drops sharply to the shoreline of Green Lake. Just beyond the Old Mill Road junction (at the bottom of the hill), turn right at a signed junction. This will take you past a bridge over Fitzsimmons Creek, over the railway tracks, and then left to parallel the tracks for a short distance. Skirt the golf course until you reach civilization again. Don't enter the golf course land, as its trail system is reserved for golf carts. Suddenly, the trail enters a parking lot where concrete barriers separate the trail from the road. Just before the end of the barriers, cross the street, and to the left side of the oncoming road, the trail continues. Soon you pass the float plane docks, and the trail turns to the left. Keep your eyes open for waterfowl, herons, and even osprey. The trail crosses two lengthy bridges over inlets to Green Lake before swinging to the right. Several interpretive signs highlight some of the area's diverse natural and human history—take the time to read them, as one of them points to an osprey nest! Each year, a nesting pair will return to use the same nest (barring some unforeseen mishap).

The trail resumes its gravel nature after crossing another bridge. It then swings right into a dark western red cedar forest. You'll notice the immense leaves of the skunk cabbage, sometimes reaching more than 1.3 m (4 feet) in length. Also present are the immense maple-style leaves of the devil's club. This plant has bright red berries and a horrific thorny character. Turn left at the next junction (the right fork merely takes you to the sports arena before dead-ending). Cross the highway at Alpine Way, and make a hard left to parallel Highway 99. Pass the swimming pool and enter Meadow Park. Along with Lost Lake, this is a wonderful place to relax on a hot day. The trail parallels the River of Golden Dreams, with homes along the right. Stay straight at a junction for Alta Lake Road. This is just another access point to the trail.

As the trail winds along the river, it turns to the left, passes under the power lines, over the railroad tracks, and then over the River of Golden Dreams. After the river, the trail makes a detour to wind around two power boxes and arrives at a residential intersection. Turn right, and then immediately left back onto the trail. This is quickly followed by another junction. At this point, you need to decide whether you want to circle the golf course on the west or the east side. The route I'm describing stays straight at this junction and follows the east side of the golf course. This allows a quicker return to the village. After this point, the trail offers the contrast of residential development on your left and golfers on your right. Two trails will come in from the left to offer early exit options.

Continue to the south end of the golf course, cross under Highway 99 via an underpass, and return to the village. Take a right at the Whistler Way junction, and the road will parallel the town development. From this point, you can either enter the main village, or return to the Marketplace via Village Gate Boulevard, Blackcomb Way, and finally Lorimar Road. This simple ride has covered approximately 15 km (9 miles). Options to extend the ride include continuing south from the golf course along the shores of Nita and Alpha Lakes.

RIDE 49 · Parkhurst Ghost Town Loop

AT A GLANCE

Length/configuration: 9-km (5.4-mile) loop

Aerobic difficulty: Moderately challenging, with total climbing of approximately 100 m (328 feet)

Technical difficulty: This is an intermediate trail with some steep climbs and loose drops

Scenery: The views open up periodically toward the rolling landscape to the north, and the trail comes out on the quiet south shore of Green Lake

Special comments: It's always neat to explore a ghost town. This ride should be on everyone's itinerary

The trail 9-km (5.4-mile) loop climbs through Douglas fir, western hemlock, and western white pine. The ride brings you along across a railroad bridge, up a moderate climb following the power lines, and then down to the ghost town of Parkhurst. The buildings are the remains of an old logging camp abandoned in the 1930s. Some of the buildings have been adopted periodically by drifters looking for inexpensive accommodation. The place has been abandoned for decades, and it still has an eerie feel about it.

When I was there, I had just begun exploring an old cabin, taking note of a stack of postcards only a few years old and a pile of cassette tape cases (no tapes) of bands like Pink Floyd, when I began to suspect that more recent travelers had taken advantage of these structures. The situation continued to get stranger. I heard the sound of running water and discovered a modern hose with water spewing forth like a magic spring. As I returned to my bike, feeling increasingly uneasy with the mystery of the place, I took a sharp branch in the left shoulder— first blood for the ride. The final straw was the discovery of a butcher knife in the tracks as I approached for the return ride. Something made me pick up the knife

RIDE 49 · Parkhurst Ghost Town Loop

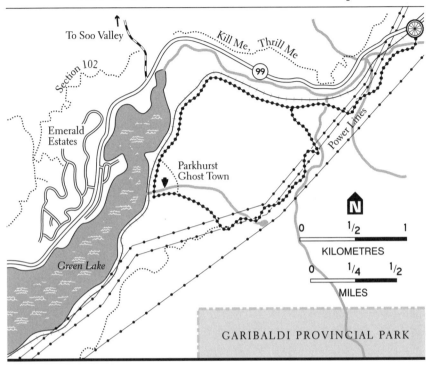

and give it a toss. The blade stuck into a railroad tie like something from a Steven Seagal Movie. This was only accentuated by the cryptic character I had passed on the way to the ghost town. Although I had made numerous greetings, he merely gave me a strange look and uttered not a word.

General location: Whistler.

Elevation change: The trail climbs little more than 100 m (328 feet) before descending down to the ghost town.

Season: April through October.

Services: All services are available in Whistler.

Hazards: The trail spends a fair bit of time riding along railroad tracks. Remember that they are also used by trains. Keep your ears open and your wits about you. The drop down the main hill is loose and sandy. At places it is becoming rutted from all the riders locking their brakes during the descent.

As you ride the rails, the rocks used to fill in the ties are very sharp, adding to the potential for a flat. Make sure you have an extra tire and tube for that unexpected eventuality.

Rescue index: This is a wilderness ride. Although you are not too far from the trailhead at any time, you may have to return all the way before you can access assistance by flagging down a vehicle. Make sure your repair kit is in order.

Land status: A mix of undeveloped private land and Crown land.

Maps: The NTS 1:50,000 topographic map for this trail is 92 J/2 Whistler, but the best map for the Whistler area is the *Whistler Area Mountain Biking & Recreation Map* produced by TerraPro GPS Surveys Ltd. (Box 1016, Whistler, B.C. V0N 1B0 or bikemap@whistler.net). The map is available from most local bike shops in Whistler.

Finding the trail: From the village, head north on Highway 99 past the watery shores of Green Lake. Shortly beyond the far end of Green Lake, you will see a Garibaldi Provincial Park sign indicating Wedge Creek. Turn right. The road will cross a bridge over the river. Immediately beyond this bridge, Wedge Creek Road climbs to the left, and a wide access road branches off to the right. Park off the road here, and ride along the high quality double-track access road.

Sources of additional information:

> Whistler Off-Road Cycling Association
> Box 3500-31
> Whistler, B.C. V0N 1B0
> (604) 938-9893

Notes on the trail: Shortly beyond the far end of Green Lake, you will see a Garibaldi Provincial Park sign for Wedge Creek. Turn right. The road will cross a bridge over the river. Immediately beyond this bridge, Wedge Creek Road climbs to the left, and a wide access road branches off to the right. Take this right junction, and follow the high quality double-track as it climbs a short, moderately steep hill on its way to the only ford of the trip at kilometre 0.8 (mile 0.5). In late summer, it is possible to cross using rocks to keep your feet quite dry. In the early season, you may have to grin and bear it. Use your judgment during the spring runoff—the water level may fluctuate dramatically. As you approach what appears to be an old gravel pit, look to your right. Do not enter the gravel wash as the trail turns right just before it to cross some soft, bogging sand before entering the woods again. If you enter the wash, you've gone too far! This trail takes you toward the railroad tracks. You need to cross the river on the railroad bridge. As you cross the bridge, a sign indicates BR 81.1. Although there is a narrow track alongside the rails, it is much easier to simply ride within the centre of the rails themselves. They have been sufficiently filled to allow moderately smooth riding. After only 100 m (328 feet) or so, a single-track takes off to the left and immediately branches. Take the left fork, which seems to backtrack toward the river. Stay the course, as it will swing to the right as it approaches.

When you see the gravel of the river coming into view, the trail will drop down a small bank. Trend right; as you pick your way through the rocks and logs, look for a narrow single-track branching off to your right. The main climbing begins here as the trail follows the power line up a steep hill. This is the principle climb of the trip. The hill is made of loose sand and rocks that will leave less experienced riders pushing. As you crest this short, steep hill, the descent is rapid and technical. It begins just beyond a junction at kilometre 3.7 (mile 2.2).

It is a simple drop for riders used to British Columbia's radical riding, but for most it will be a challenging drop down a sandy, rocky slope. It offers numerous opportunities for a tumble.

Your next major junction, unsigned like all the rest, will occur just as the single-track opens up slightly at kilometre 4.2 (mile 2.5). This is the Green Lake Loop junction; stay right. This trail opens up as it drops. The descent is beautiful as you pass under immense pine and Douglas fir trees, bordered by a prominent rock slope to your right. Beneath the rock slope, the rocks are thickly covered with a deep green moss.

An irrelevant junction appears as you drop toward the lake. Take your pick—each will bring you to the ghost town. The trail drops steadily until you begin to see the remains of old buildings. A few of the buildings have been slightly restored. This has attracted the attention of the occasional squatter who has used the buildings as a temporary residence. A wonderful old truck adds to the ambience.

The trail toward the tracks is to the south of the most well developed building. If you took the left junction to the ghost town, it was slightly before this building. Otherwise, it is slightly beyond. As you descend to the tracks, take some time to enjoy the pristine view of Green Lake. The tracks are being slowly replaced with steel ties, but they still provide good riding. A faint single-track parallels the tracks, but the best riding is right between the rails. Follow the tracks until you cross the river on the same bridge you passed on your way out. Immediately beyond the bridge, the trail forks to the right. Ford the river again, and spin your way back to your vehicle at kilometre 9 (mile 5.4).

RIDE 50 · Microwave Hill

AT A GLANCE

Length/configuration: 9-km (5.4-mile) point-to-point

Aerobic difficulty: This trail climbs 290 m (951 feet) and requires a hefty set of lungs and numerous water bottles

Technical difficulty: This is a moderate trail in terms of technical challenge. It is primarily a lung-burner

Scenery: The views are dramatic with Alpha, Nita, and Alta Lakes spread out beneath you

Special comments: As part of the Cheakamus Challenge race course, this ride should be part of any trip to Whistler

RIDE 50 • Microwave Hill

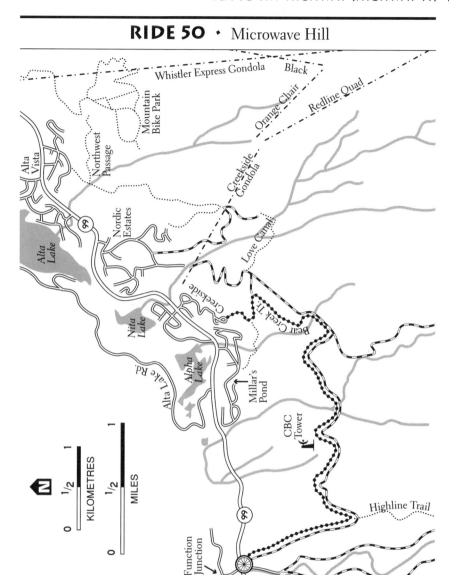

With so much of British Columbia's mountain biking focused on technical prowess, it's nice to find a trail that focuses on elevation and vantage point, with superb views being the order of the day. Forget about steep wheelie drops and sheer cliffs; this trail tests your lung capacity. Be sure to bring along a camera on this 9-km (5.4-mile) point-to-point ride. As you pass the CBC (Canadian Public Broadcasting) tower, the waters of Alpha, Nita, and Alta Lakes spread out beneath you and remind you of the swim that is a requisite part of completing any ride in the area. It also should remind you that you are just about out of drinking water, so be sure to pack an extra bottle. This is camelback country for good reason. You'll find yourself sucking the humid air until your throat screams for water.

The basic route climbs from the Whistler Interpretive Forest, passes a CBC tower, and finally drops down to finish in the Creekside Condos south of the village. Plenty of viewpoints offer a welcome rest, and several other trails may beckon en route. Should you decide to heed their call, simply select the downhill line when you've had enough.

General location: South of Whistler Townsite.

Elevation change: The trail begins at the valley bottom at 600 m (1,968 feet) and climbs steadily to a maximum elevation of 890 m (2,919 feet).

Season: April through October.

Services: All services are available in Whistler.

Hazards: Make sure you bring more water than you might usually require. This is camelback country, with most riders carrying a large reservoir. Climbing this dusty summit will immediately make the need for water quite obvious. Also, while the trail is wide, there are numerous sections of loose rock that require caution.

Rescue index: This is a wilderness ride, and you may not encounter another soul. Though the trail is a wide access road, the remote character requires extra respect.

Land status: A combination of private and Crown land.

Maps: The NTS 1:50,000 topographic maps for this trail are 92 J/3 Brandywine Falls and 92 J/2 Whistler, but the best map for the Whistler area is the *Whistler Area Mountain Biking & Recreation Map* produced by TerraPro GPS Surveys Ltd. (Box 1016, Whistler, B.C. V0N 1B0 or bikemap@whistler.net). The map is available from most local bike shops in Whistler.

Finding the trail: Traveling Highway 99 from Vancouver to Whistler, you will pass Brandywine Falls approximately 45 km (27 miles) north of Squamish. Travel north another 10 km (6 miles) to Function Junction. To the right of this major intersection is a parking lot for the Whistler Interpretive Forest. Park here. From the lot, the trail leaves from the far left corner.

Sources of additional information:

Whistler Off-Road Cycling Association
Box 3500-31
Whistler, B.C. V0N 1B0
(604) 938-9893

Notes on the trail: Right from the get-go this trail begins climbing. To enjoy this route, you need to be able to simply drop your head and grunt (DYHAG). The climbing is steady and unrelenting, with the exception of a few short flat bits, until you pass the CBC tower at kilometre 3.4 (mile 2.04). The upside is that the views become increasingly spectacular as you climb. The first main scenic view is at kilometre 1.6 (mile 1) and elevation 755 m (2,476 feet). A short spur road comes in from the right. It is worth the 100-m (328-foot) diversion to take in this view—after all, you've earned it! To the west is Metal Dome Mountain and far to its left is Mount Brew (kind of makes your mouth water, doesn't it?). Almost due south is the unmistakable summit of Black Tusk, a sharp pinnacle jutting defiantly into the sky. Adjacent to its summit are two more microwave towers.

Continue the climbing until a signed junction appears (kilometre 1.7/mile 1). The right-hand trail takes you to the Highline Trail—stay on the fire road as it switches back to the left and continues climbing. Soon the climbing becomes very challenging as loose boulders test your technical climbing prowess. You may very well find yourself pushing—I did! Be prepared for an endless number of false summits before you reach the tower—and even this is not the end of the climbing. Ignore several overgrown spur trails as you climb.

Pass the tower at kilometre 3.4 (mile 2) and elevation 885 m (2,902 feet), creating the illusion that all the climbing is done. You ain't seen nothin' yet! Shortly beyond this summit, the trail meets another old route coming in from the right. Stay straight past this and several others until you cross Bear Creek and begin climbing again. Watch for some excellent views over the lakes and condos of the many villages of Whistler.

Just beyond the 5-km (3-mile) mark is a major junction. The road you are traveling climbs to the right, while Bear Creek Trail drops to the left in a sudden switchback and continues descending. Jump at this opportunity to change gradients and take the downhill plunge. You cross the creek after a short descent; follow this wide fire road right down to the Creekside Condos at approximately the 9-km (5.4-mile) mark. Simply stay on this wide road all the way to the valley floor.

RIDE 51 · Brandywine Trail

AT A GLANCE

Length/configuration: 4.7-km (2.82-mile) point-to-point or 8.6-km (5.16-mile) loop using Highway 99

Aerobic difficulty: Beyond the short climb at the start of the trail, this is a nice easy ride

Technical difficulty: Some loose gravel, but few other challenges

Scenery: The ride passes numerous little marsh ponds and then parallels the Cheakamus River

Special comments: This is perfect for beginner riders looking for a quiet trail

If you are searching for a pleasant ride for the whole family, look no further than this 8.6-km (5.16-mile) loop. Before you actually start the ride, though, you must take the time to visit the falls for which this park is known. Spilling over a lip of hard volcanic rock, it literally pours into a picture-perfect basin like water from a pitcher. Though not massive, it is one of the most picturesque falls along the Sea to Sky corridor. Beginning in Brandywine Falls Provincial Park, this ride starts with a short, stiff climb, and then rolls its way past several marshy ponds with views toward Metal Dome and Brandywine Mountains to the northwest.

The trail becomes narrower and bumpier as it begins to parallel the Cheakamus River. This powerful river begins to roar as the Callaghan Creek joins from the north. Suddenly, its volume almost doubles and it becomes a raging torrent. Cross over Callaghan Creek on a high-quality suspension bridge, but don't forget to check out the exceptional blueberry patch before you cross. Roll your way through the South Side Campground, and join the highway at kilometre 4.7 (mile 2.82). Turn left, and you'll return to the park in a fast downhill roll of 3.9 km (2.34 miles).

General location: South of Whistler.

Elevation change: From the bridge over Brandywine Creek at 475 m (1,558 feet), the trail climbs gradually to a maximum elevation of 525 m (1,772 feet) as you cross over the railway tracks.

Season: April through October.

Services: All services are available in Whistler.

Hazards: The first climb includes some short, tricky sections for beginners. In addition, the short stretch before the suspension bridge is narrow and rooted.

Rescue index: This trail has popular campgrounds at both ends; you may not meet many riders en route, but there will always be assistance at the trailheads. At Brandywine Falls Provincial Park, there is an office/residence for park staff, and a pay phone at the highway entrance to the park.

Land status: The ride begins within Brandywine Falls Provincial Park and then rolls through a combination of private and Crown land.

Maps: The NTS 1:50,000 topographic map for this trail is 92 J/3 Brandywine Falls, but the best map for the Whistler area is the *Whistler Area Mountain Biking & Recreation Map* produced by TerraPro GPS Surveys Ltd. (Box 1016, Whistler, B.C. V0N 1B0 or bikemap@whistler.net). The map is available from most local bike shops in Whistler.

Finding the trail: From Whistler Village, head south on Highway 99 to Brandywine Falls Provincial Park. Park your car in the main day-use parking lot and follow the signs for the falls. As you cross the bridge over Brandywine Creek, the trail to the falls goes right, but you will want to turn left onto a wide doubletrack that climbs right away.

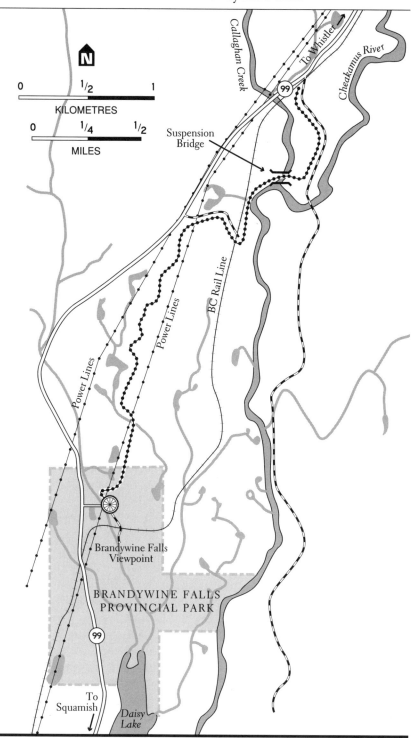

Brandywine Trail includes a suspension bridge crossing over Callaghan Creek.

Sources of additional information:

Whistler Off-Road Cycling Association
Box 3500-31
Whistler, B.C. V0N 1B0
(604) 938-9893

Notes on the trail: After you cross the bridge at Brandywine Falls day-use area, turn left and begin climbing up a wide double-track that follows the river upstream. As the trail levels off, you'll pass a sign indicating that the trail doubles as a winter cross-country ski trail called Easy Street. Roll your way along this wide trail, and pass by several marshy ponds to the left. Covered with yellow pond lilies, they make a picturesque sight. At kilometre 2.9 (mile 1.74), you'll pass some private land to the left. Stay right at a junction at this point, and follow this wide double-track as it crosses over the railroad tracks. Immediately beyond the tracks, make a hard left onto the single-track surface of the Calcheak Trail. This brings you over a small bridge surrounded by the razor-sharp spines of devil's club. As the trail approaches the Cheakamus River, it becomes a little more technical, deteriorating into a rooty roller coaster. There is a high-quality suspension bridge over Callaghan Creek just upstream of its juncture with the Cheakamus River.

Beyond the bridge, roll your way through the South Side Campground and follow the gravel access road as it heads toward the highway. At kilometre 4.7 (mile 2.82), you'll pass the Callaghan Creek Campground to your left and join Highway 99 immediately beyond. Turn left and roll your way back to Brandywine Falls Provincial Park at kilometre 8.6 (mile 5.16).

RIDE 52 · Brandywine–Function Junction

AT A GLANCE

Length/configuration: 12.7-km (7.62-mile) point-to-point

Aerobic difficulty: Moderate; a few long hills

Technical difficulty: The trail is largely double-track with a few rooted sections of single-track

Scenery: There are some great views along the river

Special comments: This great ride follows the roaring Cheakamus River over numerous bridges and through some very scenic landscape

As part of the route of the Cheakamus Challenge mountain bike race, this trail gets a lot of use. It combines wide double-track with a few single-track connectors to create at 12.7-km (7.62-mile) point-to-point ride that parallels the winding Cheakamus River. Along the way it rolls past several picturesque ponds covered with yellow pond lilies. You get to bounce your way over a suspension bridge, but only after taking some time to feast on blueberries before you go. However, don't plan on storing the berries for later. (Only guidebook authors get so preoccupied that they fill a bottle with blueberries and then ride through a garbage dump favoured by the local bear population.)

Following a short stretch of pavement, you head back onto double-track, cross the river again, and climb to the crest of a short, sharp hill. Turning back downhill, you then get a long, fast roll that takes you past several panoramas with views to Mount Sproat to the north. Finally, plug your nose and roll your way through the municipal dump to rejoin Highway 99 at Function Junction.

General location: South of Whistler.

Elevation change: From the trailhead at 475 m (1,558 feet), the trail gradually gains elevation until its second major river crossing at approximately 520 m (1,706 feet). From here, the climbing gets a little more intense, gaining 120 m (394 feet) in just 1.4 km (0.84 mile). Beyond this, it is primarily downhill all the way to Function Junction.

Season: April through October.

Services: All services are available in Whistler.

Hazards: While the trail is primarily wide single-track and double-track, there are several short rooted stretches. In addition, after the long climb, avoid the temptation to scream downhill until you've passed a drainage channel carved

RIDE 52 · Brandywine–Function Junction

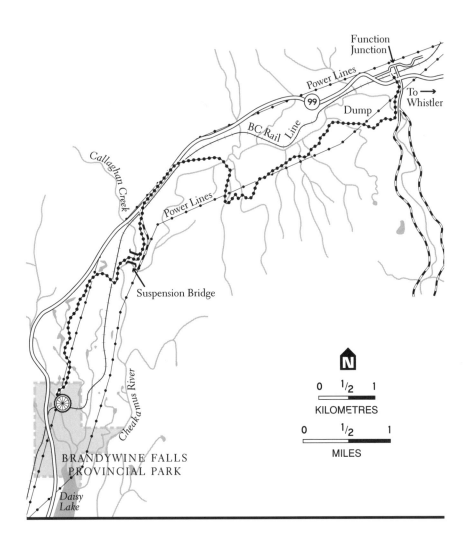

across the road. This could easily catapult a novice over the handlebars. Experts will do a quick bunny-hop and be done with it. Finally, the trail finishes by rolling through the municipal dump. Bears and dumps go together, so keep your eyes peeled for master bruin as you cross through the landfill.

Rescue index: The trail meets the highway halfway, allowing a midpoint option for getting assistance if needed. You may meet some riders along the way as well, as this is a popular trail.

Land status: A combination of private and Crown land.

Maps: The NTS 1:50,000 topographic map for this trail is 92 J/3 Brandywine Falls, but the best map for the Whistler area is the *Whistler Area Mountain Biking & Recreation Map* produced by TerraPro GPS Surveys Ltd. (Box 1016, Whistler, B.C. V0N 1B0 or email them at bikemap@whistler.net). The map is available from most local bike shops in Whistler.

Finding the trail: From Whistler Village, head south on Highway 99 to Brandywine Falls Provincial Park. Park your car in the main day-use parking lot and follow the signs for the falls. After crossing the bridge over Brandywine Creek, the trail to the falls goes right, but you will want to turn left onto a wide double-track that climbs right away.

Sources of additional information:

Whistler Off-Road Cycling Association
Box 3500-31
Whistler, B.C. V0N 1B0
(604) 938-9893

Notes on the trail: Cross the bridge over Brandywine Creek, and turn left onto a wide double-track that begins a short uphill stretch following the course of the creek upstream. As the trail levels off, you'll pass a sign indicating that the trail doubles as a winter cross-country ski trail called Easy Street. Roll along this wide trail, passing several marshy ponds to the left. At kilometre 2.9 (mile 1.74), you'll pass some private land to the left. Stay right at a junction at this point, and follow this wide double-track as it crosses over the railway tracks. Immediately beyond the tracks, make a hard left onto the single-track surface of the Calcheak Trail. This brings you over a small bridge surrounded by the razor-sharp spines of devil's club. As the trail approaches the Cheakamus River, it becomes a little more technical and deteriorates into a rooty roller coaster. There is a high-quality suspension bridge over Callaghan Creek just upstream of its juncture with the Cheakamus River.

Beyond the bridge, roll your way through the South Side Campground and follow the gravel access road as it heads toward the highway. At kilometre 4.7 (mile 2.82), you'll pass the Callaghan Creek Campground to your left and join Highway 99 immediately beyond.

Turn right and follow Highway 99 north for a few hundred metres until you see a B.C. RAIL sign to the right. You'll see a double-track branching off of Highway 99. Take this track; you'll see a gate just beyond a large volcanic rock that exhibits textbook columnar jointing. The rock has cracked in such a way as to create perfect columns. Head through the gate and across the tracks. Beyond the tracks the road heads left and follows the tracks for a short distance. It quickly narrows into a wide single-track that slowly rolls away from the river to cross the Cheakamus River on a good bridge at kilometre 6.9 (mile 4.14). Stay on the main road as an overgrown road joins in from the left beyond the bridge. The trail climbs over the next 1.2 km (0.72 mi.), crosses under the power lines, and eventually makes a hard left as it joins an overgrown road coming in from the right at kilometre 8.3 (mile 4.98). Stay left at this juncture and be cautious on the descent as a drainage channel cuts across the road. At a fork in the road at kilometre 10.2 (mile 6.12), stay left; soon you'll enter the municipal dump. You may get a whiff or two before you actually arrive, depending on the wind direction. Keep an eye open for bears—always a popular sight at a landfill—and enter the actual dump as you cross under the transmission wires.

Turn left at an access road at kilometre 11.4 (mile 6.84), and roll your way down the wide pavement to Function Junction at kilometre 12.7 (mile 7.62). Turn left on Highway 99 and head back to Brandywine Falls.

RIDE 53 · Cheakamus Challenge Race Course

AT A GLANCE

Length/configuration: 57.7-km (34.62-mile) point-to-point

Aerobic difficulty: Extreme, with an elevation gain of 944 m (3,096 feet); only the strong will survive

Technical difficulty: Though much of the trail is on forestry access roads and fire roads, the sheer length makes it a tough challenge

Scenery: This ride covers diverse landscape. Views along the Canyon Trail include the Cheakamus Canyon with its sheer walls. Later, as you climb toward the high summits of Microwave Hill, the views open up to offer a panorama of the surrounding landscape. This ride has it all. Alpha, Nita, and Alta Lakes lie at the valley bottom while to the southwest Mount Brew dominates

Special comments: Nonracers will probably do this ride in sections to make it more manageable

The race was started by Doris Burma, a longtime resident of Whistler. She operated Summit Cycle, the first bike shop in the area back when Whistler was dead quiet during the summer months. It is due to her persistence and sweat that this race came into existence. Today, Whistler is looked at as an example of how mountain bikers can integrate with other trail users to create a challenging recreational wilderness for all. This 57.7-km (34.62-mile) point-to-point ride was designed to push racers to the limit. The length is extreme, as are the climbs en route. Though this is a spectacular ride, it should *not* be taken lightly. The vehicle shuttle alone makes it a challenge for most riders. A solid day can be created

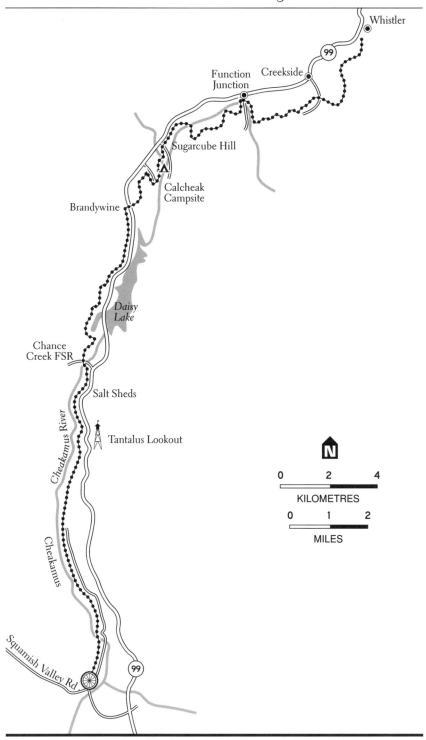

Whistler

99

Creekside

Function
Junction

Sugarcube Hill

Calcheak
Campsite

Brandywine

Daisy
Lake

Chance
Creek FSR

Salt Sheds

Cheakamus River

Tantalus Lookout

N

0	2	4

KILOMETRES

0	1	2

MILES

Cheakamus

Squamish Valley Rd

99

by riding the north section of the trail beginning at Brandywine Falls and finishing at the village. This removes the highway riding and focuses on the stretch with the most elevation gain. However you approach this ride, remember that you are following the tracks of champions.

General location: Between Squamish and Whistler.

Elevation change: From the trailhead at the Sunwolf Outdoor Centre at 46 m (150 feet), the trail climbs steadily, finally cresting on Microwave Hill at 990 m (3,247 feet) for a total elevation gain of 944 m (3,096 feet).

Season: April through October.

Services: All services are available in Whistler.

Hazards: This is an extremely long ride, designed to test the best racers. It should only be attempted by the strongest and fittest. Along the way, there are many hazards, including short hike-a-bike sections, loose rocks, roots, and sudden drops.

Rescue index: This route covers a lot of territory and passes numerous settlements, following Highway 99 periodically. It is generally not difficult to find help. The northern stretch, once you begin climbing Microwave Hill, takes you into remote territory, so you must be prepared for the fact that you may have to travel out before you can access help.

Land status: This epic trail runs through municipal and Crown land, provincial parks, and private land.

Maps: The NTS 1:50,000 topographic maps for this trail are 93 G/14 Cheakamus River, 92 J/3 Brandywine Falls, and 92 J/2 Whistler, but the best map for the northern section of this ride is the *Whistler Area Mountain Biking & Recreation Map* produced by TerraPro GPS Surveys Ltd. (Box 1016, Whistler, B.C. V0N 1B0 or bikemap@whistler.net). The map is available from most local bike shops in Whistler.

Finding the trail: From Squamish, take Highway 99 north, following signs for Brackendale. Head left off the highway, and follow this road until you see signs for the Sunwolf Outdoor Centre at Cheekeye. Park here and begin the ride by continuing up the paved Cheakamus Valley Road.

Sources of additional information:

Garibaldi/Sunshine Coast District
Alice Lake Park
P.O. Box 220
Brackendale, B.C. V0N 1H0
(604) 898-3678,
(604) 898-4171 fax
email: parkinfo@prkvctoria.elp.gov.bc.ca

Squamish Off-Road Cycling Association
Box 793
Garibaldi Highlands, B.C. V0N 1T0
(604) 898-3519

Notes on the trail: From the Sunwolf Outdoor Centre, follow the wide pavement of Cheakamus Valley Road as it follows the course of the Cheakamus River. Eventually, the pavement gives way to gravel and the road continues. When the gravel finally ends after approximately 11.5 km (6.9 miles), continue on Canyon Trail. This trail includes several hike-a-bike sections and some challenging riding. You'll finally return to Highway 99 at around the 15.3-km (9.2-mile) mark. Turn left, and continue along the highway for 5.5 km (3.3 miles) to Chance Creek Forest Service Road. Turn left onto the wide gravel and stay right at the first junction to ride around the shores of Lake Lucille. At the far end of the lake, turn right again and follow the forest service road as it makes its way northwest toward Shadow Lake. Just before the lake, turn left to circle the lake's western shoreline. As you leave the lake, a gravel road will branch to the left just before you meet Highway 99. Take this junction, and it will bring you back to the highway near the Pinecrest subdivision at kilometre 27.3 (mile 16.4).

Back on the highway, wind your way north again, this time turning to the right when you meet Brandywine Falls Provincial Park at kilometre 31.7 (mile 19). Cross the parking lot, and ride across the high-quality bridge over Brandywine Creek. Take a hard left after the bridge to begin Brandywine Trail.

The trail begins climbing right away up a wide double-track that follows the river upstream. At kilometre 34.6 (mile 20.76), you'll pass some private land to the left. Stay right at a junction at this point, and follow the wide double-track as it crosses the railroad tracks. Immediately beyond, the tracks make a hard left onto the single-track surface of Calcheak Trail. This brings you over a small bridge surrounded by the razor-sharp spines of devil's club. As the trail approaches the Cheakamus River, it becomes a little more technical and deteriorates into a rooty roller coaster. There is a high-quality suspension bridge over Callaghan Creek just upstream of its juncture with the Cheakamus River.

Beyond the bridge, roll your way through the South Side Campground and follow the gravel access road as it heads toward the highway. At kilometre 36.4 (mile 21.84) you'll pass the Callaghan Creek Campground to your left and join Highway 99 immediately beyond.

Turn right and follow Highway 99 north for a few hundred metres until you see a B.C. RAIL sign to the right. Take the double-track branching off of Highway 99, and you'll see a gate just beyond a large volcanic rock that exhibits textbook columnar jointing. The rock has cracked in such a way as to create perfect columns. Head through the gate and across the tracks. Beyond the tracks the road heads left and follows the tracks for a short distance. It quickly narrows into a wide single-track that slowly rolls away from the river to cross the Cheakamus River on a good bridge at kilometre 38.6 (mile 23.2). Stay on the main road as an overgrown road joins in from the left beyond the bridge. The trail climbs over the next 1.2 km (0.72 mile), crosses under the power lines, and eventually makes a hard left as it joins an overgrown road coming in from the right at kilometre 40 (mile 24). Stay left at this juncture, and be cautious on the descent as a drainage channel cuts across the road. As a road joins in from the left at kilometre 41.9 (mile 25.14), continue to stay left; soon you'll enter the municipal dump. You may get a whiff or two before you actually arrive, depending on the wind direction. Keep an eye open for bears—always a popular sight at a landfill—and enter the actual dump as you cross under the transmission wires.

Turn left at an access road at kilometre 43.1 (mile 25.9), and roll your way down the wide pavement to the Whistler Interpretive Forest trailhead at kilometre 44.4 (mile 26.6). To the left of the Whistler Interpretive Forest sign, Microwave Hill begins ascending. The climb is steady and unrelenting, with the exception of a few short flat bits, until you pass the CBC (Canadian public radio and television) tower at kilometre 47.8 (mile 28.7) and elevation 885 m (2,902 feet). The upside is that the views become increasingly spectacular as you climb. Ignore several overgrown spur trails.

The grind continues beyond the tower. Shortly beyond this summit, the trail meets another old route coming in from the right. Stay straight past this and several others; you pass an excellent viewpoint and begin climbing sharply again. At kilometre 49.7 (mile 29.82), turn left at a junction with a road that crosses Microwave Hill Trail. This will drop you down toward Bear Creek. Just after crossing a bridge over the creek at kilometre 50 (mile 30), take a single-track that heads down to the left. This narrow run has some very steep, tricky sections near the bottom. Turn right at a junction at kilometre 51.2 (mile 30.72), and begin climbing again up toward Love Canal. Pass through an open gate indicating DANGER, BLASTING AHEAD (which refers to winter avalanche control), and keep climbing. You'll rejoin the road you previously ditched for the single-track at kilometre 51.7 (mile 31). As you climb the wide double-track, you cross several bridges over tributaries of Whistler Creek. Beyond the crossings, you'll climb a short sharp stretch, after which a road will drop sharply to the left, while another will switchback up to the right. Take the low road left and enjoy some downhill for a change of pace.

As you pass under the Creekside Gondola at kilometre 53.4 (mile 32.04), the route you've been riding makes a sharp switchback to the left. *Do not* take this turn! Instead, ride straight ahead and the single-track of Northwest Passage will continue. This single-track rolls along a rough track and crosses a ramshackle bridge at kilometre 55.4 (mile 33.34). Beyond the bridge, look for the trail to make a hard right and begin climbing. The climb is short but so steep that many riders will find themselves pushing, particularly after the long ride they've already done. Continue climbing until kilometre 56.5 (mile 33.9); just as the trail levels off, you meet the Whistler Mountain Bike Park. Ride through the park and finish in Whistler Village at kilometre 57.7 (mile 34.62).

RIDE 54 · Cheakamus Lake Trail

AT A GLANCE

Length/configuration: 8.8-km (5.28-mile) total distance out-and-back from the Cheakamus Lake Trailhead, including 4.4 km (2.64 mile) to the shores of Cheakamus Lake. You can extend it to make a 23.8-km (14.28-mile) out-and-back by riding the length of the Eastside Main Road

Aerobic difficulty: Moderate

Technical difficulty: The narrow single-track from the Cheakamus Lake trailhead provides many technical challenges. Once you reach the lake it increases in difficulty

Scenery: Cheakamus Lake is spectacular and easily warrants time to explore and simply enjoy the magic of the place

Special comments: Some books describe a loop between the Cheakamus River and the Helm Creek Trail. This option is actually a horrific hike-a-bike and provides little virtue, not to mention imminent potential for injury

This pleasant trail brings you along the gravel of Eastside Main Road and finishes with a soft, carpeted ride toward one of the most picturesque spots in the area. As you bounce your way along the Eastside Main Road, take the time to read the interpretive signs of the Whistler Interpretive Forest. These signs and several of the short loop options are designed to teach visitors about the forest industry in British Columbia. They are extremely well done and offer options for extending this ride.

As you ride the Cheakamus Lake Trail, you enter a dark hemlock and western red cedar forest. Feel the magic of these giants of the west coast and take the time to admire their immensity. We need to respect their tenure. They were here, in some cases, long before Captain George Vancouver sailed around the island that now bears his name. When you arrive at the lake, you'll definitely want to take time to simply sit and enjoy. Although the trail deteriorates as you reach the lake, you can continue to bounce your way along a much more technical course for another 3 km (1.8 miles) or so before turning back. The lake takes its name from the native Squamish term meaning "salmon weir place," indicating the importance of this river to the early native salmon fishery. At the far end, Overlord Mountain dominates the left (north) shoreline, while Mount Davidson rules the right.

RIDE 54 · Cheakamus Lake Trail

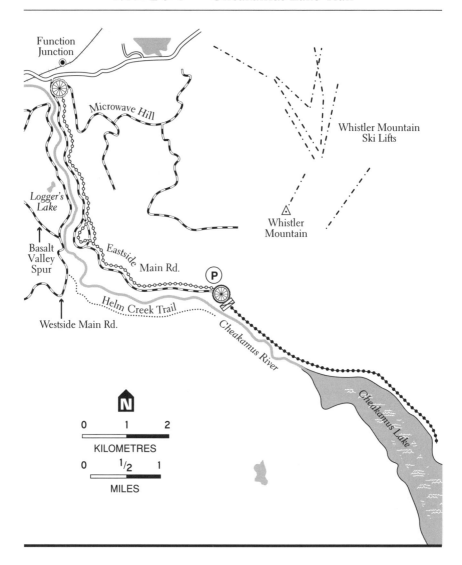

General location: South of Whistler.

Elevation change: The trail climbs gradually from the Whistler Interpretive Forest trailhead at approximately 600 m (1,968 feet) to the lake at approximately 860 m (2,821 feet).

Season: April through October.

Services: All services are available in Whistler.

Hazards: Like many areas, Garibaldi Provincial Park has had many conflicts between cyclists and other trail users. As a result, almost all of the park has been

Cheakamus Lake Trail
rolls through a stand of
ancient western redcedar.

closed to cyclists. The trail to Elfin Lakes, along with this one, represents the few
trails open to fat tires. Please yield to hikers—they have the right of way on this
trail. This will ensure that this wonderful ride will remain open for years to come.
For the park staff, this trail is a test site for integrating the two groups of users.

Rescue index: This is a very popular hiking trail, so there is always someone
around. As you reach the lake, a campground will usually have numerous tents
in residence as well.

Land status: A combination of private and Crown land, the trail enters
Garibaldi Provincial Park shortly after beginning the actual trail.

Maps: The NTS 1:50,000 topographic maps for this trail are 92 J/3 Brandywine
Falls and 92 J/2 Whistler, but the best map for the Whistler area is the *Whistler
Area Mountain Biking & Recreation Map* produced by TerraPro GPS Surveys
Ltd. (Box 1016, Whistler, B.C. V0N 1B0 or bikemap@whistler.net). The map is
available from most local bike shops in Whistler.

Finding the trail: If you do the entire ride as described here, drive north on
Highway 99, and watch for a sign for Garibaldi Park/Cheakamus Lake. It will be
directly across the Function Junction, Whistler's southern industrial centre. You

can park at the Whistler Interpretive Forest sign and ride along the access road if you want to add some length to this ride, or you can bypass the dusty access road and drive to the road's end at the Cheakamus Lake trailhead parking lot.

Sources of additional information:

> Squamish Off-Road Cycling Association
> Box 793
> Garibaldi Highlands, B.C. V0N 1T0
> (604) 898-3519

Notes on the trail: From the trailhead at the Whistler Interpretive Forest parking lot, ride the Eastside Main Road. The trailhead is approximately 7.5 km (4.6 miles) from the main parking lot. The road to this point is rolling, but it has a definite uphill trend. The trail now takes on a very different character. From wide, dusty access road to rolling single-track, this trail offers an instant change of state. The gradient is pleasant, with a downhill bias. It is a lovely roller coaster on a carpeted pathway. Pass the junction to the Cheakamus River 1.3 km (0.8 mile) from the trailhead. It drops down to a new bridge (replacing the cable car indicated on the maps of the area). Beyond the river, mountain bikes are not allowed.

A further 1.4 km (0.8 mile) will bring you across a steep sidecut above the point at which the river widens into Cheakamus Lake. Another minute or two of pedaling will bring you to the first campground. From here, the trail continues along the lake shore to another campground 3 km (1.8 miles) away. The views are exquisite along this awesome lake. When you're ready, head your bike back toward the trailhead and return at kilometre 8.8 (mile 5.28) and back to your vehicle at kilometre 23.8 (mile 14.28).

RIDE 55 · Riverside Trail

AT A GLANCE

Length/configuration: 4.6-km (2.76-mile) point-to-point, or make a 7.3-km (4.38-mile) loop using the gravel of Westside Main Road

Aerobic difficulty: Moderately rolling terrain

Technical difficulty: Quite easy along gently rolling landscape

Scenery: Pretty views focusing on the fast-flowing Cheakamus River

Special comments: This is a great trail for days when you simply want to explore

RIDE 55 · Riverside Trail

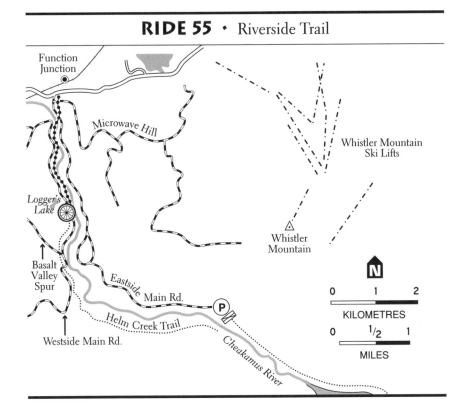

This 7.3-km (4.38-mile) loop combines a rolling single-track along the powerful Cheakamus River with a fast gravel roll to return to your car. It makes for a great half-day ride with numerous options for exploring and simply enjoying the sound of the river. Along the way, a self-guided interpretive trail offers an option to park your bike and take a short walk. Keep your eyes out for kayakers surfing the standing waves of the river.

As you roll along, the gradients are moderate but variable. A few of the hills include quick switchbacks that will challenge novice riders. Some of the climbs are also short and sharp. While the trail is easily rideable by advanced beginners, it requires some caution as you bounce your way up and down the riverbank.

General location: South of Whistler.

Elevation change: From the trailhead at approximately 700 m (2,297 feet) the trail rolls down to the Whistler Interpretive Forest trailhead at 600 m (1,968 feet).

Season: April through October.

Services: All services are available in Whistler.

Hazards: The trail makes some sharp switchbacks near the river and has some uneven angles and loose rocks. Generally, though, the gradients are good and the hazards minimal.

The author rolls past huge leaves of pungent skunk cabbage, a common plant in marshy, low-elevation locales.

Rescue index: Because the road parallels Westside Main Road, there are numerous options for making a quick exit to look for assistance. If you cannot find help, head out to Highway 99 and cross the street to Function Junction. You can get help from one of the local businesses here.

Land status: A combination of private and Crown land.

Maps: The NTS 1:50,000 topographic map for this trail is 92 J/3 Brandywine Falls, but the best map for the Whistler area is the *Whistler Area Mountain Biking & Recreation Map* produced by TerraPro GPS Surveys Ltd. (Box 1016, Whistler, B.C. V0N 1B0 or bikemap@whistler.net). The map is available from most local bike shops in Whistler.

Finding the trail: From Whistler, head south on Highway 99 to Function Junction. Turn left onto Westside Main Road and bounce your way down this road for 2.7 km (1.62 miles) until you see the Logger's Lake parking lot. This is the trailhead.

Sources of additional information:

Whistler Off-Road Cycling Association
Box 3500-31
Whistler, B.C. V0N 1B0
(604) 938-9893

Notes on the trail: From the Logger's Lake parking lot, cross Westside Main Road; the trail begins at right angles to the gravel road. The wide single-track begins with a short descent and then levels off near the river. After you ride for 1.2 km (0.72 mile), several sharp switchbacks bring you up above the river at kilometre 1.8 (mile 1.08); there is an option to rejoin the road. If you stay right at this junction, the trail will make a sharp right switchback and take you back toward the river. Take a right at the next junction, which will bring you back to water level before eventually joining back with the left junction. Another junction at kilometre 2.7 (mile 1.62) has a sign on a trail to the left for INTER-PRETIVE FOREST RECREATION TRAIL IMPROVEMENT 1983. Stay to the right at this junction. At most junctions, simply take the fork that will bring you closest to the river. This allows maximum enjoyment of the varying gradients and the calming influence of the roaring water. At kilometre 3.2 (mile 1.92), another right junction will bring you back to the water and along a series of boardwalks.

After joining the road again at kilometre 3.5 (mile 2.1), turn right onto the road and pass a cable swing that allows access to the river for water level studies. Immediately after crossing the Cheakamus River on the good-quality bridge of Westside Main Road, the trail makes an immediate right turn to leave the road.

Cross directly over the gravel of Eastside Main Road at kilometre 4 (mile 2.4) and continue along the Lower Riverside Trail on the opposite side. As you ride along this self-guided interpretive trail, the smell of the nearby dump gives you an olfactory clue that you are nearing the end of the ride. After crossing another high-quality bridge, you'll meet the trailhead at kilometre 4.6 (mile 2.76). Turn left onto the pavement and roll your way back to your car at kilometre 7.3 (mile 4.38).

RIDE 56 · Helm Creek Trail

AT A GLANCE

Length/configuration: 5.7-km (3.42-mile) point-to-point or 11.4-km (6.84-mile) out-and-back

Aerobic difficulty: Moderate to easy

Technical difficulty: With the exception of a few loose rock sections, this is a trail for riders of all levels

Scenery: Beautiful views along the Cheakamus River

Special comments: The focus on this ride is sweet, fast single-track

RIDE 56 · Helm Creek Trail

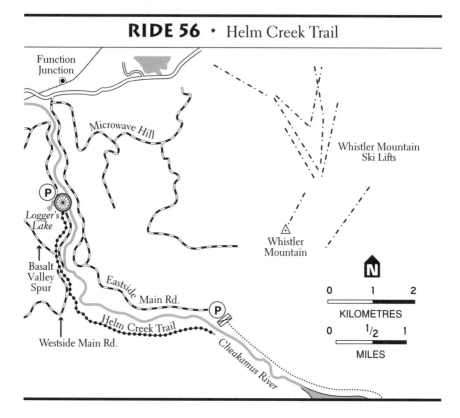

This 11.4-km (6.84-mile) out-and-back ride offers some of the sweetest single-track in Whistler. It's easy, fast, smooth, and a great break from the challenging riding that is de rigueur in the area. Beginning along Westside Main Road, the ride parallels the road through some winding single-track with high-quality bridges. The marshy water beneath the bridges is ideal for the growth of skunk cabbage, a wonder of west coast forests. With leaves up to 1.5 m (4.5 feet) in length, they are easily identifiable.

After a short stint on the gravel of Westside Main Road again, the trail leaves the gravel behind and rolls on wide single-track, where you can scream along in high gear and forget the slow grind up trails like Black Tusk and Microwave Hill. Just let the spirit move you and enjoy the ride. The trail finally ends as Helm Creek boils its way down toward its confluence with the Cheakamus River. Turn yourself around and enjoy the same ride back.

General location: South of Whistler.

Elevation change: The trail climbs approximately 100 m (328 feet).

Season: April through October.

Services: All services are available in Whistler.

Hazards: The gradient is smooth with a few short, sharp uphills; overall you need only be prepared for a few loose rocks and the occasional drainage channel.

Rescue index: Once you leave Westside Main Road behind, you will probably not meet anyone on the trail. Though the gradient is smooth and level, you'll still want to have a good repair kit along. I snapped a chain on this moderate ride and was very happy to have my chain breaker along to make repairs.

Land status: A combination of private and Crown land.

Maps: The NTS 1:50,000 topographic maps for this trail are 92 J/3 Brandywine Falls and 92 J/2 Whistler, but the best map for the Whistler area is the *Whistler Area Mountain Biking & Recreation Map* produced by TerraPro GPS Surveys Ltd. (Box 1016, Whistler, B.C. V0N 1B0 or bikemap@whistler.net). It is available from most local bike shops in Whistler.

Finding the trail: From Whistler, head south on Highway 99 to Function Junction. Turn left onto Westside Main Road and bounce your way down this road for 2.7 km (1.62 miles) until you see the Logger's Lake parking lot. This is the trailhead.

Sources of additional information:

Whistler Off-Road Cycling Association
Box 3500-31
Whistler, B.C. V0N 1B0
(604) 938-9893

Notes on the trail: From the Logger's Lake parking lot, the trail takes off at the south side of the junction of Westside Main Road and Logger's Lake Trail. The trail begins climbing gradually on a wide single-track and crosses a bridge at kilometre 0.3 (mile 0.18). Beyond the bridge the trail winds to a second bridge at kilometre 0.5 (mile 0.3). You cross the Basalt Valley Spur road at kilometre 0.9 (mile 0.54). The single-track rolls for another 0.5 km (0.3 mile) before joining with Westside Main Road. Stay on the gravel until kilometre 2.3 (mile 1.38), when Helm Creek Trail forks off to the left of Westside Main Road just as it begins its steep ascent toward the microwave towers on Black Tusk.

From the very beginning this is sweet single-track. It is worth riding this trail even though it doesn't really have a final destination. After 1.5 km (0.9 mile), the trail narrows from a slightly overgrown double-track to a smooth single-track. Two more kilometres (1.2 miles) bring you to the end of the trail at Helm Creek. At the time of this writing, there was a rough—and I mean *rough* (with imminent danger of severe personal injury, experienced firsthand by the author)— trail described in other books that continues toward the bridge over the Cheakamus River. I have not described it in this book because it is a moderately insane bushwhack/hike-a-bike. If you insist on potential pain, ask at local bike shops for directions.

RIDE 57 · Highline Trail

AT A GLANCE

Length/configuration: 2.9-km (1.7-mile) point-to-point, or a 5.6-km (3.36-mile) loop using Eastside Main Road

Aerobic difficulty: Challenging as it climbs 115 m (377 feet) in just 1.7 km (1.02 miles)

Technical difficulty: A wide, steep climb along a gravel access road for a microwave tower followed by a moderate single-track descent

Scenery: The views are spectacular as you reach several vantage points over the valley

Special comments: This short loop offers a steep, wide climb, followed by a picturesque single-track descent through the woods

SEA TO SKY HIGHWAY

This ride combines some of the climbing of Microwave Hill with a pleasant single-track descent back toward Eastside Main Road. By using the road, you can create a 5.6-km (3.36-mile) loop. As you grind your way up Microwave Hill, take the time to enjoy the views of the surrounding ranges. Metal Dome Mountain and Mount Brew dominate the western skyline, and below, the valley of the Cheakamus River is dissected by numerous forestry access roads and trails.

Leave Microwave Hill behind at kilometre 1.7 (mile 1.02) and begin the rolling descent of Highline Trail. This single-track takes you through a rainbow of wildflowers and ferns, with more views of the valley as you descend. Shortly before reaching Eastside Main Road, you'll pass some old remnants of the logging industry for which this valley is well known. Finally, rejoin Eastside Main Road, turn right, and enjoy a quick roll back to your vehicle.

General location: South of Whistler.

Elevation change: The trail climbs approximately 140 m (460 feet) to the junction with Highline Trail.

Season: April through October.

Services: All services are available in Whistler.

Hazards: As you begin to unload your car and load up your bike, you may think you've stepped on something a dog left behind. Fear not. Your shoes are clean; you're just getting a whiff of the Whistler Dump located just up the road. The climb up Microwave Hill includes some loose gravel that will allow your back tire to spin out and leave novices pushing. Once you begin the descent down the Highline Trail, watch for downed trees and roots. The trail is generally quite well kept, but it may have some rooted sections and loose gravel.

RIDE 57 · Highline Trail

Rescue index: While Microwave Hill is quite popular, you may not meet any cyclists along the Highline Trail portion. Be prepared for a wilderness journey. Assistance can usually be found along the Eastside Main Road or at one of the many businesses at Function Junction, across the highway from the trailhead.

Land status: A combination of private and Crown land.

Maps: The NTS 1:50,000 topographic map for this trail is 92 J/3 Brandywine Falls, but the best map for the Whistler area is the *Whistler Area Mountain*

The Highline Trail provides excellent views of the Cheakamus River Valley and distant Mount Brew.

Biking & Recreation Map produced by TerraPro GPS Surveys Ltd. (Box 1016, Whistler, B.C. V0N 1B0 or bikemap@whistler.net). The map is available from most local bike shops in Whistler.

Finding the trail: From Whistler, head south toward Function Junction. Turn left at a sign indicating Garibaldi Park/Cheakamus Lake, and left again right away into the WHISTLER INTERPRETIVE FOREST parking lot. The trail climbs to the left of this parking lot.

Sources of additional information:

Whistler Off-Road Cycling Association
Box 3500-31
Whistler, B.C. V0N 1B0
(604) 938-9893

Notes on the trail: The best way to enjoy this ride is to grind your way up Microwave Trail, and then descend this single-track roller coaster. The grinding begins immediately. In dry weather, the road can be dusty and loose, but your perseverance will be rewarded. Alder, willow, thimbleberry, and fireweed line your climb as you quickly run out of steam with the steepness of the incline. Around the 1-km (0.6-mile) mark, you get several short breaks from the climbing. They are short, though, so take advantage of this opportunity to rest your legs. As you pass the 1.5-km (0.9-mile) mark, a spur trail will beckon you to the right. Take this short trail for 100 m (109.4 yards) or so to a good viewpoint over the surrounding valley. As you look west, Metal Dome Mountain is to the right and Mount Brew is to the left. To the south, the defiant summit of Black Tusk is visible, along with its neighbouring microwave towers.

Return to the main trail; almost immediately you'll meet the junction with the Highline Trail as it forks to the right. This rolling downhill grade is rimmed with enormous ferns, thick alder growth, amabalis fir, and western redcedar. A quick view offers a glimpse of the surrounding landscape just before another sign indicates Valleyview Lookout, a pullout farther along Eastside Main Road.

The trail rejoins Eastside Main Road at kilometre 2.9 (mile 1.7). From here, a quick downhill spin will return you to the trailhead at approximately kilometre 5.6 (mile 3.36).

RIDE 58 · Black Tusk via Westside Main

AT A GLANCE

Length/configuration: 34.2-km (20.52-mile) total distance out-and-back

Aerobic difficulty: Extreme, including an unrelenting climb of 1,210 m (3,969 feet)

Technical difficulty: The trail includes loose rock along a wide access road

Scenery: The higher you climb, the more the valley opens up at your feet. The area around you when you reach the microwave station represents the main scenic focus of this ride. The trail ends here, but you are only a short scramble from the volcanic tooth of Black Tusk. Take the time to explore on foot and to make the extra effort to climb and touch the tusk

Special comments: Save this for excellent weather, as storms can blow over the summit without warning

Very few mountain bike rides allow you to enter the alpine, let alone climb 1,210 m (3,969 feet) in just over 17 km (10.2 miles). This 34.2-km (20.52-mile) out-and-back takes you high above the valley to a microwave tower near the jagged tooth of Black Tusk. This volcanic tower dominates the skyline, and travelers from all over the world photograph its defiant silhouette. Few of these tourists ever have the opportunity to experience its magic firsthand. Be aware, though, that this ride doesn't take you all the way to the tusk. You'll need to park your bike at the microwave station and scramble up another 185 m (607 feet) before you can actually claim bragging rights to the tusk.

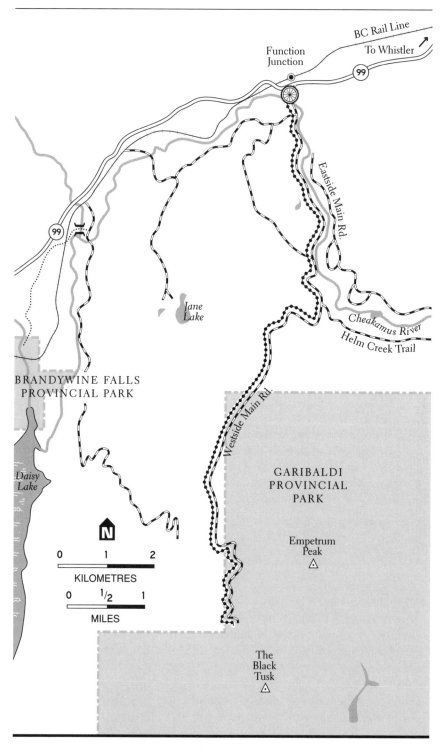

The author grinds the last hundred metres to the microwave station near the volcanic tooth of Black Tusk.

The ride follows wide roads, with the occasional four-by-four and dirt bike, but generally you'll see little sign of civilization until you reach the actual microwave station. As you break out of the trees, you'll feel the wind blasting you. Be prepared for rapid weather changes and strong winds. This is one of those rides that leaves you with a feeling of pride and accomplishment, not to mention sore legs and aching brake fingers.

General location: Whistler.

Elevation change: Rising from the trailhead at 650 m (2,132 feet), you climb steadily, finally reaching the microwave station at 1,860 m (6,100 feet) after climbing 1,210 m (3,969 feet).

Season: May or June through September.

Services: All services are available in Whistler.

Hazards: The trail is wide, but there is plenty of loose gravel. Keep your eyes and ears open for vehicles and dirt bikes, which occasionally share this trail. On the way down, be sure to rest at regular intervals, as you'll definitely feel the strain from incessantly squeezing your brakes. Finally, be prepared for changeable weather. This ride takes you far from civilization and high above the valley. Storms can blow in with little notice, and you need to have warm clothes and rain gear. If the weather takes a turn for the worse, head down immediately.

Rescue index: Remote. You will probably be completely on your own on this ride. Though Westside Main Road is a popular access point in the valley, very few people continue up toward the tusk. You will need to make your own way down in order to get help.

Land status: A combination of private and Crown land.

Maps: The NTS 1:50,000 topographic maps for this trail are 92 J/3 Brandywine Falls and 92 G/14 Cheakamus River, but the best map for the Whistler area is the *Whistler Area Mountain Biking & Recreation Map* produced by TerraPro GPS Surveys Ltd. (Box 1016, Whistler, B.C. V0N 1B0 or bikemap@whistler.net). The map is available from most local bike shops in Whistler.

Finding the trail: From Whistler, head south toward Function Junction. Turn left at a sign for Garibaldi Park/Cheakamus Lake, and left again immediately into the WHISTLER INTERPRETIVE FOREST parking lot. The parking lot is the trailhead.

Sources of additional information:

Whistler Off-Road Cycling Association
Box 3500-31
Whistler, B.C. V0N 1B0
(604) 938-9893

Notes on the trail: From the trailhead, ride your bike up the pavement, forking to the right when Eastside Main Road branches to the left. Shortly beyond this point, the pavement crosses the Cheakamus River on a good bridge. Immediately after, the Westside Main Road forks to the left onto a wide gravel road.

After 4.4 km (2.6 miles), the road runs right beside the river. The raging torrent makes beautiful company, except for the twisted mass of an old Toyota pickup lying in the ditch. Another kilometre (0.6 mile) brings Helm Creek Trail in from the left, and the climbing begins in earnest.

Shortly after you begin this steep climb, a Garibaldi Provincial Park sign indicates that snowmobiles are not allowed in the park. At kilometre 6.7 (mile 4), you get a short break from the climbing when the trail levels out and even drops a little. After a bit more climbing, you get your first view of your objective—the distant towers—still more than 600 m (2,000 feet) above you. Soon after, you ride along the river for a short distance, and the road gets quite bumpy for a bit as the gravel becomes extremely coarse. Loose rocks make it even more choppy.

A cattail marsh on your left at kilometre 9.7 (mile 5.9) signals a steep climb again, followed by a short break in the grind. Each one of these short breaks is a great opportunity to stretch and rest your legs. You won't get many chances.

At kilometre 10.4 (mile 6.2), the steep climbing begins again and doesn't relent. Several switchbacks help reduce the gradient. You still have 679 m (2,226 feet) left to climb—ouch! A final break occurs as you finally crest this set of switchbacks. For a short distance, it follows the contour of the mountain before making its final bid for the summit. Are you warmed up yet? At kilometre 11.4 (mile 6.8), the climbing resumes. A wonderful view follows as the trail traverses a steep rock slide. You get great views of Metal Dome to the north and Mount Brew to the southeast. The trail descends a bit, followed by more climbing.

Simply continue climbing, taking advantage of the rare flat stretches to loosen up your quads and tendons.

The remains of a gate are reached at kilometre 14.8 (mile 8.9). At the base of the climb, a sign stated that the road was closed to vehicles 2 km from the summit. This may have been true at one time, but this area has no gate now. There is nothing with which to close the road. Perhaps the skeleton of an old truck just beneath the gate site has something to do with it. The gate frame has a brand-new lock, but no actual gate. Another totaled vehicle appears on the left as you grunt your way to the summit. This automotive skeleton also heralds the approach of the tree line. The trees begin to give way to carpets of lupine, fireweed, cotton grass, and many others. This is also the point where the wind will smack you. When I was approaching the summit, I felt like I had stepped from the inside of a building into a hurricane.

As you approach the summit, it may feel extremely hot, but there might still be snow on the ground. Often, the snow takes on a pink colour. This is not an optical illusion, but the result of an algae that lives on the surface of summer snow. The common name for it is *watermelon snow*. You finally reach the microwave station at kilometre 17.1 (mile 10.3) and elevation 1,860 m (6,100 feet), after a climb of 1,210 m (3,969 feet).

Not completely pooped yet? Why not park your bike and scramble to the black tusk? This is an alpine environment that begs exploration. Use prudence and have fun. When you're finished, point your tires downhill and hope your brakes (or rather, your fingers) don't wear out before the trailhead. Return to your vehicle at kilometre 34.2 (mile 20.52).

RIDE 59 · Ancient Cedars

AT A GLANCE

Length/configuration: 15.3-km (9.2-mile) combination (out-and-back with a loop at the farthest point)

Aerobic difficulty: Moderate. The ride follows a wide fire road with a short, sharp push to access the Ancient Cedars loop

Technical difficulty: The fire road is easy riding, but the loop at the far end includes a short technical push followed by a loose rock descent

Scenery: Riding through a timeless stand of cedars will humble even the most jaded cyclist

Special comments: Best done in dry weather

This combination ride follows a wide fire road for 5.5 km (3.3 miles) and then takes you around a short loop beneath the dark canopy of a western red-cedar forest, finally returning you to your vehicle at kilometre 15.3 (mile 9.2). You'll begin this loop with a technical uphill push; as the landscape becomes marshy, look for the palm-sized leaves of the skunk cabbage in wet areas. Their enormous fronds can be 1.4 m (4.5 feet) in size. A club-like seed case often stands beneath the leaves. It is one impressive plant, soon to be followed by several others. After crossing a bridge, you enter the cedars. You cannot help but feel reverence for their age and majesty. The cedars are more than a metre (3.28 feet) in diametre and rule the skyline, blocking out the sunlight. Beneath their protective shade, the maple-like fronds of the devil's club create an impenetrable undergrowth. The sharp thorns of the devil's club created such a barrier to exploration that entire stretches of the Canadian Pacific Railway were re-routed to avoid some of the worst patches. Beneath the devil's club, the tiny blooms of the foam flower with its lone maple-like leaf and spike of tiny five-petaled blossoms makes a delicate addition to the immense stature of the trees here. Remember, though, this is true rain forest, with rain forest–sized mosquitoes. You may find that you don't linger as long as you might like as these aerial para-sites bombard your bare legs.

General location: North of Whistler near D'Arcy.

Elevation change: From the junction with Highway 99 at 640 m (2,100 feet), the gravel Cougar Mountain Forest Service Road climbs gradually to the beginning of Ancient Cedars Trail at 915 m (3,000 feet). After a stiff climb, the trail reaches a maximum elevation of 1,128 m (3,700 feet) within the stand of red-cedar.

Season: April through October.

Services: All services are available in Whistler.

Hazards: As this is an active logging road, look for logging trucks and other vehicles sharing this route. Some are less courteous than others. As you begin the Ancient Cedars loop at the far end of this combination ride, you will find yourself pushing up a steep, rocky trail. As you complete the loop, you will be descending this same incline. Its loose character and large boulders can easily eject you if you're not cautious. Don't forget your insect repellent.

Rescue index: While you may see other vehicles on the forest service road, you may not encounter anyone on the Ancient Cedars loop. Be prepared to make your way out to Highway 99 in an emergency. This is a popular area, but with the immensity of recreational potential in the Whistler area, even popular locations can be deserted.

Land status: A combination of private and Crown land.

Maps: The NTS 1:50,000 topographic map for this trail is 92 J/2 Whistler, but the best map for the Whistler area is the *Whistler Area Mountain Biking & Recreation Map* produced by TerraPro GPS Surveys Ltd. (Box 1016, Whistler,

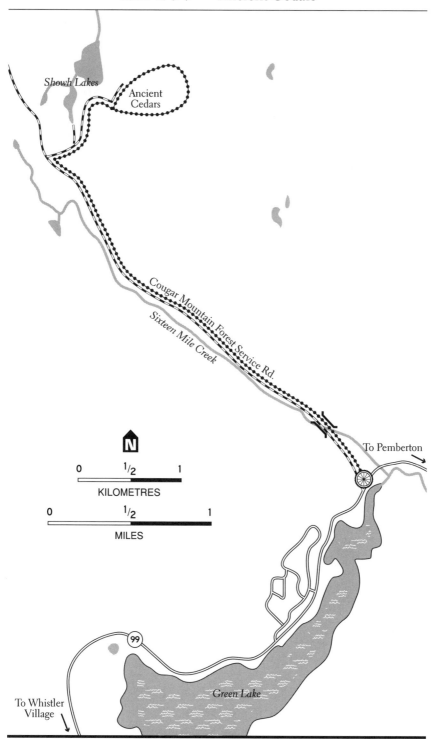

Showh Lakes

Ancient
Cedars

Cougar Mountain Forest Service Rd.

Sixteen Mile Creek

N

To Pemberton

0   1/2   1
KILOMETRES

0   1/2   1
MILES

99

To Whistler
Village

Green Lake

The highlight of Ancient Cedars Trail is the dense stand of redcedar that seems to block out the sun.

B.C. V0N 1B0 or bikemap@whistler.net). The map is available from most local bike shops in Whistler.

Finding the trail: While heading north on Highway 99, go beyond the main Whistler entrances. When you pass the intersection for Emerald Estates, continue 1.4 km (0.8 mile) and turn left onto an unsigned gravel road. Once you make the turn there will be a sign indicating Cougar Mountain and the Ancient Cedars. Park near the start of this road and begin riding.

Sources of additional information:

Whistler Off-Road Cycling Association
Box 3500-31
Whistler, B.C. V0N 1B0
(604) 938-9893

Notes on the trail: Park near the highway, and ride up this rough forestry access road. Stay right at the first junction, at kilometre 0.4 (mile 0.25). As you climb the road, you'll cross a steep rock slide before crossing the river on a good-quality bridge. The next major junction occurs at kilometre 4.3 (mile 2.6), where you will fork to the right, and the road will get a little rougher (the junction is signed). Another kilometre (0.6 mile) brings you to the trailhead. It is signed to the right of the road.

Almost immediately this trail shows its rough side. It begins with a rough, steep, rocky climb. An overgrown double-track joins the road at kilometre 6 (mile 3.6). Stay to the right. Just beyond this point, the climbing becomes difficult. Most riders will push through this collection of loose rocks. Riders descending this slope generally ride with brakes locked, and this has added to the rocky nature of this ascent. Don't be shy—push if you need to. It is worth continuing. At the top of the hill, the trail maintains its technical nature for a short distance before becoming much smoother. Crossing a good bridge at kilometre 7 (mile 4.3), you soon enter the ancient cedar forest. The trail travels through a magical stand of cedars, crosses two more bridges, and regains its technical nature before rejoining the main trail just above the first bridge. You now return on the original trail, descending down a technical but largely rideable downhill to return to the trailhead at kilometre 10 (mile 6). A quick spin down the road will bring you to your vehicle at the 15.3-km (9.2-mile) mark.

RIDE 60 · Birkenhead Loop

AT A GLANCE

Length/configuration: 52-km (31.2-mile) loop using a combination of public highway, forest service road, and single-track

Aerobic difficulty: The sheer length of the ride will challenge riders unless they have strong legs and lungs

Technical difficulty: Most of the ride is along public roadways, with the single-track along the shores of Birkenhead Lake offering a moderate challenge. Beginners will find some of the exposure above the lake disconcerting, but the trail is entirely rideable

Scenery: This is a very scenic loop, offering great views toward Sun God Mountain as you climb the forest service road, and later great panoramas of Birkenhead Lake

Special comments: Though it is long, this is an exceedingly pleasant ride with a constantly changing panorama

This loop is beautiful! As you wheel your way westward on the highway, many of the local peaks retain their snow throughout the summer months. The cabins along the way almost emanate a pioneer spirit. One in particular made

RIDE 60 · Birkenhead Loop

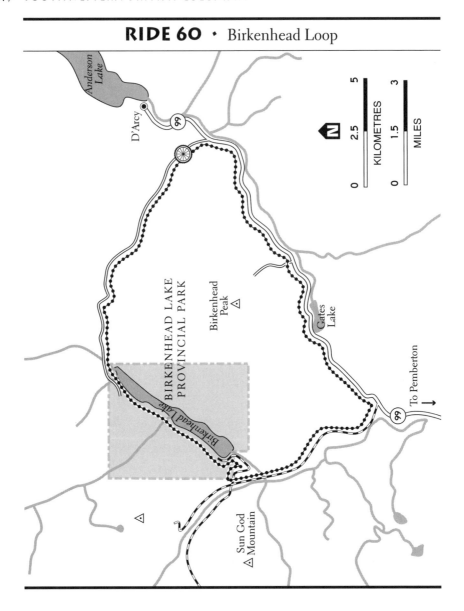

me envision a pioneer family struggling against an unforgiving and barren valley. Things have certainly changed, although the Whistler frenzy has yet to discover this area.

As families of riders find themselves pushing up the fire road, remember— the family that pushes together, pulls together. It's during outings like this that we build the strength to make it through the hard times in life. Grinding your way up the fire road, it's often easy to forget to look up. In this case, you pass wonderful views of the distant Place Glacier saddled between Mount Gardiner and

Birkenhead Loop culminates with the opportunity for a dip in the chilly waters of
Birkenhead Lake.

Gate's Peak. Before long, Sun God Mountain (2,315 m/7,593 feet), replaces this
glacial panorama.

As you reach the lake, don't pass up the opportunity for a dip in the glacial
waters of Birkenhead Lake. It's beautiful, welcoming, and reasonably warm. As
you stand in the shallows, trying to build up the courage to dive in, you may feel
a strange sensation on your toes. A plentiful supply of minnows is probably taking the opportunity to nibble at your toes. This is one of the unique characteris-
tics of this lake and doesn't hurt at all.

General location: North of Pemberton on the D'Arcy Road.

Elevation change: From the trailhead, climb along D'Arcy Road toward Pemberton Pass at 604 m (1,980 feet) along the shores of Gates Lake. Over the pass,
you drop to the junction with the Birkenhead River Tenas Creek Branch Forest
Service Road at 451 m (1,480 feet). This wide gravel road reaches a maximum elevation of 604 m (1,980 feet) before eventually joining the shores of
Birkenhead Lake. As you climb above the placid waters of the lake, you'll crest
at 756 m (2,480 feet) before dropping down to the day-use area. Once you leave
the beach, you'll climb again to 762 m (2,500 feet) before the final downhill
scream back to your vehicle.

Season: April through October.

Services: All services are available in Whistler.

Hazards: The D'Arcy Highway doesn't have a paved shoulder, so you must ride
in the traffic lane. This is not a big problem due to the low level of traffic on this

road. I did the trail on a busy August weekend and was passed by no more than six vehicles as I wheeled my way west. Once you leave the road behind and begin the trail above Birkenhead Lake, there are numerous stretches of loose gravel and a few narrow sidecuts to be negotiated.

Rescue index: Most of this route follows highway, forest service roads, or park access routes. The single-track stretch above Birkenhead Lake is one section that may be quiet; I didn't meet any other riders as I rolled my way through it. Be ready to continue toward the park in the case of an emergency. Along the busy beach and campground you will be able to access assistance. If not, pay phones are also present.

Land status: The trail runs through Birkenhead Lake Provincial Park, along with a mixed bag of private and Crown land.

Maps: The NTS 1:50,000 topographic maps for this trail include 92 J/7 Pemberton-50 and 92 J/10 Birkenhead Lake or the NTS 1:250,000 topographic map 92 J Pemberton.

Finding the trail: From Pemberton, continue east on Highway 99 for 6.5 km (4 miles) to Mount Currie. As you drive past the craft shops, the road forks with Highway 99 heading to the right. Take the D'Arcy branch to the left. After driving 17 km (10.2 miles), a sign will indicate Birkenhead Lake in 16 km (10 miles) and a gravel road will take off to the left. Take careful note of this junction, because you will be backtracking on your bike to this point. Keep driving an additional 17 km (10.2 miles) to the proper junction for Birkenhead Lake Provincial Park. Turn left here, and look for a convenient place to park your vehicle. I used a little field 0.4 km (0.25 mile) along this road on the right-hand side. Mount your saddle, drop down to the main road, turn right, and you're on your way.

Sources of additional information: Contact Birkenhead Lake Provincial Park through the Garibaldi District at:

Garibaldi/Sunshine Coast District
Alice Lake Park
P.O. Box 220
Brackendale, B.C. V0N 1H0
(604) 898-3678,
(604) 898-4171 fax
email: parkinfo@prkvctoria.elp.gov.bc.ca

Notes on the trail: From your car, descend to D'Arcy Road, turn right, and wheel your way back toward the gravel road you passed on your way out. The easy riding ends for a time as you climb between kilometres 5.5 and 10 (miles 4.9 and 6). You reach the summit of this stretch as you pass the shoreline of picturesque Gates Lake. The turnoff is at kilometre 18 (mile 10.8). You will see the gravel road you passed on your way to the trailhead. As landmarks, a large power line crosses the road immediately after the turnoff. Crank your handlebar to the right, and leave the pavement behind. Ignore the signs indicating no access to the lakes, as you will be traveling on single-track not available to cars. Almost immediately, you'll cross the railroad tracks. This is followed by a fork branching to the left. Take this turn, pass under the hydro wires, and begin the only major ascent of the trip. It's a grunt until you summit at kilometre 21 (mile 12.6) after climbing 210 m (690 feet). Soon the views toward Sun God Mountain (2,315 m/7,593 feet) grab your attention. Stay right at the junction with the Birkenhead River Tenas Creek Branch Forest Service Road. Cross the Birkenhead River on a high-quality bridge at kilometre 26.4 (mile 15.8). After this point, turn right at a junction at kilometre 26.8 (mile 16.1). When the trail seems to dead end at a gate for Birkenhead Lake Estates, follow the double-track trail that heads to the left of the closed gate. Before long, a second closed gate to your right denotes private property, and the trail seems to end at a ditch and rock barrier. Look carefully for the trail continuing beyond the barrier. Take this trail and leave the estate property behind.

As you roll your way through the lodgepole pine forest, you'll notice a poor example of selective logging; it seems certain trees have been cut, others left standing, and still others simply bulldozed over. The double-track makes a hard left at kilometre 28.3 (mile 17); however, a single-track takes off across and just left of the junction. A wooden post indicates that this trail is part of the Sea to Sky Trail project. Take this single-track and leave the double-track behind. After riding the single-track for 0.5 km (0.3 mile) the trail takes a hard left where a log seems to block the main route. A junction to the right shortly after this point takes you to a small campsite on the shore of the lake. It is worth the short detour. The main trail continues to the left at this junction. Your best view of the lake is at kilometre 30.4 (mile 18.25), where a steep rockslide to the left opens up the view as the trail crosses this steep sidecut.

Beyond this point, watch for a sudden, technical, switchbacking descent, followed by a short, steep climb back to the main trail. This is the most technical section of the trail, and its previously pleasant character will soon resume. From this point, the path climbs gradually but steadily until kilometre 31.5 (mile 18.9). After this point, you are rewarded with 2 km (1.2 miles) of downhill spinning. A few sections get quite steep and rocky, but all are easily rideable for beginners. At this point, a bridge over Sockeye Creek is so narrow that you'll need to raise your front wheel and push your bike over on its back wheel. The trail continues to descend, crossing several more rustic bridges, and the forest is replaced with western red cedar and a dense understory of devil's club.

Stay left at a junction at kilometre 34.2 (mile 20.5). The faint single-track to the right is a hiking-only trail to another campsite on the shoreline. You may have noticed that as soon as you stop, hundreds of small flies seem to come at you from all directions. If you were to look behind you as you ride, you'd probably see a black cloud of winded flies desperately trying to keep up with you. As you approach the 35-km (21-mile) mark, a short technical stretch will have beginners walking their bikes. Suddenly, at kilometre 36.3 (mile 21.8), you reach the lake access road. A short spin to the right will put you on the beach and offer you the opportunity to rinse off some of that trail dust and sweat.

From this point, the road is a hard, smooth, oil surface. Stay on this route for the rest of your ride. It climbs gently through picturesque ranching country until you take your last pedal at kilometre 45 (mile 27). From this point, it's a downhill rip to your vehicle. You won't need to expend any more energy than that required to slow your vehicle down on some of the faster stretches. Some gravel, just before the bridge at kilometre 50.8 (mile 30.5), warrants a temporary speed reduction. Beyond this point, you'll reach warp speed yet again, but this time on pavement. Your vehicle should appear at the 52-km (31.2-mile) mark.

RIDE 61 · Blowdown Creek

AT A GLANCE

Length/configuration: 31-km (18.6-mile) out-and-back

Aerobic difficulty: The total elevation gain for this ride is 1,080 m (3,542 feet) to a maximum of 2,180 m (7,150 feet). Only the very strongest riders will make it

Technical difficulty: Though the road follows former logging roads, it has loose and rocky sections

Scenery: As you gain in elevation, the rain forest begins to give way to open panoramas of the summits of the Lillooet Range, which surround you on every side. The view from the summit of Gott Pass is incredible. As you approach the pass, the Stein Valley drops to the west, descending a sinuous ridge that forms the north boundary of this picturesque valley

Special comments: This wilderness ride allows you to leave the world behind and takes you through a magical mountain landscape

This ride has it all! Options for all levels of ability and endurance, some of the most dramatic mountain scenery along the west coast, and the ability to personally tailor your trip make this one of my personal favourites. Despite my belief that no one else would travel this far, I found the valley to be surprisingly popular—at least to the pass. Make sure you get an early start on the day. This is a long trip any way you slice it. Don't let yourself run out of daylight!

The trail spends much of its time traversing large avalanche slopes. This provides prime habitat for everything from marmots to grizzly bears. Stay vigilant, but don't be so paranoid that you miss the majesty surrounding you. If the bears know you're in the area, you probably won't even encounter one if you make enough noise. A rapid exit is always their preferred course of action.

RIDE 61 · Blowdown Creek

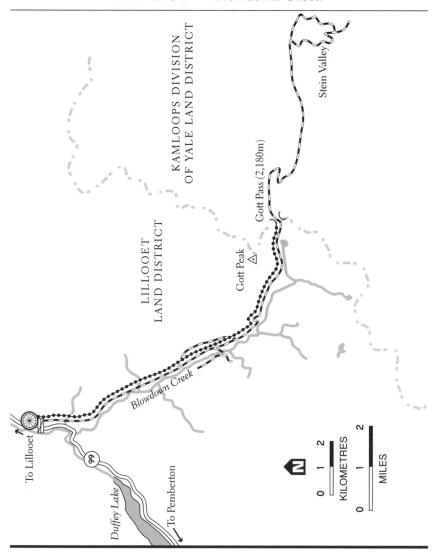

KAMLOOPS DIVISION
OF YALE LAND DISTRICT

Stein Valley

LILLOOET
LAND DISTRICT

Gott Pass (2,180m)

Gott Peak

Blowdown Creek

To Lillooet

99

Duffey Lake

To Pemberton

KILOMETRES

MILES

The main plants along the avalanche slopes are cow parsnip, alder, willow, and the beautiful purple of the edible thistle. As you climb, red paintbrush, fireweed, lupine, and yarrow become dominant. As you approach the pass, you begin to see alpine species like western anemone, valerian, phacelia, hellebore, and even white rein-orchids. Along with the fabulous wildflowers, local marmots seem to be as surprised with your arrival in their turf as you are by their sudden appearance. Their whistling call will make you aware of their presence, although you may suspect someone is trying to get your attention (their call sounds as if someone were whistling to you, and gave the town of Whistler its name). Occasionally, one will

The author cresting the summit of Gott Pass on Blowdown Creek Trail.

pop out on a rock right in front of you. Slow movement may allow you to approach within a very short distance as you try to figure each other out.

General location: North end of Duffey Lake on Highway 99 between Pemberton and Lillooet.

Elevation change: From the trailhead at 1,100 m (3,600 feet), the ride climbs constantly until you finally crest the pass at 2,180 m (7,150 feet). The total elevation gain is 1,080 m (3,542 feet).

Season: May or June through September.

Services: All services are available in Whistler.

Hazards: This is a very remote trail that passes through some excellent grizzly habitat, so vigilance is important. While the ride is mostly on good quality gravel, you will want to be cautious of loose rocks on a few sections. Remember to have a fully equipped repair and first-aid kit, along with wet weather gear. If a storm begins building, take the hint and turn around. The last place you want to be in a thunderstorm is on an isolated mountain pass.

Rescue index: You must respect the wilderness character of this ride and be fully prepared to rescue yourself should an emergency arise. Though it seems to be a popular destination for sport utility vehicles, there is still a very strong possibility that you will not encounter anyone else on this route. You may have to make your way all the way out to Highway 99, and even then it may take a few minutes before any vehicles stumble on you. Keep in mind as well that there will be no cellular signal in this remote area.

Land status: Crown land.

Maps: The NTS 1:50,000 topographic map for this route is 92 J/8 Duffey Lake.

Finding the trail: Follow Highway 99 to the resort community of Pemberton. Continue on Highway 99 to the tiny hamlet of Mount Currie. Turn right to stay on Highway 99, following the signs to Lillooet. Pass through the Lil'Wat Nation Reserve, and follow the highway as it leaves Lillooet Lake and begins the winding climb toward Duffy Lake. You will not make very good time on this exceedingly steep highway, an average of 60 kmh (36 mph) was about all I could muster. As you skirt the shores of this picturesque lake, watch for the Duffy Lake East recreation area at the far end. Just 3 km (1.8 miles) beyond this point, after you cross a good-quality bridge, you will pass a highway closure gate. These gates are used when the road conditions are too hazardous for travel. Immediately beyond this, making a hairpin right turn, is the road up Blowdown Creek. Gearheads may want to begin the ride here, while regular mortals will want to bounce their way 9.4 km (5.64 miles) up the road (and save themselves 405 m/1,328 feet of climbing).

Sources of additional information: I was unable to find any additional sources of information.

Notes on the trail: The road up Blowdown Creek is an excellent access route. It is easily passable by a two-wheel-drive vehicle, as long as caution is used at all times. The climbing is instantaneous. Views quickly open toward the glacier-studded peaks of the Joffre Group to the west and the Lillooet Range to your left and right, and the Cayoosh Range to the north (behind you). At the 3-km (1.8-mile) mark, the road begins to parallel Blowdown Creek, and the peaks further up the valley begin to invite you—or was that challenge you?—to venture further. The climbing takes on a more gradual character for the next little bit. Ignore any spur trails as you bounce your way south, and simply stay on the main route.

At kilometre 10 (mile 6), turn left on a sharp switchback and ignore the faint single-track continuing straight. For a short time it will feel like you are heading in the wrong direction, but it will crank right soon enough and all will feel fine again. At the 11-km (6.6-mile) mark, the trail begins to switchback sharply. The climbing soon tempers again until the 13-km (7.8-mile) mark, where the gradient gradually increases, but the landscape compensates with increasingly spectacular views. Soon, the road climbs to another sharp left switchback with a faint track continuing. As the switchback retaliates in the opposite direction, you begin to crest the tree line and the alpine fir begins to give way to sturdy wildflowers and inquisitive marmots.

Gott Lake appears to the right at kilometre 14.8 (mile 8.9) and seems to beckon you downward. You can return for a visit later. Soon, the trail will make its final sharp left and ascent to the summit. The pass is reached soon after at kilometre 15.5 (mile 9.3). The view toward the Stein Valley will pull you forward. Don't heed its call unless you have sufficient time and supplies. This is an extremely remote valley, and the drop from the summit is instantaneous. You

Duffey Lake, just before the trailhead of Blowdown Creek Trail.

will need to return up to the pass to exit the trail. The additional out-and-back distance for the Stein Valley loop is approximately 22.5 km (13.5 miles).

For those prepared to continue (a storm turned the author back at the pass), the trail drops off the pass and quickly branches, with a single-track taking off to the right and a double-track to the left. The single-track makes a more direct descent, but the trails soon rejoin. As you drop into the valley, make sure you have a topographic map to show you the route; you will encounter an old copper mine. Numerous artifacts may be visible, but please leave them where you discover them. The recreation area is trying desperately to preserve its cultural artifacts. The excellent-quality road visible from the pass will eventually deteriorate; drop down into the valley and then begin the climb back up toward the pass. Owners of sport utility vehicles and four-by-fours may want to make this a two-day excursion. Ride your bike up the pass one day, and then drive the pass the next, using the time (and energy) saved to descend the Stein Valley on your bike the second day. Just for your information, from the pass at 2,180 m (7,150 feet), the trail drops all the way to 1,433 m (4,700 feet), climbs again to 1,830 m (6,000 feet), drops back down to 1,463 m (4,800 feet), and then returns to the pass. You can do the math if you want, but it all adds up to an epic adventure. Few riders will be able to do this portion in addition to the original trek to the pass.

When you drop down off the pass, the trail is steep, constant, and rideable all the way. A few rough stretches will have you carefully choosing your route. Make sure you stop occasionally to give your brake fingers a rest—it's the only way they will get a break.

VANCOUVER ISLAND

Vancouver Island, the largest island on the Pacific coast of North America, stretches for 450 kilometres (270 miles) from its southern tip at Victoria, British Columbia, all the way beyond Port Hardy to its northern limit at Cape Sutil. It's bordered on the west by the Pacific Ocean, on the south by the Juan de Fuca Strait, on the north by the Queen Charlotte Strait, and on the east by the Strait of Georgia. Vancouver Island is an incredibly diverse place. Its cultural centre, Victoria, claims to be more British than the British themselves. Residential roadsides are lined with immaculate gardens. Drive to the Inner Harbour and wonder at the immense Empress Hotel, part of the great Canadian Pacific Railway line. Across from the Empress, the Parliament buildings were built between 1893 and 1897; at night, 3,300 light bulbs illuminate the exterior. Victoria is a land of culture and quiet class as well as the capital of British Columbia.

Victoria has another side as well. It has a strong population of young people looking for a way to burn off energy. Mountain biking has become a perfect way to do just that, and over the past few years the riding has continually improved. Associations like the South Island Mountain Bike Society have made great strides in ensuring access to trails for mountain bikers. They have also taken over some of the networks, like the Hartland Dump, and created a mountain biking paradise. Victoria is a land of action on the mountain bike scene. It has some great beginner rides, like the famous Galloping Goose Railroad, where you follow the route of one of the island's early railroads. Other local networks allow experts to stretch their legs a bit more. Millstream Highlands and the Hartland Dump are excellent places for riders of all abilities to test themselves against the rugged landscape of the island.

As one heads north along the Trans-Canada Highway (Highway 1) and leaves Victoria behind, the landscape becomes more rugged and the population more spread out. The city of Nanaimo offers some excellent mountain bike options. The famous Ultimate Abyss Trail demonstrates the best of Nanaimo riding. Flat rides like the Westwood Lake Loop can be broken up by a slow grind up to the summit of Westwood Ridge with views out toward the ocean.

The farther north you go, the more rugged the landscape gets. The town of Parksville hosts another biking classic, the Hammerfest. This loop challenges the strongest riders and provides a great mix of logging road and tight single-track. Local riders have also created the Top Bridge Mountain Bike Park, which provides hours of winding, moderate rides.

Not to be outdone, the communities of Courtenay and Comox have also created an excellent collection of rides. The rides in this area, including the Monster Mile on Mount Washington, tend to be a bit more rustic. Signs are a foreign concept; although rides like Boston Main, Tomato Creek, and Bear's Bait are great fun, they require a good explorer's sense to find them. Local riders have been active in trying to create more signage, but it is a slow process.

Vancouver Island offers an amazing variety of places to play with your bike. As more and more riders make the short ferry ride to the island, the fame of these areas continues to grow. With this increased popularity comes the potential for increased conflict. Please respect private land and be sure to check with local bike shops on the status of trails before riding them. Rides that may be open one day can be closed without notice. Have fun, and remember, keep the rubber down.

RIDE 62 · Galloping Goose Railroad Trail—Victoria to Glen Lake

AT A GLANCE

Length/configuration: 17.92 km (10.75-mile) point-to-point

Aerobic difficulty: Easy; perfect for the whole family

Technical difficulty: Wide path, much of it paved

Scenery: This first stretch of Galloping Goose passes through urban landscapes with limited views

Special comments: This first leg of the goose is a pleasant, paved roll

The Canadian National Railway extended its line from Victoria between 1911 and 1919. The passenger service, which ran through the 1920s, became known locally as the Galloping Goose. The rail line was finally abandoned in the 1960s as roads and highways began to reduce the necessity of the trains. Today, the Galloping Goose provides 100 km (60 miles) of wide pathways running from Victoria west to Sooke and north to Swartz Bay on the Saanich Peninsula. Because the riding is too much to do in a single day, I've divided the western portion of the railway into three separate rides, each with a slightly different focus. The three rides make up a 55.45-km (33.9-mile) point-to-point.

RIDE 62 · Galloping Goose RR Trail–Victoria/Glen Lake

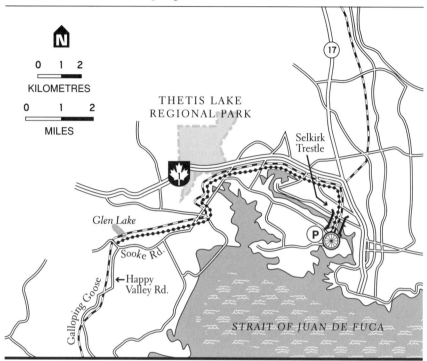

This first stretch of the railway runs through the heart of Victoria, beginning in the Upper Harbour and continuing 17.92 km (10.75 miles) to Glen Lake, a popular swimming hole. Along the way, you'll pass many other users taking advantage of this wide trail, much of which is paved. In-line skaters, skateboarders, and people out for a walk share this popular route. Be sure to stay to the right and be courteous of other users. As you work your way farther along the trail, it takes on a more rural appearance, interrupted periodically by busy street crossings. The way is lined with salmonberries and blackberries for a tasty treat. Wildflowers include the white tubular flower of the bindweed and the pink of the bleeding heart. Although a seemingly endless number of spur trails and access points join the main trail, it is always clearly defined and easy for the whole family to ride.

General location: Victoria.

Elevation change: Negligible.

Season: Year-round.

Services: All services are available in Victoria.

Hazards: The main hazard on this ride is vehicle traffic at major junctions. Be sure to use caution at all crossings.

Rescue index: With the many road crossings, help is rarely far away.

Land status: A mixture of private and municipal land.

Maps: The best map for this ride is the Victoria Cycling Map produced by the Greater Victoria Cycling Coalition (GVCC). The GVCC Web site is gvcc.bc.ca. The map is available from most local bike shops or by contacting:

Davenport Maps Ltd.
201-2610 Douglas St.
Victoria, B.C. V8T 4M1
(800) 611-6277

Finding the trail: In Victoria, make your way to the Inner Harbour area and turn west onto Yates Street, as Johnson is a one-way road eastbound. Follow Yates to Wharf Street, and then make a left turn directly onto the bridge. Cross over the harbour on the Johnson Street Bridge, which separates the Inner Harbour from the Upper Harbour. Immediately turn right onto Harbour Road and find a place to park. The parking lot at the end of the block has been turned into an overnight parking lot for motor coaches—do not park here! There may also be parking along Tyee Road, the second right-hand turn after crossing the bridge.

Sources of additional information: Contact the Greater Victoria Cycling Coalition at (250) 480-5155.

Notes on the trail: From the trailhead, ride west along Harbour Road past the bus parking lot, and you'll find the main trail beginning with smooth, wide pavement. You cross under the Point Ellice bridge and soon cross over the Selkirk Trestle bridge, which separates the Upper Harbour from the Gorge. Beyond the trestle, continue through an underpass for Gorge Street at kilometre 1.67 (mile 1); on the sides of the underpass a beautiful mural has been painted with the theme "Bridging." Beyond this, you'll cross under another bridge, this one just decorated with graffiti. The character changes as you cross Dupplin Road at kilometre 2.28 (mile 1.37) and enter a mixture of industrial and residential developments. Continue on the clearly defined trail as it crosses many side roads and finally over the Trans-Canada Highway on a large overpass. Just beyond the highway, the trail forks. Make a hard left to continue on Galloping Goose westward. The trail ahead continues toward Swartz Bay. As you ride, kilometre marker signs can be a useful guide to your location. Pass the 4-km marker at kilometre 3.86 (mile 2.32). Beyond this, you'll meet Tillicum Road. Stay to the right of the Trans-Canada Highway and avoid the obvious tendency to cross over it. The trail continues on the right. You'll soon go over a small wooden overpass and meet the three-way junction of Admiral's Road, McKenzie Avenue, and the Island Highway. Stay to the right of the highway at this junction as well. This next stretch is marked by lots of road crossings, limiting your ability to maintain any significant speed. Head over another wooden overpass at kilometre 6.6 (mile 3.96); soon the views begin to open up toward Portage Inlet.

You leave the highway behind at kilometre 7.35 (mile 4.4) and soon go under an underpass made of corrugated metal. The pavement ends at kilometre 8.22 (mile 4.93), but resumes in less than a kilometre. After crossing Atkins Road, cross another wooden overpass, and then cross Atkins Road twice more. The trail begins to lose its urban feel after passing the 12-km marker. The junction with Colwood Corners at kilometre 12.86 (mile 7.72) can be dangerous. There are traffic lights a short distance to the right and left to enable a safe crossing of the Island Highway. Avoid the temptation to race across this busy thoroughfare. You'll pass Sooke Road at kilometre 14.07 (mile 8.44). This is another potentially dangerous intersection, so please heed signs. After additional crossings at Kelly Road, Brittany Drive, and Jacklin Road, you'll cross over a narrow wooden bridge with metal highway guards to keep you from going over the edge. As you pass Glen Lake at kilometre 17.28 (mile 10.4), you may want to jump in for a cool, refreshing dip. At this point, either retrace your steps or arrange for a vehicle to pick you up at the next crossing of Sooke Road at kilometre 17.92 (mile 10.75).

RIDE 63 · Galloping Goose Railroad Trail—Sooke Road Second to Third Junction

AT A GLANCE

Length/configuration: 21.7-km (13.02-mile) point-to-point

Aerobic difficulty: Rolling landscape with minor elevation gains

Technical difficulty: Easy for the whole family

Scenery: Excellent views toward the bays of Juan de Fuca Strait

Special comments: Of the three sections of the Galloping Goose, this stretch is by far the most picturesque

Section two of the Galloping Goose railway takes you past lots of ocean views on its 21.7-km (13.02-mile) point-to-point route. From Sooke Road, it rolls through a rural landscape past farms that were homesteaded more than 100 years ago. Pioneers like Edward and Phoebe Field, after traveling the Oregon Trail in 1877, settled this area in 1878 and began one of the first sheep farms. Years later, the railway brought even more people to the area, but it has still retained much of its rustic beauty. Beyond this ranch, the trail begins to roll above the Juan de Fuca Strait, offering successive views of Pedder Inlet, Roche

RIDE 63 • Galloping Goose RR Trail–
Sooke Road Second to Third Junction

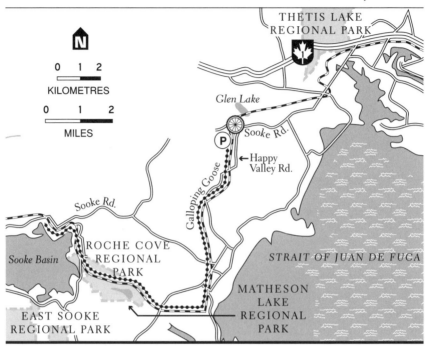

Cove, and the Sooke Basin. Take the time to imagine the tall ship of Juan de Fuca plying the strait in 1592, long before the next European arrived. Though the waters have not changed, the land has been parceled out and settled. The views along this stretch of ocean still beg thoughts of adventure.

The trail reminds you of early native claims to the area as you ride past an area known as Saseenos, after a native Salish word meaning "sunny land sloping gently up from the sea." Beyond this, the ocean view is blighted by a large industrial complex built between 1911 and 1915. A large pipeline was built to provide fresh water to Victoria. The large boilers and construction yard still sit near the waterline.

General location: Victoria.

Elevation change: Minimal.

Season: Year-round.

Services: All services are available in Victoria.

Hazards: The main hazard on this ride is related to vehicle traffic at major junctions. Be sure to use caution at all crossings.

Rescue index: With the many road crossings, help is rarely far away.

Matheson Lake reflects
the landscape surround-
ing the Galloping Goose
Railway.

Land status: A mixture of private and municipal land.

Maps: The best map for this ride is the Victoria Cycling Map produced by the Greater Victoria Cycling Coalition. The GVCC Web site is www.islandnet.com/~gnarly/gvcc. The map is available from most local bike shops or by contacting:

Davenport Maps Ltd.
201-2610 Douglas St.
Victoria, B.C. V8T 4M1
(800) 611-6277

Finding the trail: In Victoria, follow the Island Highway (Highway 1A) west until it becomes Sooke Road (Highway 14). Follow this main road to the junction of Sooke Road and Glen Lake Road. Turn right and there will be parking visible on the right side of Glen Lake Road.

Sources of additional information: Contact the Greater Victoria Cycling Coalition at (250) 480-5155.

Notes on the trail: From the parking lot along Glen Lake Road, cross Sooke Road and follow the trail as it continues to the southwest. After lots of road crossings over the next 2 km (1.2 miles) you'll cross over a wooden bridge. Pass an old barn at kilometre 2.7 (mile 1.62), and cross Happy Valley Road at kilometre 2.95 (mile 1.77). After crossing another wooden bridge at kilometre 4.48 (mile 2.69), cross Happy Valley Road and then Lindholm Road. The picturesque sheep farm across the field was founded in 1878 by Edward and Phoebe Field.

Wind along the trail as it passes more crossings and enjoy the views of Parry Bay that begin to roll into sight around kilometre 8.85 (mile 5.3). Pass the 29-km marker at kilometre 11.73 (mile 7.04) and a ravine with views to Pedder Inlet in the distance. The trail rolls into the trees again, but the views open up as you approach Matheson Lake at kilometre 14.71 (mile 8.83). Beyond the lake, the trail heads back toward the ocean with views of Roche Cove at kilometre 16.46 (mile 9.88). Beyond Roche Cove, cross Gillespie Road and enjoy views of the Sooke Basin.

At kilometre 21.25 (mile 12.75), you'll pass an area known as Saseenos. Beyond this, roll past the flow line, a concrete pipeline built to supply fresh water to Victoria. Beyond the flow line, rejoin Sooke Road at kilometre 21.7 (mile 13).

RIDE 64 · Galloping Goose Railroad Trail — Sooke Road to Terminus

AT A GLANCE

Length/configuration: This trail winds for 18.63 km (10.2 miles) to its terminus, before returning along the same trail for a total out-and-back distance of 33.66 km (20.2 miles)

Aerobic difficulty: This stretch climbs from 45 m (148 feet) to its terminus at 160 m (525 feet). Other than this minor climb, the ride is quite easy

Technical difficulty: This is a wide, smooth trail

Scenery: Views of the Sooke River and the Sooke River Potholes make this a pleasant ride

Special comments: This stretch of railway focuses on history, with an old station and two rustic trestles

RIDE 64 · Galloping Goose Railroad Trail– Sooke Road to Terminus

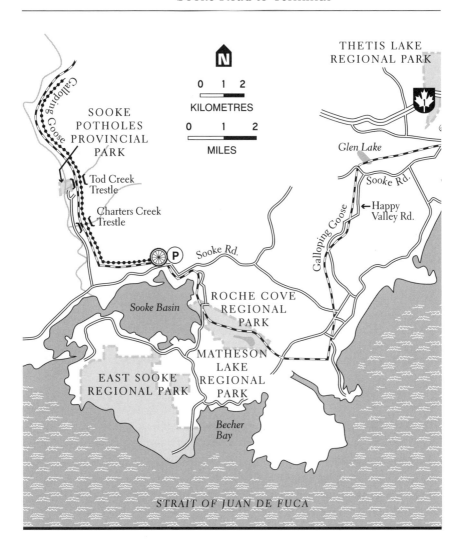

This final stretch of the Galloping Goose railway brings the history of the line into focus. Though the views change as the line moves inland, this 33.66-km (20.2-mile) out-and-back section takes you past artifacts and reminders of a different age. The line was originally built for freight, carrying lumber and other supplies to a rapidly growing Victoria, but it later began a passenger service. Nicknamed the Galloping Goose, the gas locomotive picked up passengers traveling to and from the big city. As you roll your way along this final stretch, you

The Sooke River Potholes line the final stretch of the Galloping Goose Railroad Trail.

cross two of the remaining trestles over which the train used to rumble. Beyond the Tod Creek Trestle, a rustic wooden structure high above the Sooke River, you'll pass the eerily quiet Barnes Station. The station is in surprisingly good repair—even the outhouse remains, partly camouflaged in the bushes. You can almost hear the train whistle and the cries for "all aboard!" This stretch also passes the Sooke River Potholes, a series of round pools eroded by water falling and swirling around small pieces of gravel. This swirling of debris acts like a drill, creating round potholes. As the course of the water changes slightly, the water falls on a new location and begins the process over again. These quiet ponds are a popular place for family picnics and outings. On a hot day, they offer cool relief from the heat.

The brochures describe the old gold mine site of Leechtown at the end of the ride. There is little left of this site, and the main trail ends at a gate with no sign of the old town. Beyond the gate, the trails become a labyrinth of single-track. Turn around at the gate, and roll your way back downhill to your vehicle.

General location: Victoria.

Elevation change: The trail climbs from 45 metres (148 feet) at Sooke Road to its terminus at 160 m (525 feet).

Season: Year-round.

Services: All services are available in Victoria.

Hazards: The main hazard on this ride is related to vehicle traffic at major junctions. Be sure to use caution at all crossings.

Rescue index: With the many road crossings, help is rarely far away.

Land status: A mixture of private and municipal land.

Maps: The best map for this ride is the Victoria Cycling Map produced by the Greater Victoria Cycling Coalition. The GVCC Web site is gvcc.bc.ca. The map is available from most local bike shops or by contacting:

Davenport Maps Ltd.
201-2610 Douglas St.
Victoria, B.C. V8T 4M1
(800) 611-6277

Finding the trail: In Victoria, follow the Island Highway until it joins with Sooke Road. Follow this major route until it crosses Gillespie Road. Stay on Sooke Road for an additional 2.94 km (1.76 miles) until you see the trailhead on your right. Park here.

Sources of additional information: Contact the Greater Victoria Cycling Coalition at (250) 480-5155.

Notes on the trail: Cross Sooke Road and pass the 39-km marker at kilometre 0.38 (mile 0.23). As you follow the wide path of the Galloping Goose, you'll cross over lots of roads, including a gravel access road at kilometre 3.32 (mile 2). Beyond additional crossings, including Meota Drive and Sooke River Road (twice), you'll cross the Charters Creek trestle at kilometre 6.15 (mile 3.7). Stay straight, ignoring a horse trail forking to the right at kilometre 7.93 (mile 4.76). Beyond this, cross the Tod Creek trestle at kilometre 8.29 (mile 4.97). This marks the beginning of the Sooke River Potholes. They are periodically visible off to the left and make an inviting spot for a dip. Beyond the potholes, the old Barnes Station still stands at kilometre 9.55 (mile 5.73). After passing what looks like a graveyard for old metal tanks, you'll continue climbing until the Sooke River comes into view down and to the left at kilometre 13.93 (mile 8.36). More potholes are visible along this stretch. At kilometre 16.83 (mile 10.1), the formal trail ends. Turn around here and return to your vehicle at kilometre 33.66 (mile 20.2).

RIDE 65 · Millstream Highlands

AT A GLANCE

Length/configuration: This trail network offers a variety of options. The main access along the double-track of the Mainline Trail is a 3.52 km (2.11 miles) point-to-point. From the Mainline, numerous side trails offer loops that eventually bring you back to this access trail

Aerobic difficulty: This network offers a wide spectrum of rides for all fitness levels

Technical difficulty: Variable, from beginner to extreme

Scenery: Mostly urban landscape

Special comments: This network may soon disappear as development encroaches from every direction.

Quick! Run, drive, ride—somehow get to the Millstream Highlands before it's too late. This is one fun network of interconnected trails offering everything from hairball drops to tender, rolling trails. This is a labyrinth of trails that defies mapping, but it offers oodles of opportunity to test your skills. The trail network uses a wide double-track known as the Mainline to provide access to the many side trails. The only catch is that novices have to ride all the way to the upper section of the network, while experts can dive right in. The lower slopes are composed of dark, moist, north-facing slopes. This results in a more severe, rooted, challenging network of trails. Higher up the slope, the sun bakes the hillsides and the red-barked arbutus almost seems to be peeling from sunburn. Here, the trails are smoother and drier, offering a continuum from beginner to solid intermediate (with a few expert trails hidden away for the determined rider to discover).

General location: North of Victoria.

Elevation change: The network climbs from the road at approximately 105 m (344 feet) up to 300 m (984 feet) at its highest point.

Season: Year-round.

Services: All services are available in Victoria.

Hazards: The trails vary in difficulty level so much that you need to be ready for anything, including sharp drops, roots, and rocks. The upper trails receive more sunlight and tend to have smoother gradients. The lower trails are wet, north shore–style rides popular with more expert riders.

Rescue index: Your best bet for finding help is to head back to the Mainline and begin descending toward the road. If you don't encounter any other riders, return down Millstream Road to the residential area.

RIDE 65 · Millstream Highlands

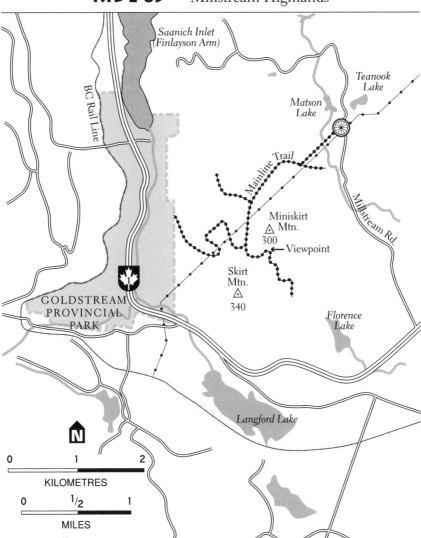

Land status: Undeveloped municipal land.

Maps: There are no good maps of this network.

Finding the trail: From Victoria, head north on the Trans-Canada Highway and take the north exit onto Millstream Road. Millstream Road crosses under a serious set of power lines 4 km (2.5 miles) from the exit. There is a pull-off on both sides of the road. On the right side is a sign warning about vehicle break-ins. Park here and cross the road; the trail begins beyond the gate.

A cyclist rolls down the wide track of the Mainline, part of the Millstream Highlands trail network.

Sources of additional information:

South Island Mountain Bike Society
Box 215, 2680 Quadra Street
Victoria, B.C. V8T 4E4
(250) 477-2455

Notes on the trail: From the roadside, go through the gate and follow the wide gravel of the Mainline Trail. This double-track allows access onto the many trails radiating away from this main artery. Along the 2.81-km (1.69-mile) length of the Mainline, many trails beckon you in varying directions. The spur trails tend to be easier as you get to the upper sections of the Mainline. This network is best experienced by simply turning when and where the spirit moves you. By riding to the upper sections of the Mainline, you can take your time rolling the side trails until you decide to head back to your vehicle.

One loop branches off to the left at kilometre 2.56 (mile 1.54), just before reaching a mini-summit on the Mainline. This is the third left junction after passing what looks like an old vehicle hood with "A12" painted on it in large black letters and occurs just after the Mainline winds to the right of the power lines and then rejoins them. This trail climbs from 245 m (804 feet) along a wide double-track with several rougher trails branching off to the left and right. It begins to level out at 300 m (984 feet) at around kilometre 3.19 (mile 1.9). Just beyond this point, you'll reach the summit in a stand of arbutus trees with views extending all the way to the Gulf Islands in the Haro Strait. The summit is at kilometre 3.52 (mile 2.11).

Deciding to take a tighter line down, I took a right fork at kilometre 3.74 (mile 2.24) and a left onto a single-track at kilometre 3.85 (mile 2.31). This single-track began to parallel a barbed-wire fence as it became a wonderful rolling slalom run through the trees. The single-track rejoined the main trail at kilometre 4.32 (mile 2.59), and then rejoined the Mainline at kilometre 4.67 (mile 2.8).

On the way down, why not go left at the vehicle hood with "A12" painted on it? This offers another option for a more technical descent. Beginning at kilometre 4.87 (mile 2.92), this trail soon joins a descending double-track. Staying left at this junction, you'll soon have the option to take a right junction onto a single-track. This trail climbs for a short distance through rougher, wetter, north-slope conditions. After crossing a log pyramid the trail becomes much more technical with some sharp verticals and large roots. The trail bottoms out at kilometre 5.71 (mile 3.43) with a trail taking off to the right. Take this and another right shortly thereafter, and rejoin the Mainline at kilometre 5.98 (mile 3.59). When you are finished exploring, turn downhill and return to your vehicle. These are only two of a seemingly infinite number of options. As you explore, keep a compass handy to make sure you don't stray too far from the Mainline. Happy hunting.

RIDE 66 · Mount Work Park—Hartland Surplus Lands

AT A GLANCE

Length/configuration: Variable. This is a convoluted network of trails

Aerobic difficulty: Moderate to very challenging depending on the route chosen

Technical difficulty: Varies from easy to extreme, with the majority of rides in the expert category

Scenery: This technical network remains within the trees with limited views. A few low summits offer views of the rolling landscape of Vancouver Island

Special comments: This is a great example of industry working with mountain bikers

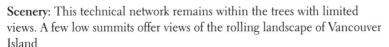

Want some great riding? Then get thee to the dump! Yes that's right—adjacent to the Hartland Landfill is one of the island's premier trail networks. It has it all, from tender to terminal. The trails act like an aggression thermometre. As you ride through the system, make a comparison of the visual character of the trails at each junction, and then go for it. At many junctions, one trail may be visibly more difficult; this typical contrast helps to make decisions easier. When you feel aggressive, the choice is obvious. When you feel more tentative, there are other, less stressful options. Generally, the lower trails are easy, with the intermediate trails taking a higher line and the expert trails working their way to the summit lines. The northwest section of trails is strictly for expert riders. With names like Harem Scarem and Dave's Dementia, they offer riders preferring the view above the handlebars an endless supply of dismounts.

The parking lot offers washroom facilities and a bike wash. This wonderful network of trails comes to us thanks to several important agencies. The two principal players are the Capital Regional District (CRD) and the South Island Mountain Bike Society (SIMBS). As a result of increased efficiency in the treatment of solid waste, and the current focus on recycling, the CRD found itself in the enviable position of having more land set aside for landfill purposes than current needs required. Through cooperation with SIMBS, the CRD opened its first multiple-use trail network. Best of all, mountain bikers are the main benefactors of this initiative. Who would have thought in this era of trail closures and restrictions that nonprofit societies and government could come together in such a way? This trail network offers hope for other locales that have yet to embrace fat-tired travel.

This network did not appear out of thin air. It is the result of countless hours of volunteer time by local riders. SIMBS regularly schedules trail maintenance days, giving you the ability to help the trails and the chance to meet other riders. Trail days are a social way to contribute to the resource that we all enjoy utilizing.

General location: Just north of Victoria.

Elevation change: Varies with route chosen.

Season: Year-round.

Services: All services are available in Victoria.

Hazards: Depending on which trails you choose, the hazards are innumerable. They include severe drops, heavily rooted sections, and even abandoned automobiles. This is a network where the rider selects the challenge level, and the hazards encountered will be reflected in these choices.

Rescue index: In the case of emergency, help may be contacted by staff at the landfill during operation hours. Otherwise, call 911 for most emergencies, but for forest fires the number is (800) 663-5555. On weekends, the network is heavily used and other riders can usually offer assistance.

Land status: Capital Regional District land.

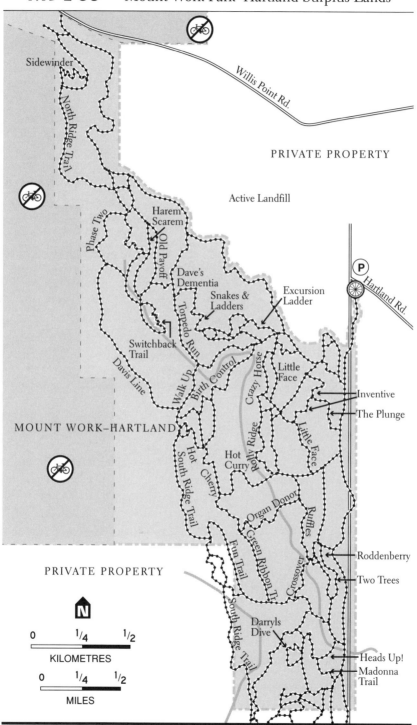

Sidewinder

North Ridge Trail

Willis Point Rd.

PRIVATE PROPERTY

Active Landfill

Phase Two

Harem
Scarem

Old Payoff

Dave's
Dementia

Snakes &
Ladders

Excursion
Ladder

P

Hartland Rd.

Torpedo Run

Switchback
Trail

Davis Line

Walk Up

Birth Control

Crazy Horse

Little
Face

Inventive

The Plunge

MOUNT WORK–HARTLAND

Holly Ridge

Little Face

Hot
Curry

Hot Cherry

South Ridge Trail

Organ Donor

Green Ribbon Tr.

Ruffles

Crossover

Roddenberry

Two Trees

PRIVATE PROPERTY

Fun Trail

South Ridge Trail

Darryls
Dive

Heads Up!

Madonna
Trail

N

0   1/4   1/2
KILOMETRES

0   1/4   1/2
MILES

The Hartland Surplus
Lands represent a moun-
tain biking success story.

Maps: Although it is of limited value, the best map of the area has been produced by SIMBS and is available at many local bike shops. Make sure to pick it
up *before* arriving, as it is not available on site. However, the trail system doesn't
require maps as it is a self-contained network, with each trail eventually leading
you back to the main access trail. You can obtain the map by contacting SIMBS
directly at (250) 477-2455.

Finding the trail: If you are coming from Victoria, head north on Highway 17
toward the ferry terminal, and turn left at onto Royal Oak Drive. If you are coming from the ferry terminal at Swartz Bay, head south on the Patricia Bay
Highway (Highway 17), and make a right at Royal Oak Drive. Follow this for a
short distance to West Saanich Road. Turn left onto Hartland Road and follow it
until you reach the entrance to the landfill. The main parking lot is to the right
of this main entrance, and the trail begins across the road from the parking lot.

Sources of additional information:

South Island Mountain Bike Society
Box 215, 2680 Quadra Street
Victoria, B.C. V8T 4E4
(250) 477-2455

Notes on the trail: Great efforts have been made to try to tame this network—not in terms of challenge, but in terms of creating an easily navigated network of trails. Along the main access trail small concrete blocks note difficulty ratings and a junction number. These numbers coincide with the trail map. In reality, beyond the tame access trail, the trail-marking system quickly breaks down. I found few junctions marked with any type of sign. This may change with time, but it did little to take away from my enjoyment of the network. The best way to enjoy this network is to begin with a copy of the trail map. There is a map at the trailhead, but it is of little use once you find yourself in a jumble of trails. It will continue to be of limited value until all the junctions shown on the map are actually marked on the ground as well. The easiest way for beginner and inter-mediate riders to approach this network is to limit themselves to the lower trails. As you climb higher from the main access trail, the difficulty grows. The upper trails are almost exclusively expert level with numerous extreme rides.

RIDE 67 · Ultimate Abyss

AT A GLANCE

Length/configuration: 4.72-km (2.83-mile) point-to-point

Aerobic difficulty: Moderate, with only limited climbing

Technical difficulty: Difficult, with some extreme obstacles

Scenery: Some spectacular views along the edge of the Harewood Plains, beautiful stretches of arbutus

Special comments: Along with its deserved fame as a technical race course, this is also one of the most pleasant trails in terms of scenery

The Ultimate Abyss takes its name from a huge fissure in the volcanic rock making up the ridge on which the trail travels. High above the Harewood Plains, the trail repeatedly crosses over this 10–20-cm (8–11-inch) opening. Mixing a high level of technical challenge with some exquisite views, this 4.72-km (2.83-mile) point-to-point ride offers equal potential as a quiet hike.

The trail rolls along the western edge of an escarpment high above the Harewood Plains. It takes you through colourful stands of arbutus and offers views to distant mountains and the ocean. Few trails can mix high technical challenge with equally tremendous views. So many of British Columbia's most

RIDE 67 · Ultimate Abyss

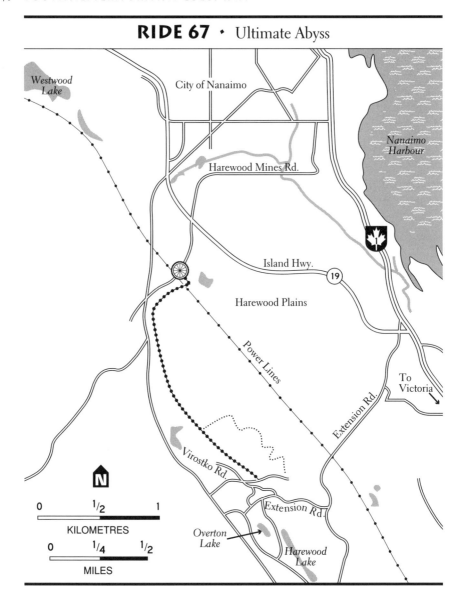

challenging rides sacrifice beauty for difficulty . . . but this trail compromises nothing. As you ride, each section has been given a descriptive name, and signs indicate the start of each section. A few, like Stu's Delight, Big Log, and Widow Maker, represent some of the very challenging sections of this ride. This is, above all, an expert technical ride. Be sure that your ability is up to the challenge, and expect to walk a few of the scarier obstacles. Please don't contribute to braiding of the trail by riding around obstacles. Get off and walk if it is beyond your comfort level.

General location: Within the city of Nanaimo.

Elevation change: From the trailhead, at 150 m (492 feet) up to a maximum of approximately 230 m (754 feet).

Season: Year-round.

Services: All services are available in Nanaimo.

Hazards: This trail was built to cultivate hazards, and the resulting mix will challenge the best of riders. There are log pyramids, high wheelie drops, big logs, narrow chutes, and any number of other challenges. Be prepared for bruises!

Rescue index: This trail is very popular, but it's also somewhat remote. It traverses a high cliff, and the only access to help is to return to the trailhead or continue to the residential area at the south end of the ride. Be sure to have a first-aid kit and repair kit along.

Land status: Municipal land.

Maps: The NTS 1:50,000 topographic map for this trail is 92 G/4 Nanaimo.

Finding the trail: In downtown Nanaimo, head west on 7th Street. This will wind south to become Harewood Mines Road. Follow this road as it passes Homestead Trail (Road), Western Acres Drive, and Rimrock Trail (Road). Soon after Rimrock Trail, the power lines will cross overhead. Park along the road at this point. The trail begins by riding to the left of the construction along the power lines on the south (left) side of the road.

Sources of additional information: Contact the Guardians of the Abyss Trail Society by fax at (250) 756-2453.

Notes on the trail: Begin the ride along the access road to the left of the power lines. This bypasses some of the construction presently going on in the area. Take the first right-hand junction and begin climbing toward the transmission towers. You want to stay to the right to head toward the tower closest to Harewood Mines Road. Just into the bush, beyond the power line, you'll see a trail. Follow this trail, and soon you'll see a sign indicating the Abyss Trail. Sections of this trail have been individually named, and signs en route identify the various sections. The main route is clearly visible throughout the ride, so avoid the temptation to take spur trails.

At kilometre 0.38 (mile 0.23), a trail forks to the left; stay straight. You'll see this trail as you enter the first section of trail, named Enigma. The trail parallels Harewood Mines Road to this point, and the sound of traffic is quite prominent. Beyond this sign, the trail begins to wind south, slowly leaving the road behind. After passing the sign for Arbutus Rock, the trail opens up with some views toward the distant firing range. At kilometre 0.89 (mile 0.53), you get your first view of the abyss, a long fault in the volcanic rock that appears as a separation of 20 to 30 cm (8 to 11 inches). As you roll along this stretch, views begin to open periodically, allowing you to see all the way to the ocean. At kilometre 1.33 (mile 0.8), the trail drops off a slickrock ledge and begins traversing the edge of a cliff dropping down to the right. There are lots of short vertical drops over the next stretch as you drop off of lava rocks, only to climb back up another one. A log pyramid at kilometre 1.9 (mile 1.14) is followed by another stretch along the ridge.

Enter the Dark Woods stretch at kilometre 2.87 (mile 1.72) as the ridge is traded for a stretch of old growth western red cedar and Douglas fir. As the canopy begins to open up, pass Big Log, where an enormous log jump awaits you (there is an option to bypass it if it's a little too large for you). Just beyond Big Log, you'll enter a clearing at kilometre 3.33 (mile 2) with a small rock cairn. Humility (Ride 68) enters from the left at this point. To continue on this ride, stay straight on the Abyss Trail. As you drop off the rocks beyond this clearing, the trail drops at an unusual angle across some lava rock and into some large roots.

Stu's Delight begins at kilometre 3.53 (mile 2.12) and takes you through a much rougher stretch of large roots and over a log pyramid. But this is just a warm-up for Widow Maker as the trail makes a serious drop down a sharp lava outcrop. There's no pretty way to do this wheelie drop; if you're not up to it, scramble down cautiously and continue from the base of the rock. As you crest the ridge again at kilometre 3.93 (mile 2.36), you'll be rewarded with views of the surrounding countryside. Enjoy this last view—the trail will begin dropping suddenly at kilometre 4.24 (mile 2.54). Once the drop begins, it is fast and furious, through a tight slalom of western red cedar. After a final set of switchbacks, you'll join the road at kilometre 4.72 (mile 2.83).

You can either return or follow this road to the left for 1.1 km (0.66 mile), and then turn left to follow the power line access back to your car at approximately kilometre 10 (mile 6). A final option is to roll left for a short distance, and then climb up Humility to make a partial loop back on the Abyss.

RIDE 68 · Humility

AT A GLANCE

Length/configuration: 2.76-km (1.66-mile) point-to-point, or make a 4.6-km (2.76-mile) loop with the lower stretch of the Abyss

Aerobic difficulty: A moderate climb with expert-level obstacles

Technical difficulty: Difficult to extreme

Scenery: Mostly dense forest with a few pleasant patches of arbutus

Special comments: This trail makes a nice loop with the lower section of the Abyss

RIDE 68 · Humility

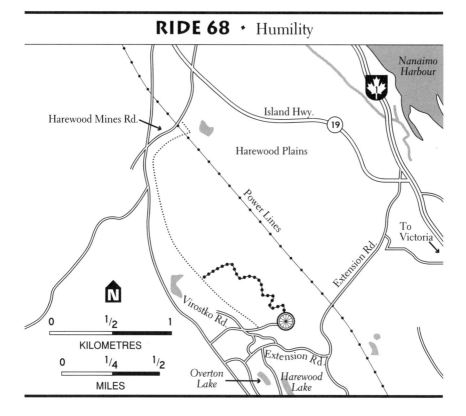

This ride, like the Ultimate Abyss, offers a strong technical challenge mixed with some pleasant patches of arbutus trees. It remains largely in the trees along its 2.76-km (1.66-mile) length, and it provides an expert-level loop option for the lower section of the Abyss. Most riders will ride the Abyss and use this to create a loop on the lower section followed by a backtrack up the upper section. This gives you the best of both worlds and adds to the variety on what would normally be an out-and-back ride. Although not well-marked, this ride is well designed and offers an expert-level extension to the classic Abyss.

From the trailhead, it climbs moderately and bounces its way over lava rock boulders and drops you down the opposite side. The challenge is steady until it rolls its way past a large lava boulder that creates a cave-like overhang. Beyond the overhang, boulders of lava rock have cracked and shattered into perfectly square blocks. Wind your way around several stacks of these boulders and finally rejoin the Ultimate Abyss Trail.

General location: Within the city of Nanaimo.

Elevation change: From the road at 140 m (459 feet), the trail climbs to its junction with the Ultimate Abyss at approximately 200 m (656 feet).

Season: Year-round.

Services: All services are available in Nanaimo.

Hazards: This is another expert ride with numerous drops off lava boulders, large roots, and log obstacles. It may also include a little bit of route finding depending on how heavily it has been used in the months prior to your arrival.

Rescue index: This is a very new trail and is not well known yet. You should assume that you will meet few riders along its length and should treat it with respect. Expect to return to the road before being able to find assistance.

Land status: Municipal land.

Maps: The NTS 1:50,000 topographic map for this trail is 92 G/4 Nanaimo.

Finding the trail: This ride is generally used as an extension of the Ultimate Abyss, creating a small loop at the end of that point-to-point ride. You can drive to the trailhead by following the Trans-Canada Highway (Nichol Street within Nanaimo) south to Cranberry Avenue. Turn right on Cranberry Avenue and right again on Extension Road. Follow this winding road past Roberta Road and Lenwood Road. At the next right junction, Extension Road makes a hard right, and White Rapids Road continues. Take the right turn, turn right again on Virostko Road, and finally turn right on Midora Road. The trailhead will be off to the left. Watch for a yellow pipe that looks like a candy cane standing up beside the road.

Sources of additional information: Contact Bastion Cycle in Nanaimo at 4196 Departure Bay Road or by phone at (250) 758-2453. You may also contact the Guardians of the Abyss Trail Society by fax at (250) 756-2453.

Notes on the trail: To find the trail, look for a yellow candy-cane pipe to the north side of the road. Behind it, the trail begins with a short technical climb, turns sharply to the right, and continues the climb on a more moderate gradient. Pass a rusted oil drum stove at kilometre 0.17 (mile 0.1) and continue climbing. While the path remains generally uphill, you drop down a lava rock boulder at kilometre 0.47 (mile 0.28). Someone has used blue-and-white flagging tape to mark sections of the trail. It doesn't continue for the entire route, though, so don't rely on it. The trail slowly climbs onto a low ridge, with some stands of arbutus mixed with darker patches of red cedar and Douglas fir. A meadow of reindeer moss—a gray, ground-hugging lichen—at kilometre 1.82 (mile 1.09) creates the illusion that the ground is covered in frost. Beyond this point, make another short drop down the lava rock, followed by an immediate left, and then head up and over a log. Beyond the log, the trail begins to wind around to the left, and the single-track gets narrower as it begins to drop off the ridge. At kilometre 2 (mile 1.2), you pass a large rock overhang that resembles a cave. The trail runs along the length of this unique feature and zigzags around several pieces of lava rock that have cracked into almost perfectly square blocks. Beyond this, it continues to wind to the left, finally rejoining the Ultimate Abyss Trail at kilometre 2.76 (mile 1.66). If you continue on the Abyss Trail to the north trailhead, add 3.33 km (2 miles), or turn left and make a 4.6-km (2.76-mile) loop with the lower stretch of the Abyss.

RIDE 69 · Westwood Lake Loop

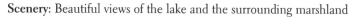

AT A GLANCE

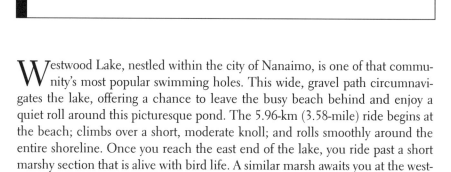

Length/configuration: 5.96-km (3.58-mile) loop

Aerobic difficulty: Generally smooth, with the exception of a moderate climb at the beginning of the trail

Technical difficulty: Generally easy, with a few narrow bridges and an occasional root during the first climb

Scenery: Beautiful views of the lake and the surrounding marshland

Special comments: This is a great ride for the entire family. Bring your bike and swimsuit and make a day of it

Westwood Lake, nestled within the city of Nanaimo, is one of that community's most popular swimming holes. This wide, gravel path circumnavigates the lake, offering a chance to leave the busy beach behind and enjoy a quiet roll around this picturesque pond. The 5.96-km (3.58-mile) ride begins at the beach; climbs over a short, moderate knoll; and rolls smoothly around the entire shoreline. Once you reach the east end of the lake, you ride past a short marshy section that is alive with bird life. A similar marsh awaits you at the western end as well. On a sunny day, a breeze off the lake helps you keep cool, and the pleasant views make this a worthwhile outing for the whole family.

General location: Within the city of Nanaimo.

Elevation change: From the trailhead, climb 45 m (147 feet) in the first 0.83 km (0.5 mile) before rejoining the lake shore. Beyond this point the trail stays quite level and smooth.

Season: Year-round.

Services: All services are available in Nanaimo.

Hazards: The first 0.83 km (0.5 mile) climbs 45 m (147 feet) as it crests a small knoll before rejoining the lake shore. Beyond this point, the main challenge is other users. This trail is used by cyclists along with hikers and families on quiet strolls. Be sure to keep your eye out and yield to other trail users.

Rescue index: This is a popular trail and beach. Help is rarely far away. There is also a pay phone at the beach for emergencies.

Land status: Municipal land.

Maps: The NTS 1:50,000 topographic map for this trail is 92 G/4 Nanaimo and a bit of the neighbouring 92 F/1.

RIDE 69 · Westwood Lake Loop

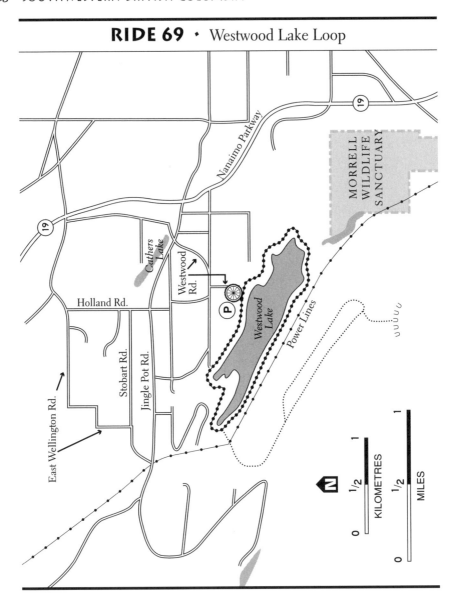

Finding the trail: In Nanaimo, follow Bowen Road to its junction with Wellington Road. Head west on Wellington, past the Nanaimo Parkway (Highway 19), and immediately left onto Westwood Road. Follow this as it winds its way across Jingle Pot Road and Arbot Road to Westwood Lake and Park. The trail begins to the left of the day use parking lot.

Sources of additional information: Contact Bastion Cycle in Nanaimo at 4196 Departure Bay Road, or by phone at (250) 758-2453.

Notes on the trail: This trail needs little description. It is a wide gravel path that rolls around a picturesque lake, through numerous gates, and returns in 5.96 km (3.58 miles). Only the first 0.83 km (0.5 mile) has any technical challenges as it climbs over a small knoll before rejoining the shoreline.

RIDE 70 · Westwood Ridge

AT A GLANCE

Length/configuration: This trail involves riding a loop around Westwood Lake; however, you'll interrupt this loop halfway around to head off to an out-and-back section with a loop at the far end. This will return you to the shores of Westwood Lake, allowing you to continue the original loop. The total ride distance is 8.55 km (5.13 miles)

Aerobic difficulty: Moderate with some steep climbing

Technical difficulty: Combination steep climb with a hike-a-bike section

Scenery: Westwood Ridge offers one of the premier views in the Nanaimo region, with panoramas stretching eastward all the way to the ocean. Beneath you, the busy shores of Westwood Lake appear deserted from this elevated vantage point

Special comments: This trail is rugged, combining a wide path, along with a steep ride and short hike-a-bike, but the views are worth it

This ride combines the smooth-rolling surface of Westwood Lake Trail (Ride 69) with a steep combination of technical riding and a short, steep hike-a-bike. The end result of this effort is a premier view of the Nanaimo region. The entire route includes the Westwood Lake Loop along with this loop for a total distance of 8.55 km (5.13 miles).

Although many riders will be tempted to forego this ride due to the hike-a-bike section, the view from the summit is without equal. Rising above the entire city, you can drink in unobstructed views all the way to Gabriola Island, the Northumberland Channel, and the Strait of Georgia. To attain the view, you must push your bike up a short, steep hill, and then park it to crest the final 60 m (197 feet) on foot.

Once you've tired of the view (if that is possible), return to your bike, continue down the ride, and finish the loop back toward Westwood Lake and then around the west end of this popular swimming hole. Don't forget your swim-

RIDE 70 · Westwood Ridge

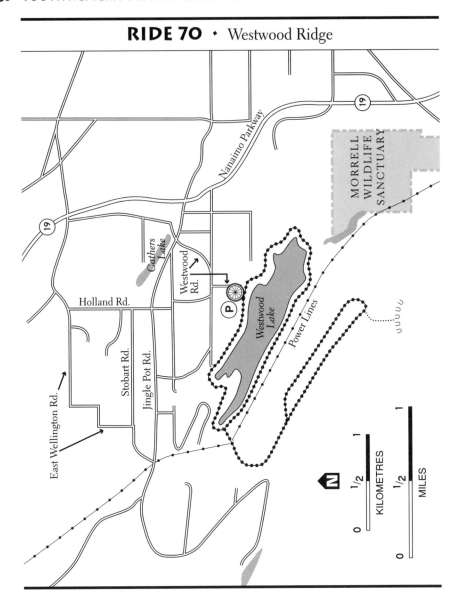

suit—a ride like this deserves a refreshing dip to add that little extra touch to an already great trip.

General location: Within the city of Nanaimo.

Elevation change: From the lakeshore at 160 m (525 feet), the trail climbs to Westwood Ridge at 360 m (1,181 feet). The final 60 m (197 feet) are done on foot.

Season: Year-round.

Westwood Ridge is one of the premier views in the Nanaimo area.

Services: All services are available in Nanaimo.

Hazards: Once you leave Westwood Lake behind, the climbing is technical, with numerous logs and other challenges. The hike-a-bike is so steep it's difficult to push your bike. The view, though, makes any amount of work worthwhile.

Rescue index: Once you leave Westwood Lake behind, be prepared to meet few hikers. Though popular, the trails are only known locally, and you may not meet any other people on this loop.

Land status: Municipal land.

Maps: The NTS 1:50,000 topographic map for this trail is 92 G/4 Nanaimo and a bit of the neighbouring 92 F/1.

Finding the trail: In Nanaimo, follow Bowen Road to its junction with Wellington Road. Head west on Wellington, past the Nanaimo Parkway (Highway 19), and immediately left onto Westwood Road. Follow this as it winds its way across Jingle Pot Road and Arbot Road to Westwood Lake and Park. The trail begins to the left of the day-use parking lot.

Sources of additional information: Contact Bastion Cycle in Nanaimo at 4196 Departure Bay Road, or by phone at (250) 758-2453.

Notes on the trail: Roll your way around Westwood Lake. If you take the long way, around the eastern shoreline, you'll roll 3.67 km (2.2 miles) before you reach the trailhead. Just before the Westwood Lake Trail makes a hard right over a bridge, a trail forks off to the left and begins climbing. Take this trail and almost immediately cross under the power lines. Beyond the power lines the trail continues into the woods. A rough sign indicates that this is the access point for several more trails. Take this trail, and begin climbing right away. A fork at kilometre 4.02 (mile 2.41) is irrelevant as both trails rejoin in a short distance. The climb is a technical single-track, moderately steep with numerous log obstacles. Cross a rickety bridge at kilometre 4.14 (mile 2.48). Continue climbing, and stay left at a junction near a bridge at kilometre 4.68 (mile 2.8). This will take you directly up to the ridge, although it includes a steep hike-a-bike. A sign at kilometre 4.8 (mile 2.94), badly chewed up by porcupines, indicates the trail to Westwood Ridge. Begin the hike-a-bike and climb up to a junction at kilometre 5.05 (mile 3.03). Park your bike here and continue hiking for a few minutes to the ridge proper. The views from here stretch to the ocean beyond and are one of the premier vantage points in the area. When you return to your bike, continue straight, following signs for Kilpatrick Trail. Take the first left junction at kilometre 5.11 (mile 3.07) and the trail begins to drop into a tight slalom through the trees. Stay to the left at another junction at kilometre 5.41 (mile 3.25) and soon rejoin the trail you originally ascended. You will get back to the lake at kilometre 6.08 (mile 3.65) and, if you continue around the lake, return to your car at kilometre 8.55 (mile 5.13).

RIDE 71 · Hammerfest Race Course

AT A GLANCE

Length/configuration: 11.2-km (6.7-mile) loop

Aerobic difficulty: Very challenging; this trail climbs 260 m (853 feet) over 6.45 km (3.87 miles)

Technical difficulty: This is an expert-level race course. There are options to avoid the most challenging stretches, but the trail is generally limited to intermediate and expert riders

Scenery: As you climb toward the upper sections of the trail, views open up to the surrounding countryside. The views reflect a rolling forest with a mixture of old growth and more recent second growth

Special comments: This is one of the premier race courses on Vancouver Island—challenging and variable

This excellent race course is one of the most popular on Vancouver Island, mixing fast logging road with narrow, technical single-track. The entire loop stretches 11.2 km (6.7 miles) to crest the upper portion of Macmillan-Bloedel's cutline before descending on a combination of technical single-track and wide fire road.

As you climb, the views open up as you crest Little Rock and Big Rock, and the entire valley spreads out beneath you. Once you leave the actively logged area behind, the ride continues climbing through a pleasant forest with stands of arbutus. The descent is tough; Fern Gully lives up to its name as it runs through a dense stand of ferns. Though beautiful, it is very challenging. Bounce down Enchanted Forest, and scream the final downhill on the fire road. This trail has a little of everything.

It's important to remember that it only exists through the goodwill of forestry giant Macmillan-Bloedel. Mountain bikers are often at odds with logging companies as they see excellent riding fall under the ax. Companies like Macmillan-Bloedel are trying to work with other users of the forest resource; this ride represents one of the success stories.

General location: South of the city of Parksville.

Elevation change: This trail climbs steadily from the trailhead at approximately 140 m (460 feet) to the summit at elevation 400 m (1,312 feet). Beyond this summit, the trend is solidly downhill.

Season: April through October. The winter months are generally very wet but sometimes passable.

Services: All services are available in Parksville.

Hazards: This is an expert-level race course with obstacles galore. These include the standard collection of verticals, roots, ruts, and log drops, plus numerous log pyramids. This is one of those rides best done with a bike computer and a compass to keep you on track. There are many unmarked junctions, and finding the proper route takes a little experimentation.

Rescue index: Don't anticipate meeting other riders unless you happen to be out on a busy weekend. Most local bike shops are discouraging the ride in order to reduce friction between the cyclists and Macmillan-Bloedel. Please respect this private property, and be prepared to return to the park for assistance.

Land status: The trail begins within Englishman Falls Provincial Park and then enters Macmillan-Bloedel private land.

Maps: The NTS 1:50,000 topographic map for this trail is 92 F/1. Your best map will probably be the one in this book—it's based on the actual race map. The race map is harder to find, but it's occasionally available at local bike shops.

Finding the trail: From Parksville, take the Alberni Highway (Highway 4A) inland and follow signs for Englishman River Falls. Park in the day-use area of the provincial park.

RIDE 71 · Hammerfest Race Course

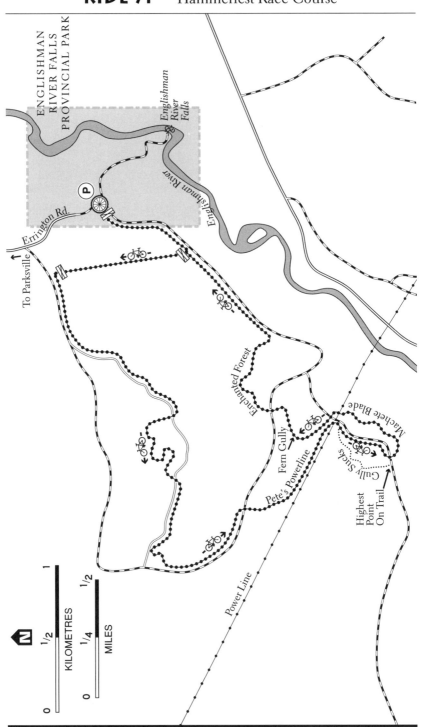

ENGLISHMAN RIVER FALLS PROVINCIAL PARK

Englishman River Falls

Englishman River

To Parksville

Errington Rd.

P

Enchanted Forest

Machete Blade

Fern Gully

Pete's Powerline

Gully Sucks

Highest Point On Trail

Power Line

N

KILOMETRES
0   1/2   1

MILES
0   1/4   1/2

One of the classic rides on Vancouver Island, the Hammerfest Race Course mixes wide climbs with narrow descents.

Sources of additional information: I was unable to find any additional sources of information.

Notes on the trail: From the day-use area parking lot, ride back up toward the campground. At the campground entrance, go left past a yellow gate along a private access road. Follow this access road until it begins to parallel a Macmillan-Bloedel clear-cut on the right. The trail is a wide double-track at this point. It makes a sharp left at kilometre 0.55 (mile 0.33). Stay right on the double-track at kilometre 0.59 (mile 0.35), and at kilometre 0.71 (mile 0.43) make a sharp right onto a wide double-track, then enter a fence gate onto Macmillan-Bloedel land. Drop down this wide track until you leave through a similar gate at kilometre 1.06 (mile 0.64). At the next junction, at kilometre 1.68 (mile 1.01), turn left onto a wide double-track. Take a left at a junction with a narrow double-track to the left at kilometre 2.16 (mile 1.3) and begin climbing. At kilometre 2.68 (mile 1.61), the trail forks with a narrow single-track going to the right. Take this trail, and although it is somewhat overgrown with thimbleberry and salmonberry, it does eventually open up. Make a left turn at kilometre 2.9 (mile 1.74) and begin the climb onto Little Rock. Dropping off of Little Rock, push your way through the thimbleberry and begin climbing at kilometre 3.21 (mile 1.93).

As you climb out of the thimbleberry, you'll soon find yourself atop Big Rock. Although this trail seems truly wild, you'll hear the sounds of big trucks in the distance. Rejoin the double-track at kilometre 3.59 (mile 2.15) after a wet stretch of mud holes and corduroy. In a race, this next stretch would be the passing lane, wide and gradually climbing. The logging road becomes rougher and continues straight at kilometre 4.09 (mile 2.45), while the trail forks off to the left onto a single-track. This stretch is a little rougher as it drops down a small depression before climbing back up to the logging road at kilometre 4.41 (mile 2.65). Turn left onto the deeply rutted and eroded double-track. The trail levels out at kilometre 4.78 (mile 2.87), just before the turnoff to Pete's Power line. While the main trail continues beyond the power line junction, it gets much rougher, and most cyclists have taken this right-hand turn. Pete's Power line is a rough, rutted, single-track climb. Rejoin the logging road at kilometre 5.41 (mile 3.25), and once again head left. Follow the power lines and take the right-hand turn at the junction at kilometre 6.13 (mile 3.68). As you climb this single-track, Gully Sucks, part of the downhill course, crosses almost immediately. Stay straight and continue climbing until you meet a small rock cairn at elevation 400 m (1,312 feet) that marks the high point of the ride. To continue on the cross-country route, head down the single-track to the left of the logging road. This is a narrow, rooted, rough single-track through some arbutus and Oregon grape. Drop down some rock steps at kilometre 6.8 (mile 4.08), followed by a serious drop down a cliff face. Head left, paralleling the cliff, and rejoin the power lines and the logging road at kilometre 7.16 (mile 4.3).

Though the downhill race course continues down the logging road, the main cross-country course turns left at the junction with the logging road and then right down onto the double-track of Fern Gully at kilometre 7.22 (mile 4.33). Stay to the left, following the power lines while a rough single-track continues straight. A stick has been placed into the centre of a rock cairn to mark this junction. For the next stretch, ignore any trail that diverts you from the power lines until the trail winds to the right at kilometre 7.57 (mile 4.54). It rapidly becomes a steep downhill slalom and climbs over a log pyramid at kilometre 7.81 (mile 4.69). This is an expert downhill, with lots of challenging obstacles, sudden drops, and sharp corners.

Cross the logging road at kilometre 8.2 (mile 4.92) and drop into the Enchanted Forest. Drop down a short, treacherous downhill with very loose gravel; follow it as it winds to the right and rejoins the fire road at kilometre 8.96 (mile 5.38).

Scream down the fire road, and pass the point at which you originally entered the Macmillan-Bloedel land at kilometre 10.38 (mile 6.23). Return to your vehicle at kilometre 11.2 (mile 6.7).

RIDE 72 · Top Bridge Mountain Bike Park

AT A GLANCE

Length/configuration: This is a rolling network of trails offering options to vary your length. The route described here totals 3.63 km (2.18 miles) and essentially circumnavigates the network. You can add distance by playing on the inner loops

Aerobic difficulty: Moderate. The network has short climbs and rolling descents

Technical difficulty: This is a perfect network for intermediate riders looking to hone their skills. The trails are challenging but moderate

Scenery: While the network remains largely in the trees, it offers limited views of the Englishman River and the busy highway that borders the trails

Special comments: This is a great network for training as it is generally clean, but it includes some moderate technical terrain and a few expert rides

This network of trails, built and maintained by the Arrowsmith Mountain Bike Club, is an excellent example of what can be accomplished when mountain bike clubs work with local authorities. The trail system is small but well developed. The entire network can be covered in a little over an hour, but it's not difficult to play for several hours.

The trails are generally moderately difficult. Trails like Reefer Ridge, Big Log, and Tower of Power are quite easy, while Highway to Hell and Zigzag offer some tight switchbacks. The sheer drops down B Trail and Full Ragin' are for solid expert riders only. When you've had enough riding, head down to the river for a dip.

This is *not* a trail network for wandering around and cutting trails to find random lines. It's located adjacent to an active firing range. When I was there, the Royal Canadian Mounted Police were out in force, blasting away at targets — luckily, none resembled mountain bikers.

General location: Parksville.

Elevation change: Limited.

Season: Year-round.

Services: All services are available in Parksville.

Hazards: Because this is a network of trails, rather than a single ride, the hazards vary with your choices. Most of the rides are well groomed, with few logs and other obstacles. A few rides, like Zigzag and Highway to Hell, have very

RIDE 72 · Top Bridge Mountain Bike Park

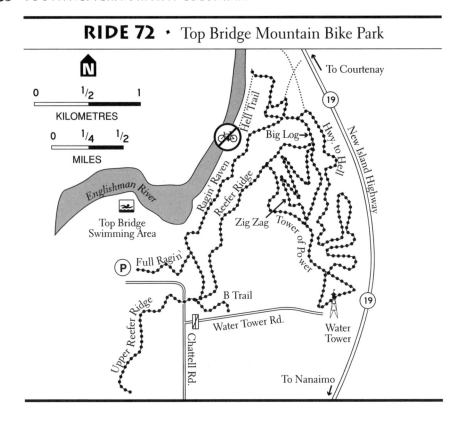

tight switchbacks. Full Ragin' is a serious drop with a gradient that would terrify any nonexpert.

Don't forget, there's an active shooting range right next to the network, so *don't* go exploring off the trails. The main network is contained between the water tower road, the Englishman River, and the Island Highway—don't stray.

Rescue index: The parking lot provides access to a popular day-use area, so there will often be other people around. The trail network is also quite popular, so you will probably see other riders. In an emergency, pop over to the shooting range (staying on the main road, of course) for assistance.

Land status: Municipal land.

Maps: The NTS 1:50,000 topographic map for this trail is 92 F/1. The map in this book shows the trails in more detail than the topographic map. The Arrowsmith Mountain Bike Club has produced a map on which the one in this book is based. Paper copies are available at local bike shops.

Finding the trail: Traveling north on the Island Highway (Highway 19), in Parksville, take the exit for the Kaye Road weight scales. As you take the exit, take an immediate right onto Chattell Road. Follow this road as it winds its way to its terminus at the trailhead.

The Top Bridge
Mountain Bike Park
offers a well-designed
network of intermediate-
level rides.

Sources of additional information: Contact the Arrowsmith Mountain Bike Club at:

c/o Arrowsmith Mountain Cycle
674 East Island Highway
Parksville, B.C. V9P 1T8
(250) 248-5575

Notes on the trail: Although this is just one potential route, it represents a good cross-section of the network. From the parking lot, ride up the good gravel road and turn left at a trailhead just before the water tower road. This circuit show-cases much of the network. As you enter the trails, take the first left and roll your way along Ragin' Raven. This moderate single-track passes the upper junction for Full Ragin', a gnarly single-track that drops straight down the fall line and spits you out at the parking lot. Beyond this junction, it rolls to the right and winds above the Englishman River. Pass another junction, this time with the Bridge Trail, at kilometre 0.69 (mile 0.41). Ragin' Raven winds to the right to become Lower Reefer Ridge. The trail meanders to the right and passes the base of Highway to Hell before meeting a more prominent three-way junction at kilometre 0.96 (mile 0.58). At this junction you can turn to the right and continue on Lower Reefer Ridge, go left and climb Big Log, or climb the narrow switchbacks of Zigzag in the middle. The preferred option is to continue on Lower Reefer Ridge to the right as it begins to parallel Ragin' Raven, and then turn left onto Tower of Power at kilometre 1.08 (mile 0.65). This gives you a more reasonable climb toward the water tower, but also gives you the option of dropping onto the tight switchbacks of Zigzag or the more direct drop of Big Log. If you continue climbing to the water tower, you have the option of the winding drop down Highway to Hell. Pass the tower at kilometre 1.5 (mile 0.9) after a pleasant climb. Wind around three long spaghetti switchbacks, which approach the highway and then swing around to move away. Rejoin Lower Reefer Ridge at kilometre 2.64 (mile 1.58). If you stay to the right and wind around Ragin' Raven until kilometre 3.4 (mile 2.04), you have the option of the sharp drop down Full Ragin', or you can stay straight until the road access at kilometre 3.44 (mile 2.06).

Turning right to drop down Full Ragin' is for solid experts only. It is a fall-line drop with no forgiveness. Expect to get ejected from the saddle at least once. If you are not sure of your ability, avoid it. It is so steep it's even challenging just to push down. Meet the parking lot at kilometre 3.63 (mile 2.18).

RIDE 73 · Monster Mile

AT A GLANCE

Length/configuration: 2.32-km (1.45-mile) point-to-point

Aerobic difficulty: This ride is straight downhill and requires little fitness — just nerves of steel

Technical difficulty: This is an extreme downhill for solid expert riders only

Scenery: From the summit, the views of the surrounding ranges are quite exceptional

Special comments: This trail is designed to beat up the best racers, and as such is strictly an expert proposition

This trail begins at the top of Mount Washington Ski Hill and literally drops straight down the mountain to the base in 2.32 km (1.45 miles). To access this madness, you can roll your way for a few kilometres up the gravel access road or hop on the new Eagle Express Quad Chairlift for an easier approach.

RIDE 73 · Monster Mile

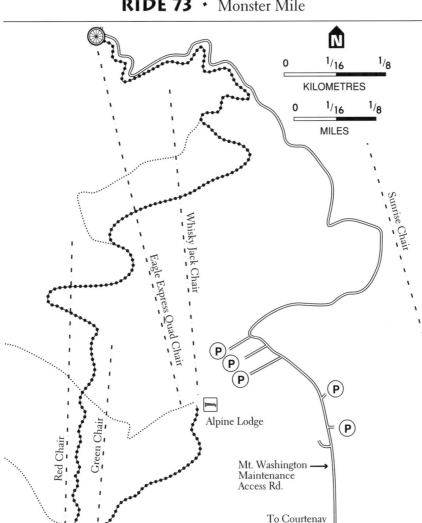

Using the chairlift, you can ride it as many times as it takes to trash your body sufficiently.

For solid riders, this trail is nirvana. It offers effortless elevation gain followed by solid downhill riding. The ability to hone your skills by continual mileage on a familiar course is one way to become a great downhiller. Expect bruises, but in between the pain, what a rush!

General location: Northeast of Courtenay.

Elevation change: From the base at 1,175 m (3,855 feet) you have the choice of winding the access road for approximately 2 km (1.2 miles) to the top of the Eagle Express Quad Chair at approximately 1,589 m (5,215 feet). The total change in elevation is 480 m (1,574 feet).

Season: June through September.

Services: All services are available in the communities of Courtenay and Comox.

Hazards: This is serious downhill country. The line is sheer, unforgiving, and lined with immovable trees. This is a ride for experts only.

Rescue index: This is a managed ski hill with staff working the lodge all summer, so help is never very far away.

Land status: Private land.

Maps: The NTS 1:50,000 topographic map for this area is 92 F/11 Forbidden Plateau and the lower part of 92 F/14. The best map (still not all that great) is a photocopied map of the ski runs with the trails marked. It is available at the ski hill or by contacting them at the address listed below.

Finding the trail: Follow the Island Highway (Highway 19) north to Courtenay. Turn left on 17th Street, and right on Willemar Avenue. Turn left after a few blocks onto Lake Trail Road and watch for signs for the Comox Logging Road. Turn right and follow this road as it swings to the left past Marsden Road. Take the next right and follow signs to Mount Washington Ski Area.

Sources of additional information:

> Mount Washington Ski Resort
> Box 3069
> Courtenay, B.C. V9N 5N3
> (250) 338-1386 or (604) 657-3275 (Vancouver)
> (250) 338-7295 fax

Notes on the trail: Once you attain the summit—most often on the Eagle Express Quad Chairlift—follow the access road down until the signs beckon you off to the right. This begins the downhill run; after a short snaking section, you traverse the mountain, cross under the Whiskey Jack and then the Eagle Express Quad Chair, then follow a series of three winding switchbacks. After the final turn, the trail takes to the fall line in earnest and heads for the final drop to the base of the Red Chair. Once you bottom out, head left and follow the access road up to the lodge.

RIDE 74 · Mount Washington — Single-Track

AT A GLANCE

Length/configuration: 2.32-km (1.4-mile) point-to-point

Aerobic difficulty: With chairlift access, this trail is aerobically quite easy as it is all downhill

Technical difficulty: Expert-level downhill, only slightly less intimidating than the Monster Mile

Scenery: The views stretch to the mountains of Strathcona Park and the waters of Lake Helen Mackenzie in the distance

Special comments: Like the Monster Mile, this trail is reserved for experts only

Though the views on this expert downhill are spectacular, stretching to the many peaks of Strathcona Provincial Park and Lake Helen Mackenzie, you won't have many opportunities to appreciate them. A lapse of concentration on this 2.32-km (1.4-mile) run will probably leave you airborne. This ride has a dual character—downhill, technical screaming, and magnificent views—just be sure to stop before you try to enjoy the panorama.

The ride follows much of the Monster Mile course, but the upper section of the trail takes a higher, slightly easier line. Along the lower section, you rejoin the Monster Mile and continue to the base. Like the Monster Mile, it is strictly for expert riders who are comfortable with steep fall-line drops with roots and numerous sudden drops.

General location: Northeast of Courtenay.

Elevation change: From the base at 1,175 m (3,855 feet) you have the choice of winding the access road for approximately 2 km (1.2 miles) to the top of the Eagle Express Quad Chair at approximately 1,589 m (5,215 feet). The total change in elevation is 480 m (1,574 feet).

Season: June through September.

Services: All services are available in the communities of Courtenay and Comox.

Hazards: This is serious downhill country. The line is sheer, unforgiving, and lined with immovable trees. This is a ride for experts only.

Rescue index: This is a managed ski hill with staff working the lodge all summer, so help is never very far away.

RIDE 74 · Mount Washington–Single-Track

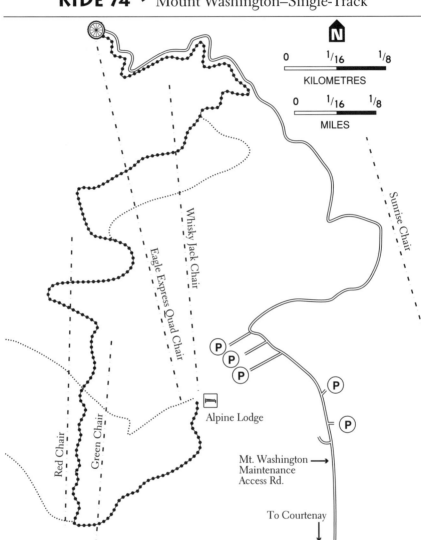

Land status: Private land.

Maps: The NTS 1:50,000 topographic map for this area is 92 F/11 Forbidden Plateau and the lower part of 92 F/14. The best map (still not great) is a photocopied map of the ski runs with the trails marked. It is available at the ski hill or at the address listed below.

Finding the trail: Follow the Island Highway (Highway 19) north to Courtenay. Turn left on 17th Street, then right on Willemar Avenue. Turn left after a few blocks onto Lake Trail Road and watch for signs for Comox Logging Road. Turn right and follow this road as it swings to the left past Marsden Road. Take the next right and follow the signs to Mount Washington Ski Area.

Sources of additional information:

Mount Washington Ski Resort
Box 3069
Courtenay, B.C. V9N 5N3
(250) 338-1386 or (604) 657-3275 (Vancouver)
(250) 338-7295 fax

Notes on the trail: Once you attain the summit—most often on the Eagle Express Quad Chairlift—follow the access road down until the signs beckon you off to the right. This begins the downhill run. The Monster Mile leaves the single-track by taking a sharp left switchback after the first winding downhill. For the single-track, stay straight at this junction and begin to traverse across the mountain and cross under the Whiskey Jack and then the Eagle Express Quad Chair. Beyond the lifts, the trail makes a sudden drop down the fall line to the access road. Head left and follow it to the marked junction for the Monster Mile, rejoining this ride as it drops straight down the fall line to the base of the Red and Green Chairs. Once you bottom out, head left and follow the access road up to the lodge.

RIDE 75 · Mount Washington—Discovery Trail

AT A GLANCE

Length/configuration: Approximately 1.75-km (1.05-mile) loop

Aerobic difficulty: Moderate climbing mixed with some pleasant downhill

Technical difficulty: Intermediate-level riding on wide track

Scenery: Some pleasant views to the southern peaks of Strathcona Provincial Park

Special comments: The only nonexpert option on Mount Washington

If you're not an expert downhiller, Mount Washington has one ride that still gives you a taste of the area while foregoing the extreme fall-line drops. This trail drops from the village in a 1.75-km (1.05-mile) loop. The loop stays near the base of the mountain, following a wide double-track across numerous ski runs

RIDE 75 · Mount Washington–Discovery Trail

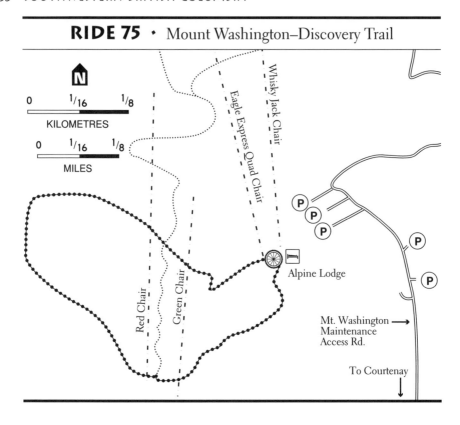

and under the Green and Eagle Express Quad Chairs. After crossing another three runs, it drops down to the left and comes out at the base of the Red Chair. A quick uphill roll will bring you back to your car.

Along the ride, periodic views to the south focus on the many peaks of Strathcona Provincial Park, along with Mount Brooks and Mount Elma. The ski hills are also a haven for wildflowers, including valerian and false hellebore.

General location: Northeast of Courtenay.

Elevation change: This ride has very limited elevation changes.

Season: June through September.

Services: All services are available in the communities of Courtenay and Comox.

Hazards: This is a moderate trail with some loose rocks and a few other obstacles.

Rescue index: This is a managed ski hill with staff working the lodge all summer, so help is never very far away.

Land status: Private land.

Maps: The NTS 1:50,000 topographic map for this area is 92 F/11 Forbidden Plateau and the lower part of 92 F/14. The best map (still not great) is a photocopied map of the ski runs with the trails marked. It is available at the ski hill or at the address listed below.

Finding the trail: Follow the Island Highway (Highway 19) north to Courtenay. Turn left on 17th Street, then right on Willemar Avenue. Turn left after a few blocks onto Lake Trail Road and watch for signs for Comox Logging Road. Turn right and follow this road as it swings to the left past Marsden Road. Take the next right and follow signs to Mount Washington Ski Area.

Sources of additional information:

> Mount Washington Ski Resort
> Box 3069
> Courtenay, B.C. V9N 5N3
> (250) 338-1386 or (604) 657-3275 (Vancouver)
> (250) 338 7295 fax

Notes on the trail: Head to the far side of the day lodge, and Discovery Trail begins to drop on a wide double-track. Crossing beneath the Green and then the Eagle Express Quad Chairlifts, it continues across the base of the mountain, crossing three more downhill runs. Following the third run, the trail drops down to the left, eventually reemerging at the base of the Red Chair. From here, follow the access road back up to the day lodge.

RIDE 76 · B-21/Boston Main

AT A GLANCE

Length/configuration: 5.53-km (3.32-mile) point-to-point or an 11.06-km (6.64-mile) out-and-back

Aerobic difficulty: The trail climbs 440 m (1,443 feet) in just 4.81 km (2.89 miles)

Technical difficulty: Although double-track for the entire distance, several sections are badly eroded

Scenery: Some pleasant views of the rolling landscape above Comox Lake open up as you near the top of the ride

Special comments: This trail is most often used to access some of the other local single-track and is less commonly ridden in its entirety

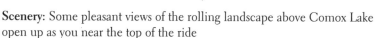

If you enjoy climbing along a wide fire road and then screaming your way back down, then this is the ride for you. It includes a moderate 440-m (1,443-foot) climb over 4.81 km (2.89 miles). At this point, a short spur trail gives you access

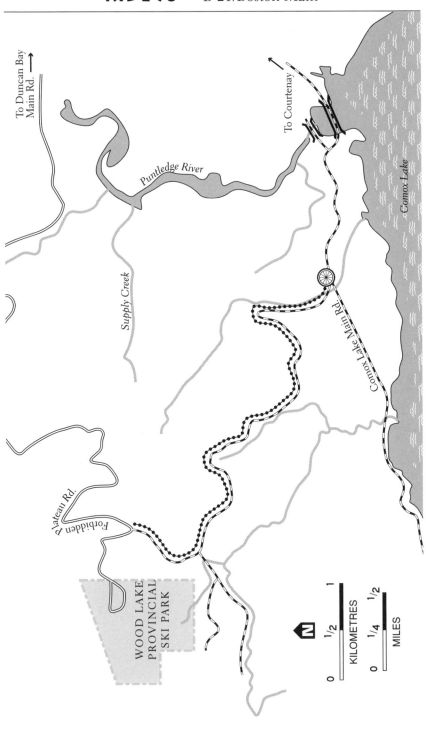

to the Forbidden Plateau Ski Hill for a total point-to-point distance of 5.53 km (3.32 miles).

The climbing also offers access to many locally defined single-track descents, all of which fall in the expert category. Many local riders use this trail as a starting point for these descents. One ride branching off from this climb is known as Arbutus, which drops to the left at kilometre 1.74 (mile 1.04). Other expert rides, like Bic's, Puntledge Plunge, and Monkey's Challenge, drop to the right. These are solid expert rides requiring local knowledge. Don't even think of taking one of these side trails without stopping at a local bike shop for advice and maps.

The mosquitoes will find you during the climb, but the trail is rimmed with vanilla leaf, a plant traditionally used to repel these determined bloodsuckers. Delicate tiger lilies with their tiny, nodding, orange heads add colour to the ride.

General location: Comox Lake west of Courtenay.

Elevation change: The trail climbs 440 m (1,443 feet) in 4.81 km (2.89 miles).

Season: May through September.

Services: All services are available in Courtenay.

Hazards: The trail is wide double-track, but several sections have been badly washed out. These make for a tricky ascent and an even more challenging descent. In addition, many of the culverts have been partially eroded, leading to potential ejections if you aren't prepared. While many spur trails leave this main route, it is critical that you get good directions from local bike shops before attempting them. This is big country, and you need a clear idea of where you're heading.

Rescue index: On weekends this is a popular ride, especially on the lower sections where locals stage for other single-tracks branching off the main trail. On many days, though, you may not meet anyone. Be prepared to return to the main road to get assistance. This is also a logging road and may be deserted.

Land status: Combination of Crown land and undeveloped private land.

Maps: The NTS 1:50,000 topographic map for this trail is 92 F/11 Forbidden Plateau.

Finding the trail: From Courtenay, follow 17th Street to Willemar Avenue. Turn right on Willemar and left on Lake Trail Road. After the power lines, make a right turn onto Miromar Road. Turn left as Miromar Road ends on Lake Trail Road. Stay left as this road forks after 1.3 km (0.78 mile). Soon you will see mile markers, for instance COLAKE MAIN CL-1 for the 1-km (0.6-mile) mark. Stay on this road until you see Comox Lake come into view on the left. Cross over the Puntledge River after rolling 9.9 km (5.94 miles) since turning onto Willemar Avenue. Continue along the gravel for an additional 2.4 km (1.44 miles) until you see a gravel road climb to the right just beyond the CL-7 sign. Park on the shoulder.

Sources of additional information:

Blacks Cycles
274A Anderton Road
Comox, B.C. V9M 1Y2
(250) 339-7011

Notes on the trail: Begin climbing the wide gravel from a starting elevation of 195 m (640 feet); the climbing is moderate but steady. Numerous single-tracks branch off this route as you climb. They are mentioned here simply to describe their location for other days' riding. They are all expert drops requiring solid skills and local knowledge. Be sure to stop at a local bike shop before taking any of these forks. For B-21, though, ignore these trails and continue on the double-track.

The first single-track forks to the right at kilometre 0.72 (mile 0.43). A second single-track branches to the right at kilometre 1.45 (mile 0.87). Beyond this trail, a culvert has partially washed out at 1.54 km (0.92 miles). The unsigned Arbutus Trail leaves from the left at 1.74 km (1.04 miles), where several rocks have been arranged to look like a false grave. Beyond this junction, the climbing continues and you'll pass several partially eroded culverts.

The forks continue with another single-track heading to the right at kilometre 2.66 (mile 1.6). There is a post with the numbers "66" visible. This is the Puntledge Plunge and drops down stiff gradient toward the creek bed. The elevation at this junction is 430 m (1,410 feet). Beyond this junction, the climbing becomes much rougher, with some very loose rocks and badly eroded areas. This poor stretch ends at kilometre 3.05 (mile 1.83), and the surface becomes smooth double-track again. A final single-track branches to the right at kilometre 3.54 (mile 2.12) and elevation 500 m (1,640 feet). The trail is marked with orange paint sprayed on one of the trees. It's locally known as Monkey's Challenge and zigzags its way down to join Puntledge Plunge. Stay straight on the double-track, and soon the trail becomes a badly eroded boulder field for 0.25 km (0.15 mile). As it improves again, you reach a fork in the gravel at kilometre 4.81 (mile 2.89). Take the right fork, and the gravel winds to the right past an old clear-cut with plenty of pink fireweed blooming. Meet the road to Forbidden Plateau Ski Area at kilometre 5.53 (mile 3.32). Either retrace your steps or arrange a vehicle pickup at the ski hill.

RIDE 77 · Tomato Creek

AT A GLANCE

Length/configuration: 3.83-km (2.3-mile) loop using the Comox Lake Road

Aerobic difficulty: Moderate, with a few short, sharp climbs

Technical difficulty: The trail is a solid intermediate ride with several small verticals and a few challenging ups and downs

Scenery: This ride crests a small knoll above Comox Lake with excellent views

Special comments: Of the rides in this area, this one has the best mix of technical fun and excellent views

This ride combines a rolling mix of intermediate challenge with the best views of any of the Comox Lake rides in this book. While the loop is short—only 3.83 km (2.3 miles)—it is the kind of ride that will make you want to stop, build a cabin, and stay forever. It leaves the road at the west end of a lava rock knoll, over which the trail then climbs, bouncing up and over fun, technical stretches of slickrock. As you crest the summit of this small outcrop, you achieve one of the premier vantage points over the lake. Its beautiful blue waters seem that much more pleasant when contrasted with the reddish, peeling bark of the arbutus trees rimming the slickrock.

The next section of the trail varies between technical ups and downs and great views. It's the kind of ride that intermediate cyclists will do over and over. Heck, it would be worth bringing a picnic and just hanging out near the best views.

General location: Comox Lake west of Courtenay.

Elevation change: The trail climbs approximately 100 m (368 feet) before dropping back down to the valley bottom.

Season: May through September.

Services: All services are available in Courtenay.

Hazards: The trail has numerous short verticals as it climbs over the lava rock outcrops. An eroded downhill chute is followed by a few technical switchbacks.

Rescue index: While the trail is accessed from a logging road, the beach at the east end of the lake is quite popular. In case of injuries or other problems, make your way out to the road and begin heading east until you reach assistance.

RIDE 77 · Tomato Creek

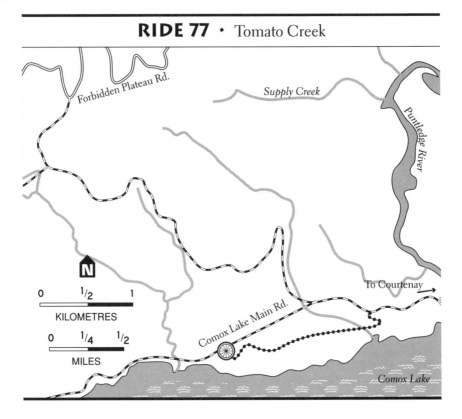

Land status: Combination of Crown land and undeveloped private land.

Maps: The NTS 1:50,000 topographic map for this trail is 92 F/11 Forbidden Plateau.

Finding the trail: From Courtenay, follow 17th Street to Willemar Avenue. Turn right on Willemar and left on Lake Trail Road. After the power lines, turn right onto Miromar Road. Turn left as Miromar Road ends on Lake Trail Road. Stay left as this road forks after 1.3 km (0.78 mile). Soon you will see mile markers, for instance COLAKE MAIN CL-1 for the 1-km (0.6-mile) mark. Stay on this road until you see Comox Lake come into view on the left. Cross over the Puntledge River after rolling 9.9 km (5.94 miles) since turning onto Willemar Avenue. Continue driving down the gravel for an additional 2.5 km (1.5 miles) to the actual trailhead. You can park anywhere along this stretch—the trail uses the road to make a loop. There are several pullouts along the left as you approach CL-7 and the B-21 trailhead. To find the proper trailhead, continue climbing beyond the B-21 trailhead, and climb over the next hill and descend the other side. Watch for the CL-8 sign. Just beyond this, you'll see Tomato Creek head into the bush on the left.

Tomato Creek crests
a small knoll above
Comox Lake.

Sources of additional information:

Blacks Cycles
274A Anderton Road
Comox, B.C. V9M 1Y2
(250) 339-7011

Notes on the trail: As the trail heads into the bush, it makes a quick switchback to the left to climb up a rock escarpment. Before long, the views to the lake begin to open up, and you grind your way up an igneous outcrop at kilometre 0.46 (mile 0.28). The main climbing ends at kilometre 0.57 (mile 0.34) as you crest another lava boulder. The next stretch is rolling and pleasant before taking two large rideable steps down at kilometre 0.86 (mile 0.52). Soon the trail begins dropping off the bench over some intermediate to expert sections with a few verticals and sharp switchbacks. At kilometre 1.04 (mile 0.62), there are several drops followed by a rutted chute.

After a breathtaking view, begin a short climb followed by a technical descent down a rutted, rocky set of five switchbacks. The switchbacks end as another trail joins in from the left at kilometre 1.58 (mile 0.95). Beyond this, the trail rapidly widens into a double-track as it makes two sharp left turns in succession. As it joins a wide access road at kilometre 1.77 (mile 1.06), stay left at this **T** intersection. Soon the trail ahead climbs steeply, but a right turn will bring you back out to the road at kilometre 2.37 (mile 1.42). Unfortunately, you still need to climb up the steep gravel back to your vehicle. Turn left and return to your vehicle at approximately kilometre 3.83 (mile 2.3).

RIDE 78 · Bevan Trail

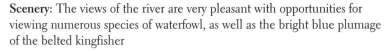

AT A GLANCE

Length/configuration: 8.46-km (5.08-mile) point-to-point

Aerobic difficulty: Moderate winding trail with limited changes in elevation

Technical difficulty: This is an intermediate ride with some wet and rooted sections

Scenery: The views of the river are very pleasant with opportunities for viewing numerous species of waterfowl, as well as the bright blue plumage of the belted kingfisher

Special comments: This is a great ride that mixes some terrific scenery with a little route finding

The sound of the kingfisher as it flies along the river is common along this trail, as is the smell of salmon on their annual upstream pilgrimage. This 8.46-km (5.08-mile) point-to-point takes you along the Puntledge River from Dam Park on Comox Lake to the river's junction with Duncan Bay Main Road. Along the way, you have many views of the lazy river's course, along with three main options for a relaxing rest at river's edge.

Factor into this pleasing ride a fair mix of route finding along with plenty of unsigned junctions. It requires confidence to wind your way along a trail with few indications that you're heading in the right direction. Generally, though, if you trust your nose, follow these directions, and backtrack a bit when necessary, you'll make your way just fine. The end result is a pleasant river roll that leaves urbanization behind and makes the return to civilization a bit of an accomplishment.

General location: Comox Lake west of Courtenay.

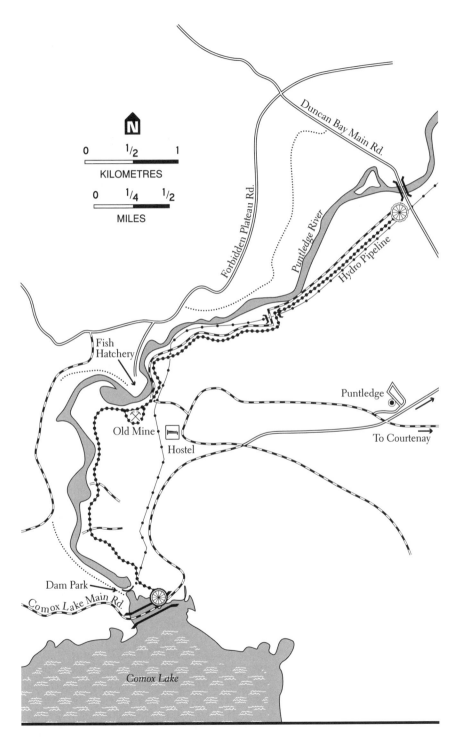

A rickety boardwalk on Bevan Trail takes the rider through a muddy stretch.

Elevation change: The trail has very small changes in elevation.

Season: May through September.

Services: All services are available in Courtenay.

Hazards: Perhaps the major challenge on this trail, like many in this area, is route finding. There are many junctions, few signs, and a constant sense of "hmm, am I on the right trail?" Be sure to bring a compass and a topographic map.

Other challenges include some rooted and muddy stretches with a multitude of bridges of varying quality.

Rescue index: Though the trail is popular, you may not meet anyone en route. You will probably need to either turn back to the trailhead or continue to the hostel if you need help.

Land status: Combination of Crown land and undeveloped private land.

Maps: The NTS 1:50,000 topographic map for this trail is 92 F/11 Forbidden Plateau.

Finding the trail: From Courtenay, follow 17th Street to Willemar Avenue. Turn right on Willemar and left on Lake Trail Road. After the power lines, turn right onto Miromar Road. Turn left as Miromar Road ends on Lake Trail Road. Stay left as this road forks after 1.3 km (0.78 mile). Soon you will see mile markers, for instance COLAKE MAIN CL-1 for the 1-km (0.6-mile) mark. Stay on this road until you see Comox Lake come into view on the left. Cross over the Puntledge River after rolling 9.9 km (5.94 miles) since turning onto Willemar Avenue. Immediately turn right into the day-use area at Dam Park. Park here. From Dam Park, head back out toward the road, turn left, and cross over the bridge. On the opposite side, you'll see a yellow-gated double-track heading into the woods. This is the trail.

Sources of additional information:

Blacks Cycles
274A Anderton Road
Comox, B.C. V9M 1Y2
(250) 339-7011

Notes on the trail: Once past the gate, follow the wide double-track until you see a sign that reads CAUTION, DAM AND PENSTOCK INTAKES DOWNSTREAM 3.7 KM. This sign is at kilometre 0.19 (mile 0.11). Beyond this, at kilometre 0.32 (mile 0.19), the trail reaches a mound of dirt. The natural tendency is to power your way over the mound and continue—but don't. The trail heads into the bushes to the left of the mound to become a single-track. This narrow single-track follows the river. Stay straight as another single-track joins in from the right at kilometre 0.7 (mile 0.42). Beyond this junction, the trail takes on a darker character, with a much rougher line and more roots and ruts. It drops toward the river until it becomes a wet, mucky rootfest. After crossing a makeshift wooden bridge, followed by a short stretch of corduroy, the trail improves and becomes a wonderful technical challenge. After leaving the river behind, the trail dries up significantly, but the root bounce continues. The trail turns hard to the left and descends to a patch of skunk cabbage before crossing a succession of three bridges (of varying quality) between kilometre 1.41 and 1.91 (mile 0.85 to 1.15).

The first indication that you are on the correct route comes at kilometre 2.04 (mile 1.22) when a piece of white cardboard with a black arrow beckons you to the left at a trail junction. Follow this sign and drop down toward the river with another bridge. Although there is a junction beyond the bridge, both trails quickly rejoin the main route. The next stretch has periodic views toward the winding river. At kilometre 2.39 (mile 1.43), the trail comes out at the river at a swimming hole. An access road comes down to the river at this point. The main trail heads to the right up this access road approximately 5 m (16 feet) before heading left into the bushes again.

The next stretch takes you over several rickety bridges and into a meadow. While the meadow is pleasant, it's also easy to lose the trail. Stay to the left at the far end of the meadow and you'll see the trail continuing. Beyond the meadow, cross a narrow plank bridge and continue until the trail joins an access road coming in from the right at kilometre 2.69 (mile 1.61). Follow this wide road as it descends to the river to a pleasant spot. One of the trees has NO FISHING spray-painted on it. Continue on the double-track as it becomes a narrower carpet of needles. At kilometre 3.34 (mile 2), head off to the right on a single-track and leave the river behind as it heads into a muddy stretch before a large marsh pond.

This next stretch circumnavigates the pond. Though the trail becomes a bit more difficult to follow, you can almost follow the mud holes. As you meet one that seems impassable, look to your right. There's an access route that bypasses it on a small bridge (well, two logs with a few cross boards). Beyond the pond, the trail crests a small rise followed by a log jump. At a junction at kilometre 4.15 (mile 2.49), stay left around a stump. Although the trail will backtrack for a short distance, this route takes you past an old mine site and numerous old building foundations. Beyond the mine site, the trail makes another left turn and rejoins the river at kilometre 4.45 (mile 2.67). Across the river, you can see the fish hatchery. Cross a small plank bridge and meet with the hostel access road at kilometre 4.54 (mile 2.72).

At the junction, there is a sign made of a white arrow on a blue sheet of paper. Head left, and follow the wide double-track until it passes a small metal shed. Soon after the shed, it narrows to return to single-track and finally meets the powerhouse on the river at kilometre 4.93 (mile 2.96). It quickly widens and becomes a gravel access road. Stay on this road until kilometre 6.56 (mile 3.94), at which point the access road crosses over the dam and swings right on the opposite side. Ride this wide road, pass through a yellow gate at kilometre 8.36 (mile 5.02), and join Duncan Bay Main Road at kilometre 8.46 (mile 5.08).

RIDE 79 · Nymph Falls

AT A GLANCE

Length/configuration: 2.94-km (1.76-mile) point-to-point

Aerobic difficulty: Moderate challenge with little change in elevation

Technical difficulty: The trail was designed as a fun technical challenge. Most of the obstacles can be bypassed by advanced beginners.

Scenery: It's a rolling trail through the woods with several pleasant, wooded environments

Special comments: This is a fun trail through a carpeted wood, down into a darker, wetter landscape, and over numerous (not to mention creative) man-made obstacles

VANCOUVER

ISLAND

RIDE 79 · Nymph Falls

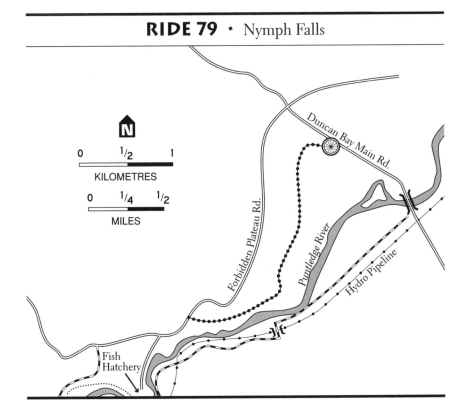

This ride is a great roller coaster through a combination of open deciduous forest and dark, damp, cedar-hemlock woods. It rolls along the Puntledge River, over several bridges of varying quality, and over a trail with a unique collection of man-made and natural obstacles. Climb over the back of an abandoned car, cross a bridge made of log cookies, and roll past an old toilet bowl mounted on an elevated wooden stump. This is B.C. backcountry, a place where anything can (and does) occur. The trail is under redevelopment as the old trail is being rerouted to stay farther away from the river. This means that the route may be a bit more nebulous over the next little while, but this description should hold for the near future. Be sure to follow any new signs that are erected and enjoy the magic.

General location: Comox Lake west of Courtenay.

Elevation change: The trail rolls along the river, so the changes in elevation are minimal. Short uphill rolls are countered by downhills, all amounting to little net change.

Season: May through September.

Services: All services are available in Courtenay.

Hazards: This trail includes the usual assortment of roots, log drops, and rickety bridges, but it adds the opportunity to climb over parts of an old car and other man-made challenges. Most of these obstacles can be bypassed if they look too

Skunk cabbage lines the ride on Nymph Falls Trail.

intimidating. Check with local bike shops on current routing; the trail was under redevelopment at the time of writing.

Rescue index: The trail begins and ends along wide, well-traveled pavement. In case of emergency, decide whether to return or continue, and flag down a vehicle on the roadway.

Land status: Combination of Crown land and undeveloped private land.

Maps: The NTS 1:50,000 topographic map for this trail is 92 F/11 Forbidden Plateau.

Finding the trail: From Courtenay, follow 17th Street to Willemar Avenue. Turn right on Willemar and left on Lake Trail Road. After the power lines, make a right turn onto Marsden Road and a left as it ends in the industrial yard. Roll through the yard, and take the first right onto Duncan Bay Main Road. As this road crosses the Puntledge River, watch for a yellow gate to the left just before meeting Forbidden Plateau Road. Park at this gate.

Sources of additional information:

Blacks Cycles
274A Anderton Road
Comox, B.C. V9M 1Y2
(250) 339-7011

Notes on the trail: To begin the trail, avoid the temptation to go past the yellow gate. The trail begins above the bank to the right of the gate. Climb up this embankment and roll your way along some pleasant single-track. Stay left as the trail joins a double-track, and continue on this wide, smooth path past a big framed shelter. Beyond the shelter at kilometre 0.38 (mile 0.23), the trail narrows to become a single-track again, winding through the woods to a bridge at kilometre 0.69 (mile 0.41). Beyond the bridge, there are a few log hops and a few rooted sections, but generally fast riding. After the first kilometre (0.6 mile), the trail begins to get rougher. Stay left at this point, then go right at a signed junction at kilometre 1.2 (mile 0.72). Beyond this junction, the trail becomes much rougher, and the route becomes a little more nebulous. At a junction at kilometre 1.4 (mile 0.84), the tendency is to head left, but they are rerouting the trail to the right. Apparently the old trail will be running through a small park, so the mountain bike route is being redeveloped. Soon after this junction, the back end of an old car has been turned into an interesting obstacle. Climb over a big log at kilometre 1.63 (mile 0.98) and soon begin turning back toward the river. Two bridges over the next stretch take you past some wonderful examples of skunk cabbage, with its leaves extending over 1 m (3.28 feet) in length. Cross over another bridge made out of log cookies and over a man-made jump. Cross a four-by-four road at kilometre 2.04 (mile 1.22); as you continue, you'll pass an old car door and the remains of a toilet bowl on top of a stump. You never know what you'll find in B.C. backcountry!

After crossing another bridge, stay to the right at a three-way junction and, after several long switchbacks, stay right at two more junctions. Join the road at kilometre 2.94 (mile 1.76). To return to your vehicle, turn right and roll down the wide pavement.

RIDE 80 · Bear's Bait

AT A GLANCE

Length/configuration: 4-km (2.4-mile) point-to-point

Aerobic difficulty: Quite easy with very little change in elevation

Technical difficulty: This trail is generally intermediate single-track with small route-finding challenges

Scenery: Generally within the forest, with few open views

Special comments: This is a short trail, best used as an extension between Nymph Falls and Comox Lake

RIDE 80 · Bear's Bait

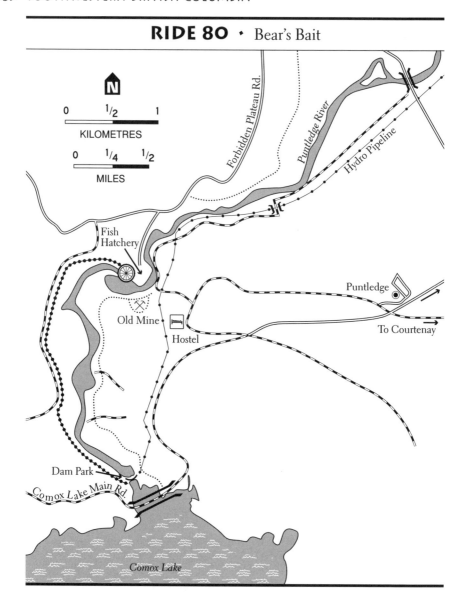

B ear's Bait is a technical bounce that combines some rooted single-track with a bit of logging road. Beginning at the Puntledge River Fish Hatchery, the trail rolls through a rough single-track along the Puntledge River before climbing up toward a meadow choked with thimbleberry. As you emerge on a logging road, it drops down wide gravel before heading back into the woods again. After another technical stretch of single-track and some pretty views along the river, the trail ends at Dam Park at the dam above Comox Lake.

This trail works well as an extension of Nymph Falls. Bear's Bait can also form the final leg of a loop with Bevan and Nymph Falls, beginning and ending at Dam Park.

General location: Comox Lake west of Courtenay.

Elevation change: The trail has little change in elevation.

Season: May through September.

Services: All services are available in Courtenay.

Hazards: The trail has some route-finding challenges, like so many of its neighbours, so be sure to have a topographic map and compass just in case. There are also numerous rutted and rooted sections that will attempt to pound you into submission.

Rescue index: Along this route, you may not meet any other cyclists. Be prepared to decide whether it is quicker to backtrack to the hatchery or continue to the terminus.

Land status: Combination of Crown land and undeveloped private land.

Maps: The NTS 1:50,000 topographic map for this trail is 92 F/11 Forbidden Plateau.

Finding the trail: From Courtenay, follow 17th Street to Willemar Avenue. Turn right on Willemar and left on Lake Trail Road. After the power lines, make a right turn onto Marsden Road and a left as it ends in the industrial yard. Roll through the yard, and take the first right onto Duncan Bay Main Road. Turn left onto Forbidden Plateau Road and left again at the sign for the fish hatchery. The trail leaves to the right of the fence around the hatchery property.

Sources of additional information:

Blacks Cycles
274A Anderton Road
Comox, B.C. V9M 1Y2
(250) 339-7011

Notes on the trail: Follow the narrow single-track along the right side of the fence line and continue as it widens somewhat as the fence ends. Pass a sign for Bear's Bait and persevere as the trail gets rougher at kilometre 0.46 (mile 0.28) as it runs along an embankment by the river. Stay right at a junction at kilometre 0.75 (mile 0.45), and push your way through the dense growth until you meet a logging road at kilometre 0.96 (mile 0.58). Turn left onto the wide gravel and drop down, staying straight as the road winds right at kilometre 1.25 (mile 0.75). As you continue on the logging road, it suddenly makes a hard right and begins climbing. The trail continues straight ahead on a single-track, leaving the cutblock behind. The single-track is good quality, with a few technical and rooted stretches. After crossing a small bridge, you get the first views of the dam and the trail's terminus. Finish at the dam at approximately kilometre 4 (mile 2.4).

APPENDIX:
METRIC CONVERSION

Though many of Canada's metric signs and measures include handy conversions for the visiting Yank, it's not something you want to count on—especially out on the trail, where missing a turn can cost you hours of backtracking.

All measurements in this book include both metric and standard values, but just in case, here's a few general conversion tips, plus some examples.

Kilometres and Miles

1 kilometre = 0.62 mile (or about two-thirds of a mile). To convert kilometres to miles, you can approximate by multiplying total kilometres by 0.6. To go back the other way and get kilometres, multiply total miles by 1.6.

Kilometres	Miles
1	0.62
2	1.24
5	3.1
10	6.2
15	9.3
20	12.4

Metres, Yards, and Feet

1 metre = 1.09 yards = 3.28 feet.

Metres	Yards	Feet
1	1.09	3.28
10	10.9	32.8
100	109	328
500	546	1,640
1,000 (1 km)	1,093	3,280

Temperature: Celsius and Fahrenheit

This is the tricky one. Strictly speaking, degrees Celsius = (degrees Fahrenheit minus 32) multiplied by $5/9$. However, unless you have a slide rule in your brain, don't stake your comfort level on your math skills. Below is a handy chart that will let the nonmetrically inclined figure out what Celsius weather forecasts mean.

°Celsius	°Fahrenheit
40	104
35	95
30	86
25	77
20	68
15	59
10	50
5	41
0 (freezing)	32 (freezing)

GLOSSARY

This short list of terms does not contain all the words used by mountain bike enthusiasts when discussing their sport. But it should serve as an introduction to the lingo you'll hear on the trails.

ATB
all-terrain bike; this, like "fat-tire bike," is another name for a mountain bike

ATV
all-terrain vehicle; this usually refers to the loud, fume-spewing three- or four-wheeled motorized vehicles you will not enjoy meeting on the trail—except, of course, if you crash and have to hitch a ride out on one

blaze
a mark on a tree made by chipping away a piece of the bark, usually done to designate a trail; such trails are sometimes described as "blazed"

blind corner
a curve in the road or trail that conceals bikers, hikers, equestrians, and other traffic

blowdown
see "windfall"

bollard
a post (or series of posts) set vertically into the ground which allow pedestrians or cyclists to pass but keep vehicles from entering (wooden bollards are also commonly used to sign intersections)

braided
a braided trail condition results when people attempt to travel around a wet area; networks of interlaced trails can result and are a maintenance headache for trail crews

buffed
used to describe a very smooth trail

Carsonite sign
a small, thin, and flexible fiberglass signpost used to mark roads and trails (often dark brown in color)

catching air	taking a jump in such a way that both wheels of the bike are off the ground at the same time
cattle guard	a grate of parallel steel bars or pipes set at ground level and suspended over a ditch; cows can't cross them (their little feet slip through the openings between the pipes), but pedestrians and vehicles can pass over cattle guards with little difficulty
clean	while this may describe what you and your bike won't be after following many trails, the term is most often used as a verb to denote the action of pedaling a tough section of trail successfully
combination	this type of route may combine two or more configurations; for example, a point-to-point route may integrate a scenic loop or an out-and-back spur midway through the ride; likewise, an out-and-back may have a loop at its farthest point (this configuration looks like a cherry with a stem attached; the stem is the out-and-back, the fruit is the terminus loop); or a loop route may have multiple out-and-back spurs and/or loops to the side; distance for a combination route is for the total distance to complete the ride
cupped	a concave trail; higher on the sides than in the middle; often caused by motorcycles
dab	touching the ground with a foot or hand
deadfall	a tangled mass of fallen trees or branches
decomposed granite	an excellent, fine- to medium-grain, trail and road surface; typically used in native surface road and trail applications (not trucked in); results from the weathering of granite
diversion ditch	a usually narrow, shallow ditch dug across or around a trail; funneling the water in this manner keeps it from destroying the trail
double-track	the dual tracks made by a jeep or other vehicle, with grass, weeds, or rocks between; mountain bikers can ride in either of the tracks, but you will find that whichever one you choose, no matter how many times you change back and forth, the other track will appear to offer smoother travel
dugway	a steep, unpaved, switchbacked descent
endo	flipping end over end
feathering	using a light touch on the brake lever, hitting it lightly many times rather than very hard or locking the brake

four-wheel-drive	this refers to any vehicle with drive-wheel capability on all four wheels (a jeep, for instance, has four-wheel drive as compared with a two-wheel-drive passenger car), or to a rough road or trail that requires four-wheel-drive capability (or a one-wheel-drive mountain bike!) to negotiate it
game trail	the usually narrow trail made by deer, elk, or other game
gated	everyone knows what a gate is, and how many variations exist upon this theme; well, if a trail is described as "gated" it simply has a gate across it; don't forget that the rule is if you find a gate closed, close it behind you; if you find one open, leave it that way
Giardia	shorthand for *Giardia lamblia,* and known as the "back-packer's bane" until we mountain bikers expropriated it; this is a waterborne parasite that begins its life cycle when swallowed, and one to four weeks later has its host (you) bloated, vomiting, shivering with chills, and living in the bathroom; the disease can be avoided by "treating" (puri-fying) the water you acquire along the trail (see "Hitting the Trail" in the Introduction)
gnarly	a term thankfully used less and less these days, it refers to tough trails
graded	refers to a dirt road that has been smoothed out by the use of a wide blade on earth-moving equipment; "blading" gets rid of the teeth-chattering, much-cursed washboards found on so many dirt roads after heavy vehicle use
hammer	to ride very hard
hammerhead	one who rides hard and fast
hardpack	a trail in which the dirt surface is packed down hard; such trails make for good and fast riding, and very painful land-ings; bikers most often use "hardpack" as both a noun and adjective, and "hard-packed" as an adjective only (the grammar lesson will help you when diagramming sen-tences in camp)
hike-a-bike	what you do when the road or trail becomes too steep or rough to remain in the saddle
jeep road, jeep trail	a rough road or trail passable only with four-wheel-drive capability (or a horse or mountain bike)
kamikaze	while this once referred primarily to those Japanese fliers who quaffed a glass of sake, then flew off as human bombs

in suicide missions against U.S. naval vessels, it has more recently been applied to the idiot mountain bikers who, far less honorably, scream down hiking trails, endangering the physical and mental safety of the walking, biking, and equestrian traffic they meet; deck guns were necessary to stop the Japanese kamikaze pilots, but a bike pump or walking staff in the spokes is sufficient for the current-day kamikazes who threaten to get us all kicked off the trails

loop
this route configuration is characterized by riding from the designated trailhead to a distant point, then returning to the trailhead via a different route (or simply continuing on the same in a circle route) without doubling back; you always move forward across new terrain but return to the starting point when finished; distance is for the entire loop from the trailhead back to trailhead

multi-purpose
a designation of land which is open to many uses; mountain biking is allowed

off-camber
a trail that slopes in the opposite direction than one would prefer for safety's sake; for example, on a side-cut trail the slope is away from the hill—the inside of the trail is higher, so it helps you fall downhill if your balance isn't perfect

ORV/OHV
a motorized off-road vehicle (off-highway vehicle)

out-and-back
a ride where you will return on the same trail you pedaled out; while this might sound far more boring than a loop route, many trails look very different when pedaled in the opposite direction

pack stock
horses, mules, llamas, etc., carrying provisions along trails

point-to-point
a vehicle shuttle (or similar assistance) is required for this type of route, which is ridden from the designated trailhead to a distant location, or endpoint, where the route ends; total distance is for the one-way trip from the trailhead to endpoint

portage
to carry your bike on your person

pummy
soil with high pumice content produced by volcanic activity in the Pacific Northwest and elsewhere; light in consistency and easily pedaled; trails with such soil often become thick with dust

quads
bikers use this term to refer both to the extensor muscle in the front of the thigh (which is separated into four parts) and to maps; the expression "Nice quads!" refers always to

	the former, however, except in those instances when the speaker is an engineer
runoff	rainwater or snowmelt
scree	an accumulation of loose stones or rocky debris lying on a slope or at the base of a hill or cliff
side-cut trail	a trail cut on the side of a hill
signed	a "signed" trail has signs in place of blazes
single-track	a single, narrow path through grass or brush or over rocky terrain, often created by deer, elk, or backpackers; single-track riding is some of the best fun around
skid road	the path created when loggers drag trees through the forest with heavy equipment
slickrock	the rock-hard, compacted sandstone that is great to ride and even prettier to look at; you'll appreciate it even more if you think of it as a petrified sand dune or seabed (which it is), and if the rider before you hasn't left tire marks (from unnecessary skidding) or granola bar wrappers behind
snowmelt	runoff produced by the melting of snow
snowpack	unmelted snow accumulated over weeks or months of winter—or over years—in high-mountain terrain
spur	a road or trail that intersects the main trail you're following
squid	one who skids
stair-step climb	a climb punctuated by a series of level or near-level sections
switchback	a zigzagging road or trail designed to assist in traversing steep terrain; mountain bikers should not skid through switchbacks
talus	the rocky debris at the base of a cliff, or a slope formed by an accumulation of this rocky debris
tank trap	a steep-sided ditch (or series of ditches) used to block access to a road or trail; often used in conjunction with high mounds of excavated material
technical	terrain that is difficult to ride due not to its grade (steepness) but to its obstacles—rocks, roots, logs, ledges, loose soil . . .
topo	short for topographical map, the kind that shows both linear distance and elevation gain and loss; "topo" is pronounced with both vowels long

trashed	a trail that has been destroyed (same term used no matter what has destroyed it . . . cattle, horses, or even mountain bikers riding when the ground was too wet)
two-track	see "double-track"
two-wheel-drive	this refers to any vehicle with drive-wheel capability on only two wheels (a passenger car, for instance, has two-wheel drive); a two-wheel-drive road is a road or trail easily traveled by an ordinary car
waterbar	an earth, rock, or wooden structure that funnels water off trails to reduce erosion
washboarded	a road that is surfaced with many ridges spaced closely together, like the ripples on a washboard; these make for very rough riding, and even worse driving in a car or jeep
whoop-de-doo	closely spaced dips or undulations in a trail; these are often encountered in areas traveled heavily by ORVs
wilderness area	land that is officially set aside by the government to remain natural—pure, pristine, and untrammeled by any vehicle, including mountain bikes
windchill	a reference to the wind's cooling effect upon exposed flesh; for example, if the temperature is minus 12 degrees Celsius and the wind is blowing at 20 miles per hour, the windchill (that is, the actual temperature to which your skin reacts) is minus 36 degrees; if you are riding in wet conditions things are even worse, for the windchill would then be minus 59 degrees!
windfall	anything (trees, limbs, brush, fellow bikers . . .) blown down by the wind

INDEX

WARD CAMERON has worked as a naturalist and interpretive guide throughout Canada's west. For many years he has brought the natural and human history of western Canada to life through a combination of speaking programs, interpretive and tour guide service, writing, and photography. This is his third book. His first, *A Kananaskis SuperGuide*, provides an overall look at one of Alberta's best known mountain playgrounds. His second book, *Mountain Bike! The Canadian Rockies*, also part of the *America by Mountain Bike* series, focuses on the vast riding potential of the mountain parks. Ward is presently working on his fourth book, an overall natural history guide to the Canadian Rockies. It is scheduled for release in the spring of 2000.

Canada's west coast has become recognized across the continent as an extremely challenging, intensely beautiful mountain biking mecca. Riders flock to its vertical trails to bounce over obstacles thought to be impossible only a few years ago. This book is the result of several years of research, numerous forced ejections and more than a few bruises. Enjoy!